DATE DUE

DEMCO 38-296

1970
The Supreme Court Review

1970
The

"Judges as persons, or courts as institutions, are entitled to
no greater immunity from criticism than other persons
or institutions . . . [J]udges must be kept mindful of their limitations and
of their ultimate public responsibility by a vigorous
stream of criticism expressed with candor however blunt."
—Felix Frankfurter

". . . while it is proper that people should find fault when
their judges fail, it is only reasonable that they should recognize the
difficulties. . . . Let them be severely brought to book,
when they go wrong, but by those who will take the trouble
to understand them."
—Learned Hand

THE LAW SCHOOL

THE UNIVERSITY OF CHICAGO

Supreme Court Review

EDITED BY

PHILIP B. KURLAND

 THE UNIVERSITY OF CHICAGO PRESS

CHICAGO AND LONDON

INTERNATIONAL STANDARD BOOK NUMBER: 0-226-46421-0

LIBRARY OF CONGRESS CATALOG CARD NUMBER: 60-14353

THE UNIVERSITY OF CHICAGO PRESS, CHICAGO 60637

THE UNIVERSITY OF CHICAGO PRESS, LTD., LONDON

TO
MILTON AND ROSEMARY,
THEIR CHILDREN, and
THEIR GRANDCHILDREN

CONTENTS

PHILIP B. KURLAND

ENTER THE BURGER COURT: THE CONSTITUTIONAL BUSINESS OF THE SUPREME COURT, O.T. 1969

Last Term, for the first time in sixteen years, the center chair of the high bench was occupied by a new Chief Justice. Warren Earl Burger, like his immediate predecessor, is a genial man. Unlike his immediate predecessor, Burger comes to the Court with long judicial experience. He is the first Chief Justice of the United States to be promoted to that office directly from a lower federal court. His earlier judicial experience may comfort the new Chief; his affability may relieve tensions that a more acidulous personality would only exacerbate. But neither the experience nor the temperament will solve the essential problems with which the Court is faced. For the Supreme Court of the United States is like no other court in the world. And its Justices are not likely to be cajoled into decisions.

Nevertheless, it must be acknowledged that, for many, the Supreme Court takes on the coloration of its presiding officer. Still others assert that, at times, if the Chief Justice is to be the leader it is he who must take on the coloration of the Court. The facts are, of course, that the processes of change are subtle and complicated. Certainly the accession to office of any new Supreme Court Justice must make a difference in how that institution works. Some of the changes are quick and visible. Others evolve slowly and are often

Philip B. Kurland is Professor of Law, The University of Chicago.

concealed from public view. Some are great and others small. A Justice's influence is felt in many ways other than through the votes that he casts or the opinions that he writes.

The opportunities for a Chief Justice to influence the Court are greater than those of the side Justices if, but only if, he has the talent and capacity to take advantage of them. For, although his legal powers are only the same as those of his brethren, his administrative position creates chances for influence not available to the others. The Chief Justice can be but one of nine—and this may be true even where the public casts him in the role of leader—or he can be first among equals. For example, one of the most important influences that a Justice can exert on the Court's work is in framing the questions to which the Court will direct itself. None who does not participate in the Friday conferences—which means none other than the Justices themselves—can completely assay the role of each Justice in this regard. The Chief Justice, because he presents each case to the conference and reveals his views first, can thereby exert a great influence. Certainly this was true of Chief Justice Hughes. Moreover, it is the Chief Justice who assigns the writing of opinions, at least where he is a member of the majority, after hearing the views that were expressed in conference by each of his brethren. In this way, too, he may have a special role in shaping the content of the Court's jurisprudence. It is obviously too early to know how the new Chief Justice is taking advantage of these opportunities.

The events about the Court that most excited the public interest during the past Term did not concern its opinions but rather the battle between the President and the Senate over the choice of a successor to Mr. Justice Fortas. The result of this long controversy was that the Court functioned with only eight Justices throughout the 1969 Term.

I. A Short Sortie into Some Simplistic Statistics

The Court has not been so deprived of its full complement for such a long period since Mr. Justice Jackson went to Nuremberg to prosecute war criminals a quarter-century ago. There are important differences between the two periods. Twenty-five years ago, the Supreme Court had 1,460 cases on its dockets. The first Term of the Burger Court saw dockets with 4,202 cases. The eight-man Court of the 1945 Term was able to hand down 136 signed opinions; the Burger Court came down with but 88.

The problem of excess of business is one to which a new Chief Justice may well direct his attention, as well as that of his brethren and Congress, in order to alleviate the undue burdens. In the past three years alone, the Supreme Court docket has increased from 3,586 cases in the 1967 Term, to 3,918 cases in the 1968 Term, to 4,202 cases in the 1969 Term. If the number of signed opinions has not been reduced proportionately, there is a downward, if temporary, turn. The 1967 Term saw 110 such opinions, the 1968 Term had 99 such opinions, and, as already mentioned, the total for the 1969 Term was 88. But, whereas the number of cases on the dockets has seen a steady increase over the years, the number of signed opinions per Term has varied from 165 in the 1940 Term to 65 in the 1953 Term, Warren's first Term in office.

The time devoted to the great number of cases on the docket necessarily limits that which can be devoted to the Court's most important function of opinion writing. Some reduction in the Court's business seems called for lest opinions more and more take on the aspect of decision by a single Justice or, worse, get intrinsically weaker and weaker, commanding less and less respect throughout the American judiciary and within the Court itself. Deterioration has been evident for some time. The attempted solutions do not seem to work. Reducing oral arguments from one hour per side to one-half hour per side is a small palliative. Nor does the increase in law clerks seem a real solution. At the time of Mr. Justice Jackson's excursion, each Justice had but a single law clerk. Today each has two or three and the number is increasing. Each Justice's office is beginning to take on the aspects of a government bureau. Such collegial activity as goes on seems to take place within a single Justice's chambers rather than among all the Justices. Responsibility for decision and for the content of the Court's opinions ought not to be a staff function nor ought it to be delegable, even to such worthy subordinates as those who become law clerks to Supreme Court Justices. Some alternative means of relief from the Supreme Court's present heavy dockets should be considered.

The 1969 Term revealed neither more nor less divisiveness within the Court than one has come to expect. Of the 88 signed opinions, only 30 called forth no dissent. In 11 cases, one Justice dissented; in 25 cases, two Justices dissented; in 23 cases, three Justices dissented. The absence of a ninth member saved the Court the embarrassment that derives from publicity usually given 5-to-4 decisions.

Unlike his immediate predecessor, the new Chief Justice revealed himself as a willing dissenter. He noted dissent in 30 percent of the cases in which he participated and was thus bracketed with Justices Douglas and Black as one of the most frequent objectors to the Court's judgments. If any substantial change among the side Justices is patent on this score, it is the proportionate increase in dissents by Mr. Justice Brennan, who lost his most consistent ally when Chief Justice Warren retired, and the great reduction in the number of dissents by Mr. Justice Harlan. Over the previous six Terms, Harlan had averaged 58 dissents per Term, while Brennan had averaged a little more than 5.

TABLE*

OPINIONS AND VOTING IN THE BURGER COURT, O.T. 1969

Votes of \ Opinions by	Burger	Black	Douglas	Harlan	Brennan	Stewart	White	Marshall	Total
Burger.......		A40	A59	A75	A40	A82	A54	A80	A61
		C20	C 0	C 0	C10	C 9	C15	C 0	C 9
		D40	D33	D25	D50	D 9	D31	D20	D30
Black........	A73		A69	A22	A40	A37	A31	A70	A51
	C 9		C 0	C22	C10	C36	C39	C 0	C17
	D18		D31	D56	D50	D27	D30	D30	D32
Douglas......	A45	A70		A45	A80	A55	A39	A40	A55
	C 9	C 0		C11	C10	C18	C13	C20	C11
	D36	D30		D44	D10	D27	D48	D40	D34
Harlan	A45	A20	A77		A70	A75	A54	A78	A61
	C55	C50	C 8		C10	C17	C14	C11	C24
	D 0	D30	D15		D20	D 8	D30	D11	D15
Brennan	A64	A60	A77	A89		A75	A70	A80	A73
	C36	C20	C 0	C 0		C17	C 0	C 0	C10
	D 0	D20	D23	D11		D 8	D30	D20	D17
Stewart	A91	A50	A62	A100	A22		A62	A80	A67
	C 0	C20	C 8	C 0	C22		C14	C 0	C 9
	D 9	D30	D30	D 0	D56		D24	D20	D24
White	A100	A60	A62	A89	A70	A83		A90	A79
	C 0	C10	C 8	C 0	C20	C17		C 0	C 8
	D 0	D30	D30	D11	D10	D 0		D10	D13
Marshall	A80	A100	A100	A100	A100	A82	A62		A88
	C20	C 0	C 0	C 0	C 0	C 9	C14		C 7
	D 0	D 0	D 0	D 0	D 0	D 9	D24		D 5
Total....	A72	A56	A73	A74	A60	A71	A53	A74	
	C19	C18	C 5	C 5	C12	C17	C16	C 5	
	D 9	D26	D22	D21	D28	D12	D31	D21	

A: joins in opinion without any separate opinion; C: concurs specially; D: dissents in whole or in part.

* The statistics are expressed in percentages. By reading across, one may determine how each of the Justices in the left-hand column voted on opinions written by each of the Justices listed at the top. By reading down, one may determine the reaction of each Justice in the left-hand column to the opinions written by those listed at the top.

It was predicted that the new Chief Justice would line up with the more "conservative" elements of the Court. But the preceding table reveals little or no pattern in the voting, perhaps because the cases are not broken down by subject matter. The table does show that Chief Justice Burger's votes most closely accord with those of Mr. Justice Stewart. And one may infer from the table a confirmation of the well-known sharp differences of point of view between Justices Black and Harlan and between Justices Brennan and Stewart. But it is difficult—at least for the amateur statistician—to discover from the table the composition of the blocs that are alleged to exist within the Court. And this effort is made no less difficult by Mr. Justice Marshall's apparent willingness to agree with the majority in almost every case, except sometimes where Mr. Justice White is the spokesman for the Court. Whether this betokens the fact that the Court is now cast in the image of Mr. Justice Marshall or he believes that it is seldom worth the trouble to indicate disagreement is a matter for speculation.

II. Reflections of the Past

The Warren Court made its reputation as interpreter of the Constitution in areas essentially different from those that had concerned its predecessors. The focus was on problems of racial conflict, of criminal procedure, of church and state, of voting rights, of obscenity and other areas of free speech. An examination of the opinions of the first Term of the Burger Court suggests that the focus has not changed, although it may be changing. The new Court's opinions afford no sharp departures from what went before, even if there were omens that, especially as the personnel continues to change as it must, differences in emphasis will result in important differences in our constitutional jurisprudence. But these will, even in this day of instant everything, take time to develop and mature.

A. RACIAL CONFLICT

The first Term of the Warren Court saw the declaration of the invalidity of state-sponsored segregation by race in public schools.[1] The first Term of the Burger Court opened with the same question before it. Despite a challenge from the Department of Justice strangely allied with Mississippi against desegregation, the Court,

---

[1] Brown v. Board of Education, 347 U.S. 483 (1954).

in *Alexander v. Board of Education*,[2] insisted that it still meant what it had said about desegregation of the public schools. Whatever second thoughts the legislative or executive branches of the national government may have, perhaps by reason of a change of administration, the Court despite a new presiding officer remains committed to the effectuation of *Brown*. In a one-paragraph, per curiam opinion, labeled by others "the immediate desegregation case," the Court ruled:[3]

> The question presented is one of paramount importance, involving as it does the denial of fundamental rights to many thousands of school children, who are presently attending Mississippi schools under segregated conditions contrary to the applicable decisions of this Court. Against this background the Court of Appeals should have denied all motions for additional time because continued operation of segregated schools under a standard allowing "all deliberate speed" for desegregation is no longer constitutionally permissible. Under explicit holdings of this Court the obligation of every school district is to terminate dual school systems at once and to operate now and hereafter only unitary schools.

As in *Brown*, the Court in *Alexander* was unanimous. Like *Brown*, the effect on desegregation of public schools remains a matter for the future. Judicial impotence in the face of overwhelming civil disobedience, exacerbated by lack of cooperation from other branches of the national government as well as those of the states, has long been demonstrated in this area. That the Court, nevertheless, still has much to do was underlined by a concurring opinion written by the Chief Justice, speaking only for himself, in *Northcross v. Board of Education*:[4]

> The suggestion that the Court has not defined a unitary school system is not supportable. In *Alexander v. Holmes County Board of Education*, . . . we stated, albeit perhaps too cryptically, that a unitary system was one "within which no person is to be effectively excluded from any school because of race or color." From what is now before us in this case it is not clear what issues might be raised or developed on argument. As soon as possible, however, we ought to resolve

---

[2] 396 U.S. 19 (1969). See also Carter v. West Feliciana School Board, 396 U.S. 226 (1969); Dowell v. Board of Education, 396 U.S. 269 (1969); Florida v. Alabama, 396 U.S. 490 (1970); Alabama v. Finch, 396 U.S. 552 (1970); Mississippi v. Finch, 396 U.S. 553 (1970).

[3] 396 U.S. at 20.　　　　　　　　　[4] 397 U.S. 232, 236–37 (1970).

some of the basic practical problems when they are appropriately presented including whether, as a constitutional matter,
any particular racial balance must be achieved in the schools;
to what extent school districts and zones may or must be
altered as a constitutional matter; and to what extent transportation may or must be provided to achieve the ends sought
by prior holdings of the Court. Other related issues may
emerge.

Quite clearly the Court—and certainly its new Chief Justice—
does not intend to abandon the problem to resolution by non-
judicial agencies alone. It is certain that the invitation to litigation
thus issued will be gratefully accepted, by the one side or the
other. The 1970 Term docket is already replete with cases presenting problems about school desegregation. It can be confidently
predicted that the United States Reports will continue to be devoted in no small part to such issues.

Just as the 1969 Term brought back to the Court the old questions of school desegregation, so too it brought other civil rights
issues with which the Court had been long familiar. None had so
bothered the Warren Court as that of defining the requirement of
"state action" under the provisions of the first section of the Fourteenth Amendment. Throughout its history the Warren Court
managed to evade direct resolution of the problem. And more
recent civil rights legislation has reduced the scope of the difficulty
by imposing duties of nondiscrimination directly on individuals.
But the question apparently will not simply go away. It arrived
again on the Court's doorstep, if slightly disguised, in *Adickes v.
S. H. Kress & Co.*[5]

The petitioner in that case was a white schoolteacher who sued
Kress for damages under 42 U.S.C. § 1983, which derived from
§ 1 of the Civil Rights Act of 1871,[6] more familiarly known as
the "Ku Klux Klan Act." Plaintiff set forth two claims. A third,
which would have raised the problem of reversing the *Civil Rights
Cases*,[7] was rejected because it was offered too late.[8] The first claim
alleged that she had entered the eating place in Hattiesburg, Missis-

---

[5] 398 U.S. 144 (1970).   [6] 17 Stat. 13 (1871).

[7] 109 U.S. 3 (1883). These cases held the Civil Rights Act of 1875, 18 Stat. 335,
unconstitutional. The cases are of doubtful viability in light of the Court's more
recent decisions.

[8] 398 U.S. at 147 n. 2.

sippi, along with six black pupils and that, although her charges were served, she was refused service "because she was a 'Caucasian in the company of Negroes.'"[9] Her second count asserted that the refusal of service and her arrest for vagrancy that subsequently followed resulted from a conspiracy between the restaurant and the police of Hattiesburg.

The statute on which she based her suit required that she show that she had been deprived of a right, privilege, or immunity "secured by the Constitution or laws," and that the deprivation had taken place "under color of any statute, ordinance, regulation, custom, or usage, of any State or territory."[10] The trial court directed a verdict for the defendant on the first count "[b]ecause petitioner was unable to prove at trial that there were other instances in Hattiesburg of a white person having been refused service while in the company of Negroes."[11] Summary judgment was entered for the defendant on the second count on the ground that plaintiff "had 'failed to allege any facts from which a conspiracy might be inferred.'"[12] Perhaps it should be pointed out that this conclusion was reached not by a district court in Mississippi but by the one sitting in Manhattan. The judgment was affirmed by the Court of Appeals for the Second Circuit.[13] The Fifth Circuit would never have reached such a conclusion.

The reversal of the summary judgment was the easier of the two actions taken by the Supreme Court. The opinion for the Court was written by Mr. Justice Harlan. Mr. Justice Black concurred separately in the judgment. Justices Douglas and Brennan each wrote their own opinions labeled "concurring and dissenting."

On the conspiracy question, the Court wrote:[14]

> Although this is a law suit against a private party, not the State or one of its officials, our cases make clear that petitioner will have made out a violation of her Fourteenth Amendment rights and will be entitled to relief under § 1983 if she can prove that a Kress employee, in the course of employment, and a Hattiesburg policeman somehow reached an under-

---

[9] *Id.* at 147.

[10] 42 U.S.C. § 1983.

[11] 398 U.S. at 147.

[12] *Id.* at 148.

[13] 409 F.2d 121 (1968). Judge Waterman dissented from the majority of Judges Moore and Hays.

[14] *Id.* at 152.

standing to deny Miss Adickes service in the Kress store, or to cause her subsequent arrest because she was a white person in the company of Negroes.

The involvement of a state official in such a conspiracy plainly provides the state action essential to show a direct violation of petitioner's Fourteenth Amendment equal protection rights, whether or not the actions of the police were officially authorized, or lawful. . . . Moreover, a private party involved in such a conspiracy, even though not an official of the State, can be liable under § 1983.

There can be little doubt that the Court, in order to upset the summary judgment, had to return to the classic standards for denying such relief contrary to the more recent trend to grant summary judgment on the basis of affidavits. Plaintiff admitted "that she had no knowledge of any communication between any Kress employee and any member of the Hattiesburg police, and was relying on circumstantial evidence to support her contention that there was an arrangement between Kress and the police."[15] There was evidence that there was a policeman in the store at the time of the refusal of service and that this was the policeman that subsequently arrested her. But defendant's affidavits from the store employees and the police were to the effect that neither had conferred with the other about the refusal of service or the arrest.

The Court ruled—and it might be hoped that the standard would be applied in other summary judgment cases where the credibility of witnesses is necessarily involved—that defendant "did not carry its burden because of its failure to foreclose the possibility that there was a policeman in the Kress store while petitioner was awaiting service, and that this policeman reached an understanding with some Kress employee that petitioner not be served."[16]

The substantive count was a bit more complicated. "We are first confronted with the issue of whether a 'custom' for purposes of § 1983 must have the force of law, or whether, as argued in dissent, no state involvement is required."[17] The answer, reached after the usual extended reading of the cases and the legislative history, was that, as Mr. Justice Douglas put it in his opinion, custom "must have 'the force of law'; and 'law,' as I read the opinion, is used in the

---

[15] *Id.* at 155–56.

[16] *Id.* at 157.   [17] *Id.* at 162.

Hamiltonian sense."[18] The "Hamiltonian sense" was derived from the *Federalist* No. 15, where Hamilton wrote:[19]

> It is essential to the idea of law, that it be attended with a sanction; or, in other words, a penalty or punishment for disobedience. If there be no penalty annexed to disobedience, the resolutions or commands which pretend to be laws will, in fact, amount to nothing more than advice or recommendation. This penalty, whatever it may be, can only be inflicted in two ways: by the agency of the courts and ministers of justice, or by military force; by the COERCION of the magistracy, or by the COERCION of arms.

It is not by any means clear that the majority adopted the Hamiltonian definition. It was clear that the majority insisted that "custom" have the force of law. The Court's conclusion, then, was:[20]

> For state action purposes it makes no difference of course whether the racially discriminatory act by the private party is compelled by a statutory provision or by a custom having the force of law—in either case it is the State that has commanded the result by its law. Without deciding whether less substantial involvement of a State might satisfy the state action requirement of the Fourteenth Amendment, we conclude that petitioner would show an abridgement of her Equal Protection right, if she proves that Kress refused her service because of a state-enforced custom of segregating the races in public restaurants.

The Court made it clear, however, that the "custom" need not be statewide and that "it might be shown on remand that the Hattiesburg police would intentionally tolerate violence or threats of violence directed toward those who violated the practice of segregating the races at restaurants."[21]

The Burger Court then, like its predecessor, continued to find the need for a showing of state action under the Fourteenth Amendment and the older Civil Rights Acts. Once again, it did so without rejecting plaintiff's claims. Once again, Mr. Justice Douglas was prepared to dispense with the notion or to find it here, there, or anywhere. This time, Mr. Justice Douglas was without the aid and comfort formerly afforded him by Justices Warren and Goldberg. But he did have Mr. Justice Brennan as an ally, with such succor as he

---

[18] *Id*. at 178.

[19] Quoted *id*. at 178, n. 1.

[20] *Id*. at 171.

[21] *Id*. at 172.

might garnish from a lengthy if unpersuasive opinion as to the meaning of history.

This is not to suggest that the Court's results were compelled, but only that reading the statute for the intention of its framers would more likely bring the reader down on Mr. Justice Harlan's side than on Mr. Justice Brennan's. This may not be much of an argument for a Court that writes and rewrites congressional legislation as easily as the Supreme Court has done in the recent past.

Like the *Adickes* case, *Sullivan v. Little Hunting Park*[22] brought back to the high court the question of the meaning now to be given to statutes enacted in an earlier era for different social conditions. The Court, in *Jones v. Mayer*,[23] had faced the problem of construing and applying 42 U.S.C. § 1982. *Sullivan* was one of the many cases that *Jones v. Mayer* may be expected to spawn.

The facts were succinctly stated in the opinion for the Court written by Mr. Justice Douglas:[24]

> Little Hunting Park, Inc., is a Virginia nonstock corporation organized to operate a community park and playground facilities for the benefit of residents in an area of Fairfax County, Virginia. A membership share entitles all persons in the immediate family of the shareholder to use the corporation's recreation facilities. Under the bylaws a person owning a membership share is entitled when he rents his home to assign the share to his tenant, subject to approval of the board of directors. Paul E. Sullivan and his family owned a house in this area and lived in it. Later he bought another house in the area and leased the first one to T. R. Freeman, Jr., an employee of the U.S. Department of Agriculture; and assigned his membership share to Freeman. The board refused to approve the assignment because Freeman was a Negro. Sullivan protested that action and was notified that he would be expelled from the corporation by the board. A hearing was accorded to him and he was expelled, the board tendering him cash for his two shares.

Sullivan and Freeman brought suit under §§ 1981 and 1982 for an injunction and damages. Because Freeman moved from the area, only the damage claim survived.

After disposing of a procedural objection to the Court's jurisdic-

---

22 396 U.S. 229 (1969).

23 392 U.S. 409 (1968).   24 396 U.S. at 234–35.

tion, the Court held that *Jones v. Mayer* compelled a judgment for the plaintiffs:[25]

> In *Jones* v. *Mayer Co.*, the complaint charged a refusal to sell petitioner a home because he was black. In the instant cases the interest conveyed was a leasehold of realty coupled with a membership share in a nonprofit company organized to offer recreational facilities to owners and lessees of real property in that residential area. It is not material whether the membership share be considered realty or personal property, as § 1982 covers both. Section 1982 covers the right "to inherit, purchase, lease, sell, hold, and convey real and personal property." There is a suggestion that transfer on the books of the corporation of Freeman's share is not covered by any of those verbs. The suggestion is without merit. There has never been any doubt but that Freeman paid part of his $129 monthly rental for the assignment of the membership share in Little Hunting Park. The transaction clearly fell within the "lease." The right to "lease" is protected by § 1982 against the actions of third parties, as well as against the actions of the immediate lessor. Respondents' actions in refusing to approve the assignment of the membership share in this case was clearly an interference with Freeman's right to "lease." A narrow construction of the language of § 1982 would be quite inconsistent with the broad and sweeping nature of the protection meant to be afforded by § 1 of the Civil Rights Act of 1866, 14 Stat. 27, from which § 1982 was derived.

The majority here, as in *Jones v. Mayer*, rejected the argument that the 1968 Civil Rights Act had replaced or limited the effectiveness of § 1982. And it was principally but not exclusively on this ground that the dissent, written by Mr. Justice Harlan, and joined by the Chief Justice and Mr. Justice White, took its stand:[26]

> In *Jones* v. *Mayer* . . . , the Court decided that a little-used section of a 100-year old statute prohibited private racial discrimination in the sale of real property. This construction of a very old statute, in no way required by its language, and open to serious question in light of the statute's legislative history, seemed to me unnecessary and unwise because of the recently passed, but then not yet fully effective Fair Housing Title of the Civil Rights Act of 1968. . . . Today, the Court goes yet beyond *Jones* (1) by implying a private right to damages for violations of 42 U.S.C. § 1982; (2) by interpreting § 1982 to prohibit a community recreation association from

25 *Id*. at 236–37.   26 *Id*. at 241–42.

withholding, on the basis of race, approval of an assignment
of a membership that was transferred incident to a lease of real
property; and (3) by deciding that a white person who is
expelled from a recreation association "for the advocacy of
[a Negro's] cause" has "standing" to maintain an action for
relief under § 1982.

Because the Fair Housing Law will become fully effective
less than three weeks from now, I think the majority even more
unwise than it was in *Jones*, in precipitately breathing still
more life into § 1982, which is both vague and open-ended,
when Congress has provided this modern statute, containing
various detailed remedial provisions aimed at eliminating racial
discrimination in housing.

It should be noted that all the Justices who participated in *Jones v.
Mayer* voted the same way in both cases. In *Sullivan*, Justices Harlan and White, who had dissented in *Jones v. Mayer*, were joined by
the new Chief Justice. *Jones v. Mayer* is likely to remain a viable
and oft-used precedent until the minority becomes a majority not
by persuasion, as is most unlikely, but by changes of personnel,
which is more likely. Perhaps it is relevant to note that it was Mr.
Justice Blackmun who wrote the opinion for the Court of Appeals
for the Eighth Circuit[27] which was reversed in *Jones v. Mayer*.

The essential issues in these cases, those of reconciling the legislative and judicial roles and of reconciling ancient legislation and contemporary legislation, have no clear and easy answers. If the Radical
sponsors of the 1866 legislation would be delighted with the Court's
behavior, at least so long as the cases came from the South, it is more
doubtful that the promulgators of the 1968 Civil Rights Act thought
that so potent a judicial remedy was already in existence. What is
clear is that a judicial remedy in the area of civil rights, dependent
upon case-by-case relief, is never so potent in fact as it appears on
the books. Litigants may get relief, at the great cost of litigation,
leaving the great majority of those imposed on still in need of an
effective champion.

Other cases raising issues deriving from racial conflict also reflected past judicial experience one or more degrees removed. The
problem of discrimination in jury selection is one of the oldest in
Supreme Court Fourteenth Amendment jurisprudence. This time
the problems were presented with several new facets in the cases of

---

[27] 379 F.2d 33 (8th Cir. 1967).

Carter v. Jury Commission[28] and *Turner v. Fouche.*[29] One difference, said the Court, which spoke through Mr. Justice Stewart in both cases, made no difference:[30]

> This is the first case to reach the Court in which an attack upon alleged racial discrimination in choosing juries has been made by plaintiffs seeking affirmative relief, rather than by defendants challenging judgments of criminal conviction on the ground of systematic exclusion of Negroes from the grand juries that indicted them, the trial juries that found them guilty, or both. The District Court found no barrier to such a suit, and neither do we. Defendants in criminal proceedings do not have the only cognizable legal interest in nondiscriminatory jury selection. People excluded from juries because of their race are as much aggrieved as those indicted and tried by juries chosen under a system of racial exclusion. Surely there is no jurisdictional or procedural bar to an attack upon systematic jury discrimination by way of civil suit such as the one brought here. The federal claim is bottomed on the simple proposition that the State, acting through its agents, has refused to consider the appellants for jury service solely because of their race. Whether jury service be deemed a right, a privilege, or a duty, the State may no more extend it to some of its citizens and deny it to others on racial grounds than it may invidiously discriminate in the offering and withholding of the elective franchise. Once the State chooses to provide grand and petit juries, whether or not constitutionally required to do so, it must hew to federal constitutional criteria in ensuring that the selection of membership is free of racial bias.

What Mr. Justice Stewart did not explain is what the Court has left unexplained throughout its dealings with the problem. If the objective is the attainment of "a body truly representative of the community,"[31] why is it only members of the excluded group who have a basis for complaint? But then he had other difficult issues to meet in these cases.

As usual, the statistics were held damning to the validity of the jury selection process as it operated. It was shown that in 1966 in the Alabama county in question, 50 percent of the white male population (women were not then included as eligible jurors) was on the jury rolls but only 4 percent of the Negro population. In 1967,

---

[28] 396 U.S. 320 (1970).

[29] 396 U.S. 346 (1970).   [30] 396 U.S. at 329–30.

[31] Smith v. Texas, 311 U.S. 128, 130 (1940), quoted 396 U.S. at 330.

after women were added, only 32 percent of the total jury list was Negro in a county where the population was 65 percent black. The burden thus put on the appellees to show reason for this disparity could not be met.

The appellants were, however, more interested in attacking the selection system than in the injunction they secured from the trial court to compel fair use of that system. The method of selection set by Alabama law called for the "commissioners to select for jury service those persons who are 'generally reputed to be honest and intelligent and . . . esteemed in the community for their integrity, good character and sound judgment.' "[32] The claim was that this left the commissioners too free to indulge their racial prejudices. They argued that the statute was, therefore, invalid on its face. This argument the Court rejected. "It has long been accepted that the Constitution does not forbid the States to prescribe relevant qualifications for their jurors. The States remain free to confine the selection to citizens, to persons meeting specified qualifications of age and educational attainment, and to those possessing good intelligence, sound judgment, and fair character."[33] Whether the states are to be equally free to specify qualifications for their general electors is a matter that the Court will have to decide during the coming Term when the eighteen-year-old enfranchisement is presented for validation.

Indeed, the electoral process was not far from the center of the controversy in these two jury cases. Another of the appellants' claims was that the selection system was invalid because the jury commission, appointed by the governor, was always made up wholly of white commissioners. The issue was handled gingerly:[34]

> For present purposes we may assume that the State may no more exclude Negroes from service on the jury commission because of their race than from the juries themselves. But the District Court found the appellants had shown only that for many years the jury commission had been composed entirely of white men, and concluded that without more the appellants' attack failed for want of proof. We think that ruling was correct. Quite apart from the problems that would be involved in a federal court's ordering the Governor of a State to exercise his discretion in a particular way, we cannot say on this record that the absence of Negroes from the Greene County jury

---

[32] 396 U.S. at 331.   [33] *Id*. at 332.   [34] *Id*. at 338.

commission amounted in itself to a prima facie showing of discriminatory exclusion.

What the Court will do when the next case presents it with the fact that never since Reconstruction has a governor of Alabama appointed a black jury commissioner remains for the future to reveal.

The appellants were not satisfied to stop at the point of discrimination however. And again they met a negative reply:[35]

> Nor can we uphold the appellants' present contention that apart from the question of discrimination in the composition of the jury commission, the absence of Negroes from the Commission compelled the District Court to order the appointment of Negro commissioners. The appellants are no more entitled to proportional representation by race on the jury commission than on any particular grand or petit jury.

It was the matter of the composition of the jury commission rather than the jury that aroused separate opinions of contradictory themes by Mr. Justice Black on the one hand and Mr. Justice Douglas on the other. Seeking to make doubly sure that he was not misrepresented by joining the Court's opinion, Mr. Justice Black wrote:[36]

> I concur in the judgment and opinion of the Court except insofar as it may leave an implication that this Court has the power to vacate a state governor's appointment of jury commissioners or the power to compel the governor of a State to appoint Negroes or any other persons to the office of jury commissioner. In my judgment the Constitution no more grants this Court the power to compel a governor to appoint or reject a certain individual or a member of any particular group than it grants this Court the power to compel the voters of a State to elect or defeat a particular person or a member of a particular group.

Mr. Justice Douglas found that there was far more evidence of impropriety in the process of selection of commissioners than a mere showing that none but white commissioners had been appointed for a period of a dozen years. For, he properly asserted, there was also the showing with which the Court concurred that the commissioners had discriminated in the selection of jurors. Unlike any of his brethren he was prepared to swallow the camel if not the gnat:[37]

---

[35] *Id.* at 339.   [36] *Id.* at 341.   [37] *Id.* at 345.

Where the challenged state agency, dealing with the rights and liberties of the citizen, has a record of racial discrimination, the corrective remedy is proportional representation. Under our Constitution that would indeed seem to be the only effective control over the type of racial discrimination long practised in this case.

I would not write a decree that requires a governor to name two Negroes out of three commissioners. I would go no further than to strike down this jury commission system, because it does not provide for proportional representation of the two races.

It will be most interesting to see what happens when Mr. Justice Douglas' proportional representation system collides, as it must, with his one man–one vote rationale. But again sufficient unto the day is the evil thereof.

The *Turner* case, in addition to raising the same problems about jury selection and jury commissioners, attacked the method for selecting school board members. The relevant Georgia statute here in question provides that school board members should be selected from "freeholders." The Court found merit in this attack:[38]

It cannot be seriously urged that a citizen in all other respects qualified to sit on a school board must also own real property if he is to participate responsibly in educational decisions, without regard to whether he is a parent with children in the local schools, a lessee who effectively pays the property taxes of his lessor as part of his rent, or a state and federal taxpayer contributing to the approximately 85% of the Taliaferro County annual school budget derived from sources other than the board of education's own levy on real property.

Nor does the lack of ownership of realty establish a lack of attachment to the community and its educational values. . . . Without excluding the possibility that other circumstances might present themselves in which a property qualification for office-holding could survive constitutional scrutiny, we cannot say on the record before us, that the present freeholder requirement for membership on the county board of education amounts to anything more than invidious discrimination.

Thus do the decisions regulating limitations of the voting franchise[39] get carried over to appointive office. And, it should be noted,

---

[38] 396 U.S. at 363–64.

[39] See Kramer v. Union Free School District, 395 U.S. 621 (1969); Cipriano v. City of Houma, 395 U.S. 701 (1969).

with the acquiescence of a unanimous Court. The implications of these cases will certainly be broader than their origins in the jury selection process would suggest.

The other major racial conflict case of the 1969 Term was not merely a reflection of cases that had come before the Court at earlier periods but was, in fact, the ultimate stage of a litigation that had already once called for Supreme Court adjudication. In 1911, Senator Augustus Bacon of Georgia, to assure his claim on posterity, devised certain real property in the city of Macon to that city to be used as a park but only by whites. According to the devise the park —called Baconsfield, no relation to Beaconsfield—was to be managed for the city by a board of seven white managers. After Bacon's death, Baconsfield was refurbished with WPA funds and other government moneys, and it drifted into use by both blacks and whites. The park's managers sued to remove the city as trustee on the theory that the segregation could be restored only if the park was privately held. The Supreme Court of Georgia approved the transfer of legal title so that the park could revert to its segregated status. In *Evans v. Newton*,[40] the Supreme Court reversed the Georgia court and ruled that the change of trustees could not change the nature and function of the park as a public institution that had to be desegregated.

On remand from the Supreme Court, the Georgia courts held that the purpose of the bequest had failed and, despite the absence of a provision for reverter, ordered that the property be restored to the heirs of the Bacon estate. Once again the case came to the Supreme Court. In *Evans v. Abney*[41] the Court affirmed the action of the state courts as not violating the Constitution. The opinion for the Court was written by Mr. Justice Black. The majority in *Abney* consisted of each of the four Justices who had dissented in *Newton*, plus the Chief Justice, whose vote was not, however, needed to make a majority. Mr. Justice Douglas, who had written for the Court in *Newton*, dissented along with Mr. Justice Brennan. The other Justices from the *Newton* 5-to-4 majority had either retired or resigned. Thus is the mandate of the Constitution revealed.

Mr. Justice Black regretted the loss of the park, to be suffered he said by white and black equally. But the Constitution did not yet tell a private citizen that he could not indulge his prejudices in pass-

---

40 382 U.S. 296 (1966).   41 396 U.S. 435 (1970).

ing on his property. Mr. Justice Douglas thought that the intent of the testator would better be carried out through an integrated park than through return of the property to the estate. Mr. Justice Brennan found many bases for invalid state action that violated the Fourteenth Amendment.

Ever since *Shelley v. Kraemer*,[42] constitutional law professors have been asking their students whether a state court could enforce a will that discriminated in its disposition of property solely on the basis of race or religion. The answer provided by the students generally was that they could. But they couldn't say why. The Supreme Court has now given us the same answer with the same paucity of explanation.

In terms of voting patterns during the 1969 Term on civil rights cases, one could discern, if one had to, three blocs. The one most sympathetic to the utilization of the judicial process for aiding black equality included only Justices Douglas and Brennan. The one least willing to write social policy inhibiting individual racial discrimination would contain the new Chief Justice and Justices Harlan and White. In the middle, but leaning toward the second group, would be Justices Black, Stewart, and Marshall, with the last recusing himself in most of the cases. It should be seen, however, that these blocs emerge only on the fringe questions. For the most part, the Court is pretty well unanimous in insisting that all clearly governmental action must be cleansed of any racial bias against minorities.

B. THE ELECTORAL PROCESS

Next to school desegregation, the reputation of the Warren Court rests most on its one man–one vote cases. Indeed, it was Chief Justice Warren's opinion, as he looked back with pride, that *Baker v. Carr*[43] and its offspring were the prime accomplishments of his tenure. The Warren Court made the simplistic formula implicit in *Baker v. Carr* explicit in its application to an ever widening ken. But it remained for the Burger Court to apply the coup de grace.

The classic issue of districting was raised in *Hadley v. Junior College District*[44] in terms of equalizing the votes in the selection of junior college district trustees. For it seemed that a statutory for-

---

[42] 334 U.S. 1 (1948).

[43] 369 U.S. 186 (1962).   [44] 397 U.S. 50 (1970).

mula, based on an apparently acceptable measure of the number of children of school age in the district, resulted in 60 percent of those schoolchildren having only 50 percent of the adult-elected adult trustees. Redistricting was commanded to assure equality of electoral power, even when not measured by the electorate but by those whom the electorate represented.

Mr. Justice Black, writing for a badly divided Court, held that the mathematical formulas developed in legislative redistricting cases were, indeed, equally applicable to all elections, no matter the office, because there was no satisfactory way of drawing lines between important and unimportant offices or between administrative agencies and legislative agencies. If the state chooses to utilize the elective process for filling state or local offices it must abide the command of the one man–one vote cases. And, on the Court's reasoning, this rule is as applicable to the judges elected to high state courts as to the local ward alderman.

Mr. Justice Harlan, the only remaining member of the *Baker v. Carr* era who recognized the words MENE, MENE, TEKEL, UPHARSIN when he saw them, continued his role of dissent. He was joined by the Chief Justice and Mr. Justice Stewart. They could not understand why the local governments of the states had to be straitjacketed in this way or why the existing representational formula did not satisfy the requirements of the rule in any event.

The conclusion in *Hadley* came as no surprise. Speculation had long shifted to problems other than the all-inclusiveness of the one man–one vote rule. One of the bigger problems opened by the Warren Court, but not fully extrapolated, was to determine the members of the electorate whose equality of voting power had been assured by the descendants of *Baker v. Carr*.

The Court held, in *Evans v. Cornman*,[45] that the residents of the National Institutes of Health enclave in Maryland could not be deprived of their votes in Maryland elections as "non-residents." There was no reasonable basis, said Mr. Justice Marshall, for a legislative conclusion that such persons lacked the interests or attachments that qualified other persons living within the borders of the state to vote. Mr. Justice Marshall's opinion for the Court did not evoke a single dissent.

The agreement about the necessary qualifications of an elector

---

[45] 398 U.S. 419 (1970).

that was revealed in *Evans v. Cornman* was totally absent in *Phoenix v. Kolodziejski.*[46] There Mr. Justice White delivered the opinion of the Court, but Mr. Justice Black concurred only in part, while the Chief Justice and Justices Harlan and Stewart were in dissent. During its last Term the Warren Court had ruled that the vote in school district elections could not be confined to owners and lessees of real property and the parents of schoolchildren.[47] The same Term, the Court had said that voting in elections to approve revenue bonds for financing local improvements could not be confined to property taxpayers.[48] The question in the *Phoenix* case, as stated by Mr. Justice White, was: "Does the Federal Constitution permit a State to restrict to real property taxpayers the vote in elections to approve the issuance of general obligation bonds?"[49]

The answer to the question was no. The case could not be distinguished from those of the earlier Term even if the burden of the bond issue in *Phoenix* would fall exclusively on property owners, where revenue bonds would be paid by those utilizing the facilities constructed. Certainly, as the Court noted, the real property tax was indirectly shouldered by others than real property owners, at least in the case of nonresidential property. In any event, we have passed the stage where there is any validity to the notion that the person who pays the piper has the right to call the tune. Mr. Justice White wrote:[50]

> We thus conclude that, although owners of real property have interests somewhat different from the interests of nonproperty owners in the issuance of general obligation bonds, there is no basis for concluding that nonproperty owners are substantially less interested in the issuance of these securities than are property owners. That there is no adequate reason to restrict the franchise on the issuance of general obligation bonds to property owners is further evidenced by the fact that only 14 States now restrict the franchise in this way; most

---

[46] 399 U.S. 204 (1970).

[47] Kramer v. Union Free School District, 395 U.S. 621 (1969). The opinion written by Chief Justice Warren drew a dissent by Mr. Justice Stewart, who was joined by Justices Black and Harlan.

[48] Cipriano v. City of Houma, 395 U.S. 701 (1969). This time the opinion was per curiam. Justices Black and Stewart concurred in the judgment but not the opinion. Mr. Justice Stewart concurred because he felt compelled to do so by the holding of the one man–one vote cases with which he continued to disagree.

[49] 399 U.S. at 205.   [50] *Id.* at 212–13.

> States find it possible to protect property owners from exces-
> sive tax burdens by means other than restricting the franchise
> to property owners.

The argument that what is good for General Motors is good for
the United States has little more appeal when stated in terms of
what is good for California is necessarily good for Arizona. The
Constitution clearly does not require uniformity among the states,
especially when it is not possible to assert that the classification of
those who pay the bonds is not an unreasonable one. Arizona might
have chosen a poor system, but it clearly wasn't an unconstitutional
system until the Supreme Court decided the *Phoenix* case. For the
Court ruled that "our decision in this case will apply only to au-
thorizations for general obligation bonds which are not final as of
June 23, 1970, the date of this decision."[51] And it was the prospective nature of the judgment to which Mr. Justice Black took exception, while that was the only part that secured acquiescence from
Justices Stewart and Harlan and the Chief Justice. The dissenters
would distinguish *Cipriano* and leave the matter to the discretion of
the state, especially since this case did not "really involve an 'election', that is, a choice by popular vote of candidates for public office
under a system of representative democracy."[52] The distinction between real elections and others hardly contributed to the resolution
of the problem, except to suggest the irrelevancy of *Baker v. Carr*
and its retinue.

Two hard questions, presented at the beginning of the 1969
Term, were avoided because of mootness. In *Hall v. Beals*,[53] an attack was leveled against the Colorado six-month residency requirement for voting in presidential elections. The per curiam dismissal
was objected to by Justices Brennan and Marshall, both of whom
thought that the case was not moot and that the residency requirement was invalid because there was "no compelling interest" to require any period of residency beyond that necessary for the me-
chanics of the electoral process. In *Brockington v. Rhodes*,[54] the
question arose as to the validity of the requirement that a candidate,
to secure a place on the ballot, must secure a statutorily specified
percentage of the voters' signatures on a petition. Although the

---

[51] *Id.* at 214.

[52] *Id.* at 215.

[53] 396 U.S. 45 (1969).

[54] 396 U.S. 41 (1969).

mootness of *Brockington* depended on a rather technical construction of the pleadings, it evoked no dissent.[55]

The Court is certainly not yet out of the political thicket. It is certainly not likely to come out at the place it went in. But it hasn't yet worked its way through to the other side. The principal issue that will bedevil it in this area is that of the gerrymander. For the reapportionment cases have done little to limit the power of the political organizations and will continue to do little unless and until some means of removing the capacity of the gerrymander is also conjured up. Since every district line is one that favors one side or the other, this device will have to be an extraordinary one indeed. The 1970 Term may well present the opportunity to deal with the question. Perhaps the Court can accomplish this end by helping contribute to the demise of the two-party system. Cases affording that opportunity will certainly be available. Meanwhile, immediately on the horizon is the problem of the congressional ipse dixit on the eighteen-year-old vote. The Burger Court will not want for thorny problems so long as it remains in the bramble bushes.

The indications of bloc voting on the electoral cases suggest only a deep dissatisfaction with the one man–one vote by the Chief Justice and Justices Harlan and Stewart. The others remain convinced of their mandate under the Equal Protection Clause to protect the majority from imposition by the minority.

C. CRIMINAL PROCEDURE

It says something about American society that the largest portion of the business of the United States Supreme Court is devoted to problems of criminal law. Indeed, it says different things to different people. On the one hand, this fact is looked on as revealing the over-niceties of criminal procedure that permit the guilty to go unpunished or even unarrested. To others, it documents the unfairness of the administration of our system of criminal prosecutions, threatening the innocent no less than the guilty with the grossness of police misbehavior. Either way, crime is our major domestic problem, whether it is regarded as an ailment of its own or merely the symptom of other diseases of our society.

---

[55] Dismissal of an action by a three-judge court that had granted a temporary injunction to add Communist candidates to the ballot was also held not reviewable directly by the Supreme Court. Mitchell v. Donovan, 398 U.S. 427 (1970).

Throughout its life the Warren Court was busily occupied in the role of supervisor of the administration of criminal justice, for the state courts no less than for the federal. This role was not created during the Warren tenure, but it was certainly much expanded during that time. There are no indications from the cases of the 1969 Term that the Court is about to retrench, although there is some showing that the new code of criminal procedure it will write will differ in marked degree from the older one.

1. *Search and seizure.* The anomaly faced by the Court in its Fourth Amendment cases derives from the need to frame rules for inhibition of government invasion of individual privacy in petty cases that concern the seizure of contraband from "squalid hucksters" of liquor, dope, guns, etc. Moreover, we live in a society in which the government is given or has taken a larger and larger role in everyone's life, at the same time that we seek to keep it out of some hard-to-define portions of our activities. The problem of preserving both individual freedom and the viability of the service state is not easily resolved. Then, too, the Constitution speaks to this subject in relative rather than absolute terms, in terms of "reasonableness." All these factors have contributed to the less than satisfactory rationalization of the cases on the subject. And, on this score, the future looks no brighter than the past. The "dirty business" of invalid searches and seizures and the protection of society from criminals who, no less than the state, deprive persons of life, liberty, and property must be reconciled. So far it has been done only on a case-by-case basis. The Burger Court, too, has made its contribution to these cases.

The first of the Burger Court cases was atypical. A civil action to recover seized liquor and suppress its use in evidence, the case was resolved on statutory rather than constitutional grounds. In *Colonnade Corp. v. United States*,[56] the Court divided 5 to 3 in favor of the return of the liquor to its former owner. Mr. Justice Douglas spoke for the Court. The facts showed that the petitioner was a catering establishment serving whiskey and under suspicion by IRS agents of violating the liquor laws. The IRS agents searched the basement without permission and then sought access to a locked room, which was denied them. They broke into the locked room

---

[56] 397 U.S. 72 (1970).

and seized the bottles of liquor that they had reason to suspect had been illegally refilled.

The Court held that a federal statute making it an offense punishable by a $500 fine to refuse entry to IRS officers for purposes of inspection precluded forcible entry without a warrant. The fine was, in effect, held the exclusive remedy chosen by Congress to punish those who inhibited proper inspection. (Mr. Justice Douglas had come a long way since he wrote the opinion for a similarly divided Court in *Davis v. United States.*)[57] The Chief Justice thought that the provision for a fine was only cumulative and not alternative to forcible inspection where the evidence warranted it, as it did here. And Mr. Justice Black, with some emphasis on the nature of the liquor business, agreed that the search was legal. "I am confident that when Congress said that federal liquor agents could search without a warrant and further provided for fines if the owner refused to permit such a search, it also intended to authorize forcible entry and seizure if that became necessary."[58] The Chief Justice and Mr. Justice Stewart joined the Black opinion. But the Chief Justice also filed a dissenting opinion of his own.

In fact, of course, Congress had not considered the question raised by the case. And Congress is free to change the rule at will, since both majority and minority conceded congressional power here. It is, therefore, unlikely that the *Colonnade* case will prove of importance, except to those who are now free to use the seized whiskey.

In this day, an additional one-day delay in the delivery of first-class mail could probably be regarded as de minimis. Even where the delay resulted not from the inefficiency of the post office but rather from the efficiency of the police. But this was not the reason given by Mr. Justice Douglas in his opinion for a unanimous Court in *United States v. Van Leeuwen.*[59] "The rule of our decisions is certainly not that first-class mail can be detained 29 hours after mailing in order to obtain the search warrant needed for its inspection."[60] On the other hand, he did say; "The significant Fourth Amendment interest was in the privacy of this first-class mail; and that privacy was not disturbed or invaded until the approval of the magistrate was obtained."[61] Obviously this case, like most search and seizure

---

[57] 328 U.S. 582 (1946).

[58] 397 U.S. at 81.

[59] 397 U.S. 249 (1970).

[60] *Id.* at 253.

[61] *Ibid.*

cases, turned on its facts. Suspicion of federal crime was appropriately engendered by the manner of mailing of two packages. And it was held, specifically "on the facts of this case," that the authorities were permitted to stop the package at the place of its shipment to get a warrant for inspection rather than let it go through and have the warrant applied at the end or in the course of its travels. Again, a judgment that does not suggest far-reaching consequences or even, as *Colonnade* did, some judicial attitudes.

The contraband was liquor in *Colonnade*, gold coins in *Van Leeuwen*, and, in more contemporary idiom, heroin in *Vale v. Louisiana*.[62] And here the case was more typical of many that clog the criminal courts. Vale, a multiple offender against the narcotics laws, received a stiff sentence for possession of heroin. He claimed that the heroin was improperly seized and improperly used in evidence against him. A majority of the Supreme Court agreed with him and reversed his conviction in an opinion written by Mr. Justice Stewart.

It seems that after surveillance by police, in the course of which they witnessed what appeared to be a narcotics sale by Vale in the street immediately outside his home, Vale was arrested. The police, there were three of them, then entered the house, where a search revealed the heroin that was used in evidence to convict Vale. The Court held that the search was invalid: it was not incident to an arrest; there was no consent; there was no emergency; there was no "hot pursuit"; the contraband was not in immediate danger of destruction. It followed that there was no reason why the police could not have secured a warrant for the search of the house.

Mr. Justice Black, joined by the Chief Justice, dissented: "This case raises most graphically the question how does a policeman protect evidence necessary to the State if he must leave the premises to get a warrant, allowing the evidence to be destroyed. The Court's answer to that question makes unnecessarily difficult the conviction of those who prey upon society."[63]

The difference between the majority and minority is apparently a difference over the inferences to be drawn from the facts. The larger number agreed that the search warrant could have been secured without substantial risk; the minority disagreed. The case, thus, affords no doctrinal illumination, merely the resolution of a particular case on its own facts.

---

[62] 399 U.S. 30 (1970).   [63] *Id.* at 41.

Chambers v. Maroney[64] also afforded familiar material. Quick police work after a gasoline station holdup resulted in the arrest of petitioner and his companions in a station wagon that had been seen near the place of commission of the crime. After the arrest, the station wagon was taken to the police station, where it was searched and incriminating evidence was discovered, seized, and used at the trial. Petitioner contended that the search of the auto without a warrant was invalid. Here the Supreme Court, expressing itself through an opinion by Mr. Justice White, disagreed.

The search of the car, said the Court, need not be justified as an incident to arrest. The fact that it was an automobile put it into a different category for purposes of the rules against unreasonable searches and seizures, so that the delayed search was justified. There was probable cause to search the car immediately upon arrest. The delay in searching the car was unimportant. The opinion, resting on the two-court rule,[65] gave short shrift to petitioner's complaint about a different search. It also cursorily rejected petitioner's claim of inadequate counsel.

Mr. Justice Stewart concurred, announcing that he continued to prefer his own dissenting position "that the admission at trial of evidence acquired in alleged violation of the Fourth Amendment standards is not of itself sufficient grounds for collateral attack upon an otherwise valid criminal conviction, state or federal."[66] He bowed to the majority's unwillingness to acquiesce in that doctrine.

It was Mr. Justice Harlan who dissented. For him the Court had too casually dismissed the claim of inadequacy of counsel; petitioner had offered sufficient grounds to justify a hearing on the question. He also found the conclusion on the validity of the search of the auto inconsistent with prior authority and without adequate justification. "The Court now discards the approach taken in *Preston*,[67] and creates a special rule for automobile searches that is seriously at odds with generally applied Fourth Amendment principles."[68] Certainly Mr. Justice Harlan was right in suggesting the inconsis-

---

[64] 399 U.S. 42 (1970).

[65] The Court cited Harrington v. California, 395 U.S. 250 (1969), as precedent for this position. *Id.* at 53.

[66] *Id.* at 54–55.

[67] Preston v. United States, 376 U.S. 364 (1964).

[68] 399 U.S. at 65.

tency with the *Preston* case. He was also right in his conclusion that the suggested precedents for the Court's judgment were inadequate because they were concerned with moving vehicles that could disappear while the police sought a search warrant. The car in *Chambers* was clearly in the safe custody of the police.

All in all, then, the search and seizure cases saw the Court continue in its role as a court of errors and appeals, deciding individual cases while affording little guidance to the other courts that have to administer the rule. Perhaps, against a constitutional standard of "reasonableness," it can do no more, although under equally amorphous provisions, it has found authority for harder rules. Perhaps the division in the Court, one of long endurance, prevents the formulation of adequate guidelines. Certainly this area of the law remains in flux and it won't be helped by continued ad hoc decisions by the Supreme Court.

2. *Coerced confessions.* Clearly the Court's business in coerced confession cases is falling off. The new vogue is to connect them with some other aspect of criminal procedure rather than offer them in the pure form that the Court first knew.

The most notorious of the coerced confession cases for the 1969 Term was one that had long claimed the attention of New York newspaper readers: *Morales v. New York.*[69] The factual situation is only too familiar to any dweller in a major American city. A passenger in an apartment house elevator was found stabbed to death. The petitioner's mother lived in an apartment in the building and he was informed through her that the police wanted to see him. He agreed to meet them at his mother's place of business. They took him from there to the police station, where, within fifteen minutes of his arrival, he confessed to the murder. He then repeated the confession. The trial court found the confessions voluntary and admitted them in evidence. The jury convicted, rejecting the defense of alibi supplied by defendant's mother.

Petitioner's contention was that there was no probable cause for his arrest and that the confession was consequently illegal. The Supreme Court agreed that the confession was voluntarily made. But it remanded the case to the state courts to determine the basis for the arrest. The Court said that it was not yet prepared to decide

---

[69] 396 U.S. 102 (1969).

whether a "State may detain for custodial questioning on less than probable cause for a traditional arrest."[70] This is obviously one of the important questions of criminal procedure that the Burger Court will be called upon to answer. It is justified in waiting for an appropriate record and lower court opinions on which to base its judgment. Only Mr. Justice Black disagreed. He dissented from the per curiam opinion because he would affirm the validity of the conviction.

Jackson v. Denno[71] continued to plague the Court. There the Court, according to the arch-enemy of the case, Mr. Justice Black, held "that the question of voluntariness of a defendant's alleged confession must be made by the trial judge in a separate proceeding prior to the submission of the confession to the jury, and that insofar as federal questions concerning coercion under the Fifth Amendment were involved the decision of the trial court judge forecloses the jury from passing upon the voluntariness question."[72] The rule, desirable or not, created little difficulty of administration for future trials. It played havoc, however, with cases already tried under a different rule. *Sigler v. Parker*[73] was one of them.

On petition for habeas corpus after exhausting state court remedies, petitioner succeeded in convincing the court of appeals that his confession, not separately evaluated by the trial court judge at the time of his trial, was involuntary. That court ordered a new trial on the merits for him unless the state was prepared to let him go. The Supreme Court rejected this position, saying that "it was error for the Court of Appeals to pass judgment on the voluntariness of the respondent's confession without first permitting a Nebraska court to make such an evaluation uninfluenced by the apparent finding of voluntariness at the 1956 trial."[74] The notion that a meaningful inquiry into fourteen-year-old facts could be made attests the Court's optimism or naïveté. But it is a prospect that the Court frequently indulges rather than face the difficulties that would otherwise result.

Mr. Justice Black dissented because he still thought *Jackson v. Denno* an abomination to be destroyed at the earliest possible moment. He was joined by Chief Justice Burger. Mr. Justice Douglas

---

[70] *Id.* at 104.   [71] 378 U.S. 368 (1964).

[72] Sigler v. Parker, 396 U.S. 482, 484–85 (1970).

[73] Note 72 *supra*.   [74] 396 U.S. at 484.

agreed with their desire to submit the issue of voluntariness to the trial court jury but, so long as the matter was to be determined by a judge, he was more ready to accept the conclusion of the court of appeals than to send it back for further state court proceedings.

Two major confession cases moved the focus to the area that is most likely to provide continuing problems for the Court. They were concerned with pleas of guilty that followed on confessions. The importance of the problem is established by the recognition that a very great proportion of the courts' criminal business is concerned with guilty pleas. Without refinement, something in the nature of 90 percent of the criminal cases in the state and federal systems are disposed of on pleas of guilty. Any step that would reduce this number considerably would endanger the capacities of the courts to continue the present system of administration of criminal justice. What would replace it could be better, but more likely would be worse.

In *McMann v. Richardson*,[75] *Jackson v. Denno* again raised its ugly head. Each of the three petitioners alleged, *inter alia*, that his plea of guilty was induced by a coerced confession, entered before the *Jackson v. Denno* case was decided. The Court of Appeals for the Second Circuit decided in favor of the petitioners: ". . . if in a collateral proceeding a guilty plea is shown to have been triggered by a coerced confession—the plea is vulnerable at least in cases coming from New York where the guilty plea was taken prior to *Jackson v. Denno*."[76] The respondent's pleas had been entered in 1956, 1959, and 1963, respectively; *Jackson v. Denno* was decided in 1964.

In an opinion by Mr. Justice White, the Supreme Court reversed:[77]

> A more credible explanation for a plea of guilty by a defendant who would go to trial except for his prior confession is his prediction that the law will permit his admissions to be used against him by the trier of fact. At least the probability of the State's being permitted to use the confession as evidence is sufficient to convince him that the State's case is too strong to contest and that a plea of guilty is the most advantageous course. Nothing in this train of events suggests that the defendant's plea, as distinguished from his confession, is an involuntary act. His later petition for collateral relief asserting that a *coerced* confession induced his plea is at most a claim that

---

[75] 397 U.S. 759 (1970).   [76] *Id.* at 766.   [77] *Id.* at 769.

the admissibility of his confession was mistakenly assessed and that since he was erroneously advised, either under the then applicable law or under the law later announced, his plea was an unintelligent and voidable act. The Constitution, however, does not render pleas of guilty so vulnerable.

Mr. Justice Black concurred in the opinion, adding his now usual damnation of *Jackson v. Denno.* Mr. Justice Brennan wrote a dissent for himself and Justices Douglas and Marshall. They thought the court of appeals right, especially in the New York situation, that respondent was entitled to a hearing on the question of the voluntary nature of the plea in light of prior confessions.

The *McMann* case is one of the few examples from the 1969 Term where it could be said that a decision was probably different because Burger had succeeded Warren as Chief Justice. The former Chief Justice would probably have voted with Mr. Justice Brennan in this case, with the result that, instead of a reversal, the case would either have been affirmed by an equally divided Court or held over for a new Term.

Parker v. North Carolina[78] presented a similar question to the Court, along with another, and the Court divided as it had in *McMann.* The different issue resulted from a challenge to the validity of a conviction based on a guilty plea where the statute provided that a higher penalty could be imposed after trial than after plea. The second question was whether a prior confession tainted a plea of guilt. On the first point, the Court had just resolved the issue against the petitioner's contention in *Brady v. United States.*[79] On the second, the Court rested on *McMann.*

In *Brady,* the Court held that a plea of guilty under the Lindbergh law was not necessarily coerced because the death penalty could have been assessed after a trial but not on a guilty plea. Subsequent to Brady's plea of guilt, the Supreme Court had held, in *United States v. Jackson,*[80] that the statute was invalid insofar as it drew this distinction between penalties with and without trial. Again speaking through Mr. Justice White, the Court said that the *Jackson* case afforded no succor to *Brady:* "Plainly, it seems to us, *Jackson* ruled neither that all pleas of guilty encouraged by the fear of a possible death sentence are involuntary pleas nor that such

[78] 397 U.S. 790 (1970).

[79] 397 U.S. 742 (1970).   [80] 390 U.S. 570 (1968).

encouraged pleas are invalid whether involuntary or not."[81] The Court was unanimous in its judgment in *Brady*.

Certainly the Court has not seen the last of the problems resulting from plea bargaining, and the close division within the Court in the *Parker* and *McMann* cases suggests that it will be some time, if ever, before an adequate rationale is forthcoming.

3. *Right to counsel.* Certainly *Gideon v. Wainwright*[82] occupies a high place in the Warren Court pantheon. And so too do the series of right-to-counsel cases that followed so hard on the heels of their leader. The roll is too long to call. Nevertheless, when the Burger Court first approached the right-to-counsel problem in still one more of its aspects, its unanimity if not its equanimity was shattered. There was no opinion for the Court in *Coleman v. Alabama*.[83] Mr. Justice Brennan wrote the opinion that announced the judgment of the Court; Justices Black, Douglas, and White, wrote concurring opinions; the Chief Justice and Justices Harlan and Stewart wrote dissents. The continued division in the Court on the issue was thoroughly revealed.

The right-to-counsel question was raised with reference to a preliminary hearing in the Alabama criminal procedure:[84]

> The preliminary hearing is not a required step in an Alabama prosecution. The prosecutor may seek an indictment directly from the grand jury without a preliminary hearing. . . . [U]nder Alabama law the sole purposes of a preliminary hearing are to determine whether there is sufficient evidence against the accused to warrant presenting his case to the grand jury and if so to fix bail if the offense is bailable.

Mr. Justice Brennan, not surprisingly, found that lawyers could be useful to defendants at such preliminary hearings and, therefore, these were a "critical stage" of the adjudicatory process for which the Constitution required appointment of counsel.

Mr. Justice Brennan ran into one difficulty. "[T]he prohibition against use by the State at trial of anything that occurred at the preliminary hearing was scrupulously observed."[85] The Court, therefore, unable to find prejudicial error on the record, remanded

---

81 397 U.S. at 747.

82 372 U.S. 335 (1963).   84 *Id*. at 8.

83 399 U.S. 1 (1970).   85 *Id*. at 10.

the case to the Alabama courts to determine "whether the denial of counsel at the preliminary hearing was harmless error under *Chapman* v. *California*, 386 U.S. 18 (1967)."[86]

Mr. Justice Black, in his separate opinion, rode his *Adamson v. California*[87] horse again, once more decrying the notion that what was at stake was a "fair trial" rather than the enforcement of the particulars spelled out in the right-to-counsel provision of the Sixth Amendment, incorporated by the Fourteenth. Mr. Justice Douglas, too, put in a claim for "strict construction." He found inspiration for this in his Russian travels:[88]

> I was impressed with the need for that kind of strict con-
> struction on experiences in my various Russian journeys. In
> that nation detention *incommunicado* is the common practice,
> and the period of permissible detention now extends for nine
> months. Where there is custodial interrogation, it is clear
> that the critical stage of the trial takes place long before the
> courtroom formalities commence. That is apparent to one who
> attends criminal trials in Russia. Those that I viewed never put
> in issue the question of guilt; guilt was an issue resolved in the
> inner precincts of a prison under questioning by the police.
> The courtroom trial concerned only the issue of punishment.
>   Custodial interrogation is in practice—here and in other na-
> tions—so critical that we would give "criminal prosecutions"
> as used in the Sixth Amendment a strained and narrow mean-
> ing if we held that it did not include that phase.

That the proceedings involved in *Coleman* might not be properly labeled "custodial interrogation" did not seem to occur to the good Justice. In any event, the Justices were as concerned with *Miranda*[89] and *Wade*[90] and other "custodial interrogation" cases as they were with *Coleman*. And, if nothing else, the opinions of Justices Black and Douglas underline once again that one man's "strict construction" is another's "personal predilections."

Mr. Justice White hesitatingly joined what he called the "opinion of the Court," fearful that such a requirement as assignment of counsel at the preliminary hearing stage would cause bypassing or "eliminating the preliminary hearing system entirely."[91] Mr. Justice Harlan agreed with the right-to-counsel conclusion only because

---

[86] *Id.* at 11.   [87] 332 U.S. 46, 68 (1947).   [88] 399 U.S. at 15–16.

[89] Miranda v. Arizona, 384 U.S. 436 (1966).

[90] United States v. Wade, 388 U.S. 218 (1967).   [91] 399 U.S. at 18.

he felt compelled to do so by the more recent precedents of the Court in this area. He dissented on another issue, the propriety of the identification procedure, again only because he felt obligated by stare decisis. The Chief Justice felt no such inhibitions.

The Chief Justice's dissenting opinion served notice that his views about criminal procedure had not changed since his elevation to the Supreme Court from the Court of Appeals for the District of Columbia. He gave every indication that he would try to muster judicial forces at least to stop if not to turn back the imposition of a federal criminal code on state criminal procedures. Certainly his opinion is portentous: [92]

> Certainly as MR. JUSTICE HARLAN and MR. JUSTICE WHITE suggest, not a word in the Constitution itself either requires or contemplates the result reached; unlike them, however, I do not acquiesce in prior holdings that purportedly, but nonetheless erroneously, are based on the Constitution. That approach simply is an acknowledgment that the Court having previously amended the Sixth Amendment now feels bound by its action. While I do not rely solely on 183 years of contrary constitutional interpretation, it is indeed an odd business that it has taken this Court nearly two centuries to "discover" a constitutional mandate to have counsel at a preliminary hearing. Here there is not even the excuse that conditions have changed; the preliminary hearing is an ancient institution.
>
> With deference, then, I am bound to reject categorically MR. JUSTICE HARLAN's and MR. JUSTICE WHITE's thesis that what the Court said lately controls over the Constitution. While our holdings are entitled to deference I will not join in employing recent cases rather than the Constitution, to bootstrap ourselves into a result, even though I agree with the objective of having counsel at preliminary hearings. By placing a premium on "recent cases" rather than the language of the Constitution, the Court makes it dangerously simple for future Courts, using the technique of interpretation, to operate as a "continuing Constitutional convention."

It is obvious that one can find his strict constructionist on either side of a constitutional question. They are usually identifiable by their ready resort to hyperbole in support of their literalness.

Mr. Justice Stewart, in dissent, took exception to a mandate of reversal in the absence of any showing or indeed of any allegation of prejudice to the fairness of the trial by reason of the absence of counsel at the preliminary hearing.

---

[92] *Id.* at 22–23.

4. *Jury trial.* The tendency of the Warren Court to treat the jury, especially in criminal cases, as the palladium of justice again had its repercussion in the work of the 1969 Term. In *Baldwin v. New York*,[93] the issue was whether a state could require nonjury trials for prosecutions involving possible sentences of more than six months' incarceration. The Court again was scattered in the expression of its views. Mr. Justice White wrote the opinion announcing the Court's judgment that a jury trial was required. Justices Black and Douglas concurred separately. The Chief Justice, Mr. Justice Harlan, and Mr. Justice Stewart each wrote a dissenting opinion.

Mr. Justice White put the issue simply:[94]

> In *Duncan* v. *Louisiana*, 391 U.S. 145 (1968), we held that the Sixth Amendment as applied to the States through the Fourteenth, requires that defendants accused of serious crimes be afforded the right to trial by jury. We also reaffirmed the long-established view that so-called "petty offenses" may be tried without a jury. Thus the task before us in this case is the essential if not wholly satisfactory one . . . of determining the line between "petty" and "serious" for purposes of the Sixth Amendment right to jury trial.

Apparently in this age of conformity, the uniqueness of the New York City system that was under review was sufficient to condemn it:[95]

> It is true that in a number of these States the jury provided consists of less than the 12-man, unanimous-verdict jury available in federal cases. But the primary purpose of the jury is to prevent the possibility of oppression by the Government; the jury interposes between the accused and his accuser the judgment of laymen who are less tutored perhaps than a judge or panel of judges, but who at the same time are less likely to function or appear as but another arm of the Government that has proceeded against him. Except for the criminal courts of New York City, every other court in the Nation proceeds under jury trial provisions which reflect this "fundamental decision about the exercise of official power," . . . when what is at stake is the deprivation of individual liberty for a period exceeding six months. This near-uniform judgment of the Nation furnishes us with the only objective criterion by which a line could ever be drawn—on the basis of the possible penalty alone—between offenses which are and which are not regarded as "serious" for purposes of trial by jury.

---

[93] 399 U.S. 66 (1970).   [94] *Id.* at 68.   [95] *Id.* at 72–73.

Justices Black and Douglas concurred specially because they would reject the six-month penalty rule. For them, "the Constitution itself guarantees a jury trial '[i]n all criminal prosecutions' and 'in all crimes.' "[96] Chief Justice Burger agreed with the Black-Douglas reading of the Constitution, but not that the rule was applicable to the states through the Sixth Amendment. It is somewhat of a mystery how the Chief Justice could assert this position here and also join Mr. Justice White's opinion in *Williams v. Florida*.[97] But that is not an unusual kind of problem for Court-watchers.

Mr. Justice Harlan's dissent, joined by Mr. Justice Stewart, presented a mystery of its own. Despite his stalwart adherence to earlier opinions in *Coleman v. Alabama*,[98] he wrote of *Baldwin:* "I cannot, in a matter that goes to the very pulse of sound constitutional adjudication, consider myself constricted by *stare decisis*."[99] He would allow the states the right to nonjury trials in appropriate cases without regard to the six-month penalty sanction.

The *Baldwin* case was tied together, at least in dissent, with *Williams v. Florida*.[100] Mr. Justice Harlan's dissent as well as Mr. Justice Stewart's concerned both cases. *Williams* had, however, not only a jury issue but a Fifth Amendment problem as well. Although the Court remained divided in its views, this time Mr. Justice White was able to announce an opinion for the Court as well as its judgment. The Chief Justice and Justices Harlan and Stewart filed concurring opinions; Mr. Justice Black filed a concurring and dissenting opinion in which Mr. Justice Douglas joined. And Mr. Justice Marshall broke silence to object to the Court's judgment on the jury issue.

The nonjury issue referred to Florida's notice-of-alibi rule:[101]

> . . . in essence a requirement that a defendant submit to a limited form of pre-trial discovery by the State whenever he intends to rely at trial on the defense of alibi. In exchange for the defendant's disclosure of the witnesses he proposes to use to establish that defense, the State in turn is required to notify the defendant of any witnesses it proposes to offer in rebuttal to that defense. Both sides are under a continuing duty

---

[96] *Id*. at 75.

[97] 399 U.S. 78 (1970). See text *infra*, at notes 100–06.

[98] See text *supra*, at notes 83 *et seq*.   [100] 399 U.S. 78 (1970).

[99] 399 U.S. at 118.   [101] *Id*. at 80.

promptly to disclose the names and addresses of additional witnesses bearing on the alibi as they become available. The threatened sanction for failure to comply is the exclusion at trial of the defendant's alibi evidence—except for his own testimony—or, in the case of the State, the exclusion of the State's evidence offered in rebuttal to the alibi.

The Court in reaching its conclusion put much emphasis on the fact that Florida afforded "liberal discovery" to the defendants, "as has apparently every other court which has considered the issue, that the privilege against self-incrimination is not violated by a requirement that the defendant give notice of an alibi defense and disclose his alibi witnesses."[102] The Court decided that, in effect, the defendant surrendered nothing that he would not have had otherwise to surrender by different and more cumbersome processes, except possibly the element of surprise. "We decline to hold that the privilege against compulsory self-incrimination guarantees the defendant the right to surprise the State with an alibi defense."[103]

The jury question was whether Florida could use a six-man jury rather than a twelve-man jury consistently with the requirements of the Sixth Amendment. The Court found no intrinsic values in a twelve-man jury. It thereupon overruled a Supreme Court opinion that held the twelve-man jury a necessary ingredient in a Sixth Amendment jury trial[104] and sustained the Florida procedure as consistent with the requirements of the Sixth Amendment. Few were startled by the permission to the states to use juries of less than twelve. The reduction of the federal requirements in order to accommodate the state procedures within the Sixth Amendment, however, did come as something of a surprise.

The Court closed its opinion with an imperious grant of permission to the national and state legislatures to insist on twelve-man juries if that was their wont:[105]

> We conclude, in short, as we began: the fact that the jury at common law was composed of precisely 12 is a historical accident, unnecessary to effect the purposes of the jury system and wholly without significance "except to mystics." [So much for the Age of Aquarius.] . . . To read the Sixth Amendment as forever codifying a feature so incidental to the real purpose of the Amendment is to ascribe a blind formalism to the

---

102 *Id*. at 83.

103 *Id*. at 86.

104 Thompson v. Utah, 179 U.S. 343 (1898).

105 399 U.S. at 102–03.

Framers which would require considerably more evidence than we have been able to discover in the history and language of the Constitution or in the reasoning of our past decisions. We do not mean to intimate that legislatures can never have good reasons for concluding that the 12-man jury is preferable to the smaller jury, or that such conclusions—reflected in the provisions of most States and in our federal system—are in any sense unwise.

Mr. Chief Justice Burger joined the Court's opinion, happy with the thought that the alibi-notice rule would help prevent cases from needlessly going to trial. Mr. Justice Black also agreed with the six-man jury rule but objected to the alibi rule on the ground that it was the first step in broad pretrial discovery against defendants which he found inconsistent with the Fifth Amendment. Mr. Justice Marshall dissented only on the jury question. For him, the twelve-man jury was a constitutional requirement for both state and federal courts.

Mr. Justice Harlan's dissent found a desirable result on the jury question but at an exorbitant cost:[106]

> The decision evinces, I think, a recognition that the "incorporationist" view of the Due Process Clause of the Fourteenth Amendment, which underlay *Duncan* and is now carried forward into *Baldwin*, must be tempered to allow the States more elbow room in ordering their own criminal systems. With that much I agree. But to accomplish this by diluting constitutional protections within the federal system itself is something to which I cannot possibly subscribe. Tempering the rigor of *Duncan* should be done forthrightly, by facing up to the fact that at least in this area the "incorporation" doctrine does not fit well with our federal structure, and by the same token that *Duncan* was wrongly decided.

Mr. Justice Harlan's opinion was a full-blown attack on the incorporation theory. Both he and Mr. Justice Black seem to have recognized that the replacement of Warren by Burger removed an "incorporationist" and added an *Adamson* jurist. The controversy may well expand with Mr. Justice Blackmun's arrival in place of Fortas, just as it did when the picture changed in the other direction at the time Arthur Goldberg was appointed to try to fill Felix Frankfurter's place.

5. *Right of confrontation.* The right-of-confrontation cases do

---

106 *Id.* at 118.

not augur a latitudinarian reading by the Burger Court of the Sixth Amendment, even where Warren Court decisions could be read to that end. *California v. Green*[107] was one of those cases. Again it was Mr. Justice White who wrote for the Court and again a number of minority opinions were contributed.

Green again reveals a criminal case typical of our time. The defendant was charged with supplying marihuana to a minor in violation of California law. The minor had reported the transaction to the police at the time of his arrest for a drug sale. At defendant's pretrial hearing, the minor, subject to cross-examination by defendant's counsel, told a variant on the original story. At the trial, the witness turned recalcitrant, alleging that he couldn't remember what had taken place in his dealing with the defendant because he was on LSD at the time. The prosecution then introduced the witness' prior statement at the preliminary hearing, as authorized by California law.[108] Defendant was convicted. But the California appellate courts upset the conviction on the ground that decisions of the Supreme Court "impelled" a holding that the statute violated the Confrontation Clause.

The Supreme Court of the United States read its own precedents differently. Mr. Justice White carefully separated the question whether the evidence was inadmissible hearsay from the question of the right of confrontation. There is no congruence between the two rules, even if there was "similarity of the values protected."[109] The Court concluded that "the Confrontation Clause is not violated by admitting a declarant's out-of-court statements, as long as the declarant is testifying as a witness and subject to full and effective cross-examination."[110] The declarant need not have been, as he was in this case, subject to cross-examination at the time of the pretrial declaration. Earlier cases, the Justice pointed out, concerned the very different question of admitting out-of-court statements by persons not amenable to the trial court as witnesses.[111]

---

[107] 399 U.S. 149 (1970).

[108] "Section 1235 of the California Evidence Code . . . provides that 'evidence of a statement made by a witness is not made inadmissible by the hearsay rule if the statement is inconsistent with his testimony at the hearing." *Id*. at 150.

[109] *Id*. at 155.   [110] *Id*. at 158.

[111] Pointer v. Texas, 380 U.S. 400 (1965); Douglas v. Alabama, 380 U.S. 415 (1965); Barber v. Page, 390 U.S. 719 (1968); Bruton v. United States, 391 U.S. 123 (1968).

The pretrial statement in the *Green* case would have been admissible even if the witness were not available because the "statement at the preliminary hearing had already been given under circumstances closely approximating those that surround the typical trial,"[112] including defendant's right of cross-examination.

Chief Justice Burger's opinion again emphasized his desire for loosening the reins the Supreme Court had drawn so tightly on the state courts' power to control their own criminal procedure:[113]

> I add this comment only to emphasize the importance of allowing the States to experiment and innovate especially in the area of criminal justice. If new standards and procedures are tried in one State their success or failure will be a guide to others and to the Congress.

Mr. Justice Harlan concurred in a lengthy opinion justifying his two conclusions:[114]

> First, the Confrontation Clause of the Sixth Amendment reaches no farther than to require the prosecution to *produce* any *available* witness whose declarations it seeks to use in a criminal trial. Second, even were this conclusion deemed untenable as a matter of Sixth Amendment law, it is surely agreeable to Fourteenth Amendment "due process," which, in my view, is the constitutional framework in which state cases of this kind should be judged. For it could scarcely be suggested that the Fourteenth Amendment takes under its umbrella all common-law hearsay rules and their exceptions.

Strangely enough, Mr. Justice Brennan dissented by himself. He concluded:[115]

> In sum, I find [the witness'] real or pretended lapse of memory about the pertinent events casts serious doubt upon the reliability of his preliminary hearing testimony. It is clear that so long as a witness . . . cannot or will not testify about these events at trial, the accused remains unable to challenge effectively the witness' prior assertions about them. The probable unreliability of the prior testimony, coupled with the impossibility of its examination during trial, denies the accused his right to probe and attempt to discredit incriminating evidence. Accordingly, I would hold California Evidence Code, § 1235 in violation of the Confrontation Clause to the extent that it permits the substantive use at trial of prior statements, whether

[112] 399 U.S. at 165.

[113] *Id*. at 171.

[114] *Id*. at 174.

[115] *Id*. at 202–03.

extrajudicial or testimonial, when the declarant is present at trial but unable or unwilling to be questioned about the events with which the prior statements dealt.

Thus, even Mr. Justice Brennan retreated to a narrow position essentially based on the facts of this case rather than the usual broadside that he indulged with Chief Justice Warren and Justice Goldberg as his close allies.

The *Green* case is likely to be of some importance despite the fact that it arrived unheralded. It is far more likely to make a difference at the pretrial stages than the overblown *Miranda* has done. And its weight is on the opposite side of the scale.

The other confrontation case evoked more notoriety because of its peculiarly contemporary ambience. In *Illinois v. Allen*,[116] the question was, as Mr. Justice Black put it, "whether an accused can claim the benefit of this constitutional right to remain in the courtroom [to confront the witnesses against him] while at the same time he engages in speech and conduct which is so noisy, disorderly, and disruptive that it is exceedingly difficult or wholly impossible to carry on the trial." The answer was a resounding negative. "We think there are at least three constitutionally permissible ways for a trial judge to handle an obstreperous defendant like Allen: (1) bind and gag him, thereby keeping him present; (2) cite him for contempt; (3) take him out of the courtroom until he promises to conduct himself properly."[117] Mr. Justice Black didn't think the contempt sanction would be very effective against a person in danger of a very long prison term. But he was certain about the need to maintain courtroom decorum. He concluded his opinion, from which only Mr. Justice Douglas dissented on nonsubstantive grounds, in this way:[118]

> It is not pleasant to hold that the respondent was properly banished from the court for a part of his own trial. But our courts, palladiums of liberty as they are, cannot be treated disrespectfully with impunity. Nor can the accused be permitted by his disruptive conduct indefinitely to avoid being tried on the charges brought against him. It would degrade our country and our judicial system to permit our courts to be bullied, insulted and humiliated and their orderly process thwarted and obstructed by defendants brought before them

---

[116] 397 U.S. 337, 338 (1970).

[117] *Id*. at 343–44.   [118] *Id*. at 346–47.

charged with crimes. As guardians of the public welfare, our state and federal judicial systems strive to administer equal justice to the rich and the poor, the good and the bad, the native and the foreign born of every race, nationality, and religion. Being manned by humans, the courts are not perfect and are bound to make some errors. But, if our courts are to remain what the Founders intended, the citadels of justice, their proceedings cannot and must not be infected with the sort of scurrilous, abusive language and conduct paraded before the Illinois trial judge in this case. The record shows that the Illinois judge at all times conducted himself with that dignity, decorum, and patience that befit a judge.

Mr. Justice Brennan's concurring opinion exhibited no disagreement, only a distaste for binding and shackling and a hope that if a defendant had to be removed some provision might be made so that he could hear and possibly see as well as hear the proceedings, even if from a distant vantage.

Only Mr. Justice Douglas thought this an inappropriate "case to establish the appropriate guidelines for judicial control."[119] The trial occurred in 1957. It was too late now really to determine the defendant's state of mind at that time. The case was "stale." Of course, many cases that reach the Supreme Court by the federal habeas corpus route, equally "stale," are not unacceptable to the Justice for that reason.

Obviously Mr. Justice Douglas was concerned about something other than staleness. He thought the guidelines for proper conduct might differ for two different kinds of cases. The first—he used the example of the trial of William Penn—he called political cases, where obviously the defendants are to be protected from the tyrannies of "law and order" judges. The second:[120]

> . . . are trials used by minorities to destroy the existing constitutional system and bring on repressive measures. Radicals on the left historically have used those tactics to incite the extreme right with the calculated design of fostering a regime of repression from which the radicals on the left hope to emerge as the ultimate victor. The left in that role is the provocateur. The Constitution was not designed as an instrument for that form of rough-and-tumble contest. The social compact has room for tolerance, patience, and restraint, but not for sabotage and violence. Trials involving that spectacle strike at the very heart of constitutional government.

---

119 *Id*. at 351.   120 *Id*. at 356.

Of course, the *Allen* case fell in neither of Mr. Justice Douglas' two categories.

The judicial process, like a university, is a fragile institution. It can be readily destroyed by those who indulge in sabotage and violence unless it is protected against the left, not by the right, but by the "vital center." The possible alternatives to the present judicial process are not pleasant to contemplate.

6. *Juvenile courts.* It was the Warren Court that acknowledged the failure of the mission of the juvenile court experiment. On paper the juvenile courts were to be social agencies for the treatment of wayward youth rather than criminal courts. But the promise was never kept. And the questions of what special procedures could be justified by the facts rather than the hopes had to be resolved by the Supreme Court. It is fairly certain that so long as the juvenile courts mete out punishment rather than treatment, they will be analogized, for purpose of constitutional protections, to the criminal courts dealing with adult offenders.

Twice in the 1969 Term the Court aborted cases, both times over dissents, raising constitutional questions about the propriety of juvenile proceedings.[121] In one case, the Court faced the issue of the standard of proof to be required in juvenile proceedings.

In *In re Winship*,[122] the question was whether, in a juvenile proceeding charging a twelve-year-old boy with commission of an act that would have constituted larceny if done by an adult, proof by a "preponderance of the evidence" rather than proof "beyond a reasonable doubt" would satisfy the constitutional standards. The Court, in an opinion by Mr. Justice Brennan, held that the lesser standard of proof was not acceptable.

Mr. Justice Brennan had first to establish that the Constitution compelled the use of the reasonable doubt standard in cases of adult offenders tried under the ordinary criminal laws:[123]

> Lest there remain any doubt about the constitutional stature of the reasonable doubt standard, we explicitly hold that the Due Process Clause protects the accused against conviction except upon proof beyond a reasonable doubt of every fact necessary to constitute the crime with which he is charged.

---

[121] De Backer v. Brainard, 396 U.S. 28 (1969); Monks v. New Jersey, 398 U.S. 71 (1970).

[122] 397 U.S. 358 (1970).   [123] *Id.* at 364.

Having thus announced a new but not surprising constitutional standard for state and federal criminal proceedings generally, he proceeded to insist that the same standard was demanded in juvenile cases: [124]

> In sum, the constitutional safeguard of proof beyond a reasonable doubt is as much required during the adjudication stage of a delinquency proceeding as are those constitutional safeguards applied in *Gault*—notice of charges, right to counsel, the rights of confrontation and examination, and the privilege against self-incrimination. We therefore hold, in agreement with Chief Judge Fuld in dissent in the Court of Appeals, "that, where a 12-year old child is charged with an act of stealing which renders him liable to confinement for as long as six years, then, as a matter of due process . . . the case against him must be proved beyond a reasonable doubt."

Mr. Justice Harlan, in his concurring opinion, asserted what many have doubted: that there is a real difference between the two standards of proof. Then, adhering to his belief in the chimera of the special nature of juvenile proceedings, he suggested that none of the purposes of the special juvenile proceedings would be adversely affected by the higher standard of proof: [125]

> I wish to emphasize, as I did in my separate opinion in *Gault*, 387 U.S. 1, 65, that there is no automatic congruence between the procedural requirements imposed by due process in a criminal case, and those imposed by due process in juvenile cases. It is of great importance, in my view, that procedural strictures not be constitutionally imposed that jeopardize "the essential elements of the State's purpose" in creating juvenile courts, *id*., at 72. In this regard, I think it worth emphasizing that the requirement of proof beyond a reasonable doubt that a juvenile committed a criminal act before he is found to be a delinquent does not (1) interfere with the worthy goal of rehabilitating the juvenile, (2) make any significant difference in the extent to which a youth is stigmatized as a "criminal" because he has been found to be a delinquent, or (3) burden the juvenile courts with a procedural requirement that will make juvenile adjudications significantly more time consuming, or rigid. Today's decision simply requires a juvenile judge to be more confident in his belief that the youth did the act with which he has been charged.

The fact is, of course, that there are few, if any, of the constitutional procedural requirements imposed on adult cases that would

---

[124] *Id*. at 368.   [125] *Id*. at 374–75.

fall afoul of the three requirements suggested by Mr. Justice Harlan as the distinguishing features of juvenile cases.

The Chief Justice, joined by Mr. Justice Stewart, dissented. His belief in the dream remained unabated:[126]

> My hope is that today's decision will not spell the end of a generously conceived program of compassionate treatment intended to mitigate the rigors and trauma of exposing youthful offenders to a traditional criminal court; each step we take turns the clock back to the pre-juvenile court era. I cannot regard it as a manifestation of progress to transform juvenile courts into criminal courts, which is what we are well on our way to accomplishing. We can only hope the legislative response will not reflect our own by having these courts abolished.

Mr. Justice Black also dissented. But his attack was on the major premise of the Brennan opinion that the Constitution required proof beyond a reasonable doubt in criminal cases generally. He could find no language in the Constitution to support such a conclusion and he was not prepared to find any such requirement in the vagaries of the Due Process Clause:[127]

> I admit a strong persuasive argument can be made for a standard of proof beyond a reasonable doubt in criminal cases— and the majority has made that argument well—but it is not for me as a judge to say for that reason that Congress or the States are without constitutional power to establish another standard that the Constitution does not otherwise forbid. It is quite true that proof beyond a reasonable doubt has long been required in federal criminal trials. It is also true that this requirement is almost universally found in the governing laws of the States. And as long as a particular jurisdiction requires proof beyond a reasonable doubt, then the Due Process Clause commands that every trial in that jurisdiction must adhere to that standard. . . . But when, as here, a State through its duly constituted legislative branch decides to apply a different standard, then that standard, unless it is otherwise unconstitutional, must be applied to insure that persons are treated according to the "law of the land." The State of New York has made such a decision, and in my view nothing in the Due Process Clause invalidates it.

Unless and until the juvenile courts can be demonstrated to be really different in their nature from other criminal courts, the road

---

[126] *Id*. at 376.   [127] *Id*. at 385–86.

on which the Court embarked in *In re Gault*[128] is not likely to be abandoned.

7. *Double jeopardy.* It was late in its tenure that the Warren Court turned its attention to the Double Jeopardy Clause as a basis for inhibiting state criminal prosecutions.[129] But the seeds it sowed promised to be productive and some of their growth was to be seen in the Court's efforts during the 1969 Term.

Waller v. Florida[130] offered an easy problem quick of solution. Petitioner had been convicted of violating two municipal ordinances and was sentenced to jail for destruction of city property and breach of the peace. The acts that were the bases for these convictions were the removal of a mural from the local city hall and carrying it through the streets, with a resultant confrontation with the local police, in the course of which the mural was damaged. Thereafter an information was filed against the petitioner alleging these same acts as a violation of the state's grand larceny statute. Petitioner was tried and convicted of grand larceny and sentenced to a longer term than that imposed under the municipal ordinances, with credit for the time served on the earlier convictions.

The Supreme Court, in an opinion by the Chief Justice, held that the second conviction was a violation of the double jeopardy provisions of the Constitution. It rejected the assertion of separate sovereignties, the municipality and the state. But the opinion's conclusions were narrowly drawn:[131]

> We decide only that the Florida courts were in error to the extent of holding that—
>
> "even if a person has been tried in a municipal court for the identical offense with which he is charged in a state court, this would not be a bar to the prosecution of such person in the proper state court."

Justices Black and Brennan each filed a short concurring opinion, reserving their position of a broader barrier to multiple prosecutions by separate sovereignties.

In the next application of the Double Jeopardy Clause, the Chief Justice's opinion was a dissent, and he stood alone.

---

[128] 387 U.S. 1 (1967).

[129] Benton v. Maryland, 395 U.S. 784 (1969); North Carolina v. Pearce, 395 U.S. 711 (1969).

[130] 397 U.S. 387 (1970).   [131] *Id.* at 395.

Petitioner, in *Ashe v. Swenson*,[132] had been charged as one of three or four men who had robbed six card players convened at a poker game. At the trial for robbery of one of the players, defendant was found not guilty by the jury "due to insufficient evidence." Petitioner was then brought to trial again for robbery of one of the other players. The evidence of defendant's identity at the second trial, adduced through the same witnesses, was much stronger. This time he was convicted.

Prior to the Warren Court's "incorporation" of the Double Jeopardy Clause, the Supreme Court had held in very similar circumstances that the second trial was not a violation of due process of law.[133] The Supreme Court now reversed that position in an opinion by Mr. Justice Stewart. The basis for the change was the ruling that[134]

> collateral estoppel . . . is a part of the Fifth Amendment's guarantee against double jeopardy. And if collateral estoppel is embodied in that guarantee, then its applicability in a particular case is no longer a matter to be left for state court determination within the broad bounds of "fundamental fairness," but a matter of constitutional fact we must decide though an examination of the entire record.

The Court then stated the test of collateral estoppel and found that it clearly barred the second prosecution in this case:[135]

> The federal decisions have made clear that the rule of collateral estoppel in criminal cases is not to be applied with the hypertechnical and archaic approach of a 19th century pleading book, but with realism and rationality. Where a previous judgment of acquittal was based upon a general verdict, as is usually the case, this approach requires a court to "examine the record of a prior proceeding, taking into account the pleadings, evidence, charge, and other relevant matter, and conclude whether a rational jury could have grounded its verdict upon an issue other than that which the defendant seeks to foreclose from consideration." The inquiry "must be set in a practical frame and viewed with an eye to all the circumstances of the proceedings." *Sealfon* v. *United States*, 332 U.S. 575, 579. Any test more technically restrictive would, of course, amount to a rejection of the rule of collateral estoppel in criminal proceedings, at least in every case where the first judgment was based on a general verdict of acquittal.

---

[132] 397 U.S. 436 (1970).

[133] Hoag v. New Jersey, 356 U.S. 464 (1958).

[134] 397 U.S. at 442–43.

[135] *Id.* at 444–45.

Straightforward application of the federal rule to the present case can lead to but one conclusion. For the record is utterly devoid of any indication that the first jury could rationally have found that an armed robbery had not occurred, or that Knight had not been a victim of that robbery. The single rationally conceivable issue in dispute before the jury was whether the petitioner had been one of the robbers. And the jury by its verdict found that he had not. The federal rule of law, therefore, would make a second prosecution for the robbery of Roberts wholly impermissible.

Mr. Justice Black's concurring opinion was typical of many he wrote during the 1969 Term. He wanted to be sure that the judgment rested on the Double Jeopardy Clause and not some amorphous "so-called due process test of 'fundamental fairness.'"[136] Mr. Justice Harlan, bowing to precedent with which he disagreed, concurred, but sought assurance that the Court was not buying the suggested "same transaction test" of the Brennan opinion.

Mr. Justice Brennan, speaking for himself and Justices Douglas and Marshall, would hold that "successive prosecutions for offenses growing out of the same criminal episode" are barred by the Double Jeopardy Clause "at least in the absence of a showing of unavoidable necessity for successive prosecutions in the particular case."[137] The choice of these Justices was a "same transaction test" rather than what they called the "same evidence" test utilized by the Court in its opinion.

The Chief Justice was adamant, if alone:[138]

Nothing in the language or gloss previously placed on this provision of the Fifth Amendment remotely justifies the treatment which the Court today accords to the collateral-estoppel doctrine. Nothing in the purpose of the authors of the Constitution commands or even justifies what the Court decides today; this is truly a case of expanding a sound basic principle beyond the bounds—or needs—of its rational and legitimate objectives to preclude harassment of the accused.

His position rested on the proposition that a second prosecution was barred only if it was for the same offense and here the victims were different and, therefore, the offenses were different. After a parade of horribles, the Chief Justice concluded:[139]

---

136 *Id*. at 447.

137 *Id*. at 460.

138 *Id*. at 460–61.

139 *Id*. at 469.

> What the Court is holding is, in effect, that the second and
> third and fourth criminal acts are "free," unless the accused
> is tried for the multiple crimes in a single trial—something
> defendants frantically use every legal device to avoid, and
> often succeed in avoiding. This is the reality of what the Court
> holds today; it does not make good sense and it cannot make
> good law.

One thing certain about the Court's opinion is that by placing
judgment on the "constitutional fact" notion, the Court has started
down the same path in its double jeopardy cases that it once traveled
with regard to the right-to-counsel cases, and still travels in the
coerced confession cases. Each case must remain unresolved until
the Supreme Court has evaluated the facts. The principles of collateral estoppel, even in the twentieth century, are not easily comprehended or applied, as those who have wrestled with them will attest.
The Court may soon see an ant trail of cases in which it will attempt
to resolve difficult factual questions none of which will afford any
precedent for those that must follow.

A second fount of cases deriving from the Warren Court's decision in *North Carolina v. Pearce*[140] began to affect the Court's
docket. In *Pearce*, the Court had held that after reversal of a first
conviction, a higher sentence after retrial would be invalid if the
higher sentence was attributed to judicial vindictiveness. In *Moon
v. Maryland*,[141] where a second trial did result in a higher sentence,
the Court dismissed the writ of certiorari as improvidently granted.
The dismissal rested on a supplementary statement by the trial
judge, explaining the reasons for the increased sentence and a statement by petitioner's counsel that he had not suggested vindictiveness as a basis for the increased sentence.

From this per curiam disposition, Mr. Justice Black abstained
and concurred separately, obviously because the Court was talking
of a "due process" standard. Mr. Justice Harlan dissented, apparently because he thought that the "due process" standard had been
violated. And Mr. Justice Douglas dissented because of his view
that the Double Jeopardy Clause meant that the sentence on the
first trial set the outside limit and could not be exceeded under any
circumstances by the sentence after retrial.

Once again these cases are not resolvable except by ascertainment
of the facts, facts as elusive as the trial judge's state of mind. Once

---

140 395 U.S. 711 (1969).   141 398 U.S. 319 (1970).

again the ruling necessarily means a major contribution to the Court's business because of what Mr. Justice Stewart called the necessity for the high court to determine for itself issues of "constitutional fact."

Price v. Georgia,[142] on the other hand, was a simple extension to the state courts of a principle theretofore applied in the federal courts. The opinion was written by the Chief Justice. Petitioner, charged with murder, was found guilty of the lesser-included offense of voluntary manslaughter. After that conviction was reversed, defendant was again tried for murder and again found guilty of voluntary manslaughter. Quite clearly, since *Green v. United States*,[143] a similarly situated defendant in the federal courts could not have been tried a second time for murder, on the theory that the conviction of the lesser-included offense was equivalent of a finding of not guilty on the higher offenses. Since the Double Jeopardy Clause was now also applicable to the states, it was agreed that the same rule would be applied there.

The complication in *Price* derived from the fact that the second conviction was for no greater a crime than the first had been. The Court, nevertheless, rejected the claim that this made the indictment for a higher crime "harmless error." The Court recognized the capacities of juries to compromise on a lesser-included offense and that the compromise might have been lower down the scale if the maximum was voluntary manslaughter rather than murder. The Court passed on to the lower courts the question whether defendant could be tried again for voluntary manslaughter. Since, however, the first trial took place in 1962 and the sentence on the voluntary manslaughter charge was ten years' imprisonment, defendant is certainly likely to have completed his sentence before he can be put through still a third trial for the killing of which he was accused, unless, of course, he has been out on bail during the interim.

The *Price* decision is notable for its unanimity but also because it establishes a rule of law that other courts can follow. It is not likely, therefore, to contribute further to the Supreme Court's own business, unless of course the Court should choose to change its collective mind as it has been known to do.

8. *Self-crimination.* The 1969 Term saw three major self-crimination cases decided. One was unanimous; in the other two Justices

---

142 398 U.S. 323 (1970).   143 355 U.S. 184 (1957).

Black and Douglas dissented. The cases may indicate a new trend for the judicial exegesis of one of the Court's most intractable problems.

Minor v. United States[144] was the title applied to two cases concerned—as is so much of the Court's recent business—with the narcotics traffic. In the first of the two cases, James Minor was convicted of selling heroin on two different occasions without a written order on an official form, in violation of the Harrison Act. The second involved similar sales, but of marihuana, by Michael Buie, without the forms required by the Marihuana Act. Both defendants argued that the limitation of sales to those presenting official forms violated the seller's privilege against self-crimination because the form is required to record the seller's name and address. The argument was based on the Court's earlier decisions holding that the obligation imposed on a buyer of narcotics to secure a purchase form and to pay the tax required him to incriminate himself under laws other than that which compelled the registration.[145]

The Court, in an opinion by Mr. Justice Stewart, held that the earlier cases were inapposite. Attempting a "realistic" approach, he asserted that there really was no compulsion under the law to reveal the seller's name because buyers on the illegal market never —hardly ever?—require the completion of the form:[146]

> The situation of the buyer is this: if he applies for the order form he must announce his intention to purchase marihuana— a transaction which, if he is unregistered, will involve a tax of $100 for each ounce of marihuana involved in the impending sale and which is illegal under both federal and state law. We have great difficulty in believing, and nothing in this record convinces us, that one who wishes to purchase marihuana will comply with a seller's request that he incriminate himself with federal and local authorities and pay $100 per ounce in taxes in order to secure the order form. The possibility is particularly unlikely in view of the fact that the Fifth Amendment relieves unregistered buyers of any duty to pay the transfer tax and secure the incriminating order form. . . .
> . . . There is no real and substantial possibility that the

---

[144] 396 U.S. 87 (1969).

[145] Leary v. United States, 395 U.S. 6 (1969); Marchetti v. United States, 390 U.S. 39 (1968); Grosso v. United States, 390 U.S. 62 (1968); Haynes v. United States, 390 U.S. 85 (1968).

[146] 396 U.S. at 92–93.

§ 4742(a) order form requirement will in any way incriminate
sellers for the simple reason that sellers will seldom, if ever,
be confronted with an unregistered purchaser who is willing
and able to secure the order form.

Because, then, the order form is not a real element in the sales of
dope, the seller's name will never be placed thereon so that he will
not have been required to create evidence of his own guilt.

The Court's argument does not seem to meet the objection of
the dissenters, which, incidentally, sounds very much like a due
process argument of the kind usually anathema to Mr. Justice
Black: [147]

As I view the case, the Government is punishing an individual for failing to do something that the Government has
made it impossible for him to do—that is, obtain an order form
from the prospective purchaser prior to making a sale of heroin.
Petitioner did, of course, have the option not to sell the heroin,
and in that sense his compliance with the statute was indeed
quite possible.
. . . it is the order form—not the mere sale—that constitutes
the heart of the offense for which this petitioner was convicted.

It is not quite clear why the two dissenting Justices limited their
dissents to the heroin case. Certainly the argument of the majority
is applicable to both; so, too, is the argument of the dissent. There
are, as the majority points out, differences in the requirements of
the different statutes, but they are not differences of any importance
to either set of arguments.

The difficulty in these cases, as both sets of opinions recognize,
derives from the earlier deviousness of both the Congress and the
Court. Seeking to place a limit on drug sales at a time when the
national power over commerce was not deemed to reach such sales,
the legislature framed the statutes as tax measures. This over-
reaching was sustained by the Court as valid exercise of the taxing
power. And so the Court and Congress are dealing with one problem in terms of an entirely different one. It would have been better
had the Court assumed the necessary boldness to tell Congress, as
Mr. Justice Frankfurter would have had it do in the case of the
gambling tax,[148] that Congress too had an obligation to truth and
honesty.

---

[147] *Id*. at 100.

[148] See United States v. Kahriger, 345 U.S. 22, 37 (1953).

Surely the time has now come for Congress to bail the Court and itself out of the hypocritical situation in which they are placed. There is little doubt that the Congress can regulate the drug traffic directly. It ought to abandon the tax ruse and do its business properly.

United States v. Knox[149] is concerned with the same kind of double-talk in government regulation by taxation of gambling. Knox was charged in a series of counts with violation of the federal law by engaging in gambling proscribed for those who have not registered and with filing false forms when he did get around to compliance with the registration and tax requirements. Again, earlier decisions of the Court had held that the provisions compelling registration and payment of the tax violated the self-crimination provision.[150] And it was appellee's contention that he could not be punished for falsifying forms that the government was forbidden to extract from him. He claimed that he was compelled by the government to do an illegal act for which he was then punished.

On the same day that *Knox* was decided, the Court decided *Bryson v. United States*,[151] which "reaffirmed the holding of *Dennis* v. *United States*, 384 U.S. 855 (1966), that one who furnishes false information to the Government in feigned compliance with a statutory requirement cannot defend against prosecution for his fraud by challenging the validity of the requirement itself."[152] The Court held that the *Bryson-Dennis* rule was equally applicable to *Knox*.

Both the *Bryson* and *Knox* opinions were written by Mr. Justice Harlan. In both cases, Mr. Justice Douglas wrote dissents, joined by Mr. Justice Black. In *Bryson*, where the statute required a "non-Communist affidavit" from union officers, Mr. Justice Douglas concluded:[153]

> In this case, . . . Congress installed an unconstitutional barrier to receipt of the benefits administered by the Labor Board. Since § 9(h), in light of *Brown*, was plainly unconstitutional, petitioner's union was entitled to those services without the filing of any affidavit. Therefore, unlike prior cases, the United

---

[149] 396 U.S. 77 (1969).

[150] Marchetti v. United States, 390 U.S. 39 (1968); Grosso v. United States, 390 U.S. 62 (1968).

[151] 396 U.S. 64 (1969).

[152] 396 U.S. at 79.   [153] 396 U.S. at 76.

States had been deprived of nothing and defrauded of nothing by the filing of any affidavit or other form of claim.

His conclusion was the same in *Knox:* ". . . if the Internal Revenue Service had no constitutional authority to require Knox to file any wagering form at all, his filing of a form which included false information in no way prejudiced the Government and is not, in my view, a matter 'within the jurisdiction' of the Internal Revenue Service."[154]

The majority in *Knox* did, however, concede that if the invalidity of the tax statutes could not be set up in defense of a charge of filing a false return, the question of the "duress" exerted by the statute was a factual matter that would have to be resolved at the trial itself:[155]

> Knox argues that the criminal sanction for failure to file, coupled with the danger of incrimination if he filed truthfully, was more coercive in its effect than, for example, the prospect that the petitioners in *Dennis* would lose their jobs as union officers unless they filed non-Communist affidavits. While this may be so, the question whether Knox's predicament contains the seeds of a "duress" defense, or perhaps whether his false statement was not made "willfully" as required by § 1001, is one that must be determined initially at his trial. It is not before us on this appeal from dismissal of the indictment, and we intimate no view on the matter.

A less controversial issue of self-crimination was presented by *United States v. Kordel,*[156] where the Court unanimously rejected the claim and reversed the lower court judgment. The defendants had been convicted of violation of the Food and Drug Act. The criminal proceeding had followed upon the initiation of a civil proceeding against the corporation of which the defendants were officers. In the civil proceeding, the Government had submitted interrogatories to the corporation. The answers, filed by defendants, had been incriminating. The Court, in an opinion by Mr. Justice Stewart, held that the defendants had not been compelled to supply incriminating answers to the interrogatories. A claim of the privilege against self-crimination would have protected them. They could have asserted the privilege even though the corporation could not. And, if the corporation was required to answer by an officer who would not invoke the privilege, the defendants could have refused to answer at all, if there were no knowledgeable officials who could

---

154 396 U.S. at 86.   155 *Id.* at 83–84.   156 397 U.S. 1 (1970).

not do so without incriminating themselves as individuals. The Court concluded:[157]

> Overturning these convictions would be tantamount to the adoption of a rule that the Government's use of interrogatories directed against a corporate defendant in the ordinary course of a civil proceeding would always immunize the corporation's officers from subsequent criminal prosecution. The Court of Appeals was correct in stating that "the Government may not use evidence against a defendant in a criminal case which has been coerced from him under penalty of either giving the evidence or suffering a forfeiture of his property." But on this record there was no such violation of the Constitution, and no such departure from the proper administration of criminal justice.

Thus, *Knox, Bryson*, and *Kordel* each dealt with a variation of a theme on coercion of testimony and the privilege against self-crimination. Certainly they present questions on the fringes of the self-crimination problem. But then it was the extension of the boundaries of the privilege that was the accomplishment of the Warren Court. These cases are small evidence that the expansion of the privileges has come to a stop. They afford no evidence that a rollback is forthcoming. But the possibility must now be kept in mind by the lower courts and the litigants who appear before them.

9. *Sentencing*. One of the areas into which the Court may be expected to delve more deeply in the future is that of sentencing in criminal cases. Sentencing has been a source of many evils that presently exist in the administration of criminal justice. One of them derives from the fact that the federal appellate courts have no authority to review the propriety of sentences. They have, therefore, quite naturally, looked for other errors in order to eliminate what they believe to be an inappropriately harsh sentence. This has been especially true in capital cases.

The question of the validity of the death sentence was expected to be one of the major issues disposed of by the Burger Court in its first Term. At least the opportunity was there for a landmark decision if the Court chose to take it. But, possibly because of the absence of one Justice whose vote could be determinative, the question was evaded.

Maxwell v. Bishop[158] was on review from a judgment of the

---

[157] *Id.* at 12–13.   [158] 398 U.S. 262 (1970).

Eighth Circuit, whose opinion had been written by Judge Blackmun. It was argued twice before the Supreme Court; once in March,
1969, and again in May, 1970. The defendant had been convicted of
rape and sentenced to death. The attack on the death sentence was
not a direct confrontation. The argument was that the jury had decided the question of guilt and the question of sentence at the same
time and the judge had given the jury no guidance on the appropriate standards for fixing sentence. The Court, after two Terms—and
after the new Justice was commissioned—suddenly realized that the
requirements of *Witherspoon v. Illinois*[159] in the selection of a jury
had not been applied in this case. Jurors were excluded for cause
who announced that they had scruples against the imposition of the
death sentence. The Court, therefore, vacated the grant of certiorari
and remanded to the lower courts to wrestle with the problem of the
application of the *Witherspoon* standards. Lest its public have
thought that it was ducking the question, the Court noted in a footnote that the issue presented by *Maxwell v. Bishop* would be presented again in the 1970 Term in two cases in which certiorari had
been granted.[160]

Sooner or later the death sentence will be abolished. For if the
sanction itself does not constitute cruel and unusual punishment
even in this day of enlightenment, then the extraordinarily long
periods during which convicts must remain in death row awaiting
execution must fall in that category. The ongoing war against the
police and other violence in the streets may militate against a quick
response of the kind suggested. For only the legislature can distinguish cop killers and bomb throwers from other murderers. But it is
to be hoped that this form of violence, too, will pass and that when
the country becomes more civilized, its government will have to be.

The Chief Justice wrote of another aspect of the sentencing problem, the imposition of imprisonment for those unable to pay fines.
The entire Court agreed that in some circumstances this kind of
quid pro quo is unconstitutional, however classic this form of punishment might have been in the past. Strangely the Chief Justice was
not here concerned about "original meaning" and Mr. Justice Black
said nothing about strict construction. But strict construction is only
for due process cases and apparently is not relevant when the Court
is speaking about "equality."

---

159 391 U.S. 510 (1968).   160 398 U.S. at 267 n.4.

Williams v. Illinois[161] did not bar all imprisonment for unpaid fines. Chief Justice Burger was insistent on the limited nature of the holding:[162]

> It bears emphasis that our holding does not deal with a judgment of confinement for nonpayment of a fine in the familiar pattern of alternative sentence "$30 or 30 days." We hold only that a State may not constitutionally imprison beyond the maximum duration fixed by statute a defendant who is financially unable to pay a fine. A statute permitting a sentence of both imprisonment and fine cannot be parlayed into a longer term of imprisonment than is fixed by the statute since to do so would be to accomplish indirectly as to an indigent that which cannot be done directly. We have no occasion to reach the question whether a State is precluded in any other circumstances from holding an indigent accountable for a fine by use of penal sanction. We hold only that the Equal Protection Clause of the Fourteenth Amendment requires that the statutory ceiling placed on imprisonment for any substantive offense be the same for all defendants irrespective of their economic status.

The Chief Justice was not unapologetic for his ruling:[163]

> We are not unaware that today's holding may place a further burden on States in administering criminal justice. Perhaps a fairer and more accurate statement would be that new cases expose old infirmities which apathy or absence of challenge have permitted to stand. But the constitutional imperatives of the Equal Protection Clause must have priority over the comfortable convenience of the status quo. "Any supposed administrative inconvenience would be minimal, since . . . [the unpaid portion of the judgment] could be reached through the ordinary processes of garnishment in the event of default." *Rinaldi v. Yeager*, 384 U.S. 305, 310 (1966).

Mr. Justice Harlan, in a concurring opinion, slashed back at the Black position that demanded specific language in the Constitution to justify action under the Due Process Clause of the Fourteenth Amendment but tolerated broad judicial rulemaking where the reference is to equal protection:[164]

> The "equal protection" analysis of the Court is, I submit, a "wolf in a sheep's clothing," for that rationale is no more than a masquerade of a supposedly objective standard for *sub-*

---

[161] 399 U.S. 235 (1970).

[162] *Id*. at 243–44.

[163] *Id*. at 245.

[164] *Id*. at 259–60, 261–62.

jective judicial judgment as to what state legislation offends notions of "fundamental fairness." Under the rubric of "equal protection" this Court has in recent times effectively substituted its own "enlightened" social philosophy for that of the legislature no less than did in the older days the judicial adherents of the now discredited doctrine of "substantive" due process. I, for one, would prefer to judge the legislation before us in this case in terms of due process, that is, to determine whether it arbitrarily infringes a constitutionally protected interest of this appellant. Due process . . . is more than merely a procedural safeguard; it is also a " 'bulwark . . . against arbitrary legislation.' . . ."

The matrix of recent "equal protection" analysis is that the "rule that statutory classifications which either are based upon certain 'suspect' criteria or affect 'fundamental rights' will be held to deny equal protection unless justified by a 'compelling' governmental interest," . . . I attempted to expose the weakness in the precedential and jurisprudential foundation upon which the current doctrine of "equal protection" sits. . . . I need not retrace the views expressed in these cases, except to object once again to this rhetorical preoccupation with "equalizing" rather than analyzing the *rationality* of the legislative distinction in relation to the legislative purpose.

An analysis under due process standards, correctly understood, is, in my view, more conducive to judicial restraint than an approach couched in slogans and ringing phrases, such as "suspect" classification or "invidious" distinctions, or "compelling" state interest, that blur analysis by shifting the focus away from the nature of the individual interest affected, the extent to which it is affected, the rationality of the connection between legislative means and purpose, the existence of alternative means for effectuating the purpose, and the degree of confidence we may have that the statute reflects the legislative concern for the purpose that would legitimately support the means chosen. . . .

. . . If equal protection implications of the Court's opinion were to be fully realized, it would require that the consequence of punishment be comparable for all individuals; the State would be forced to embark on the impossible task of developing a system of individualized fines, such that the total disutility of the entire fine, or the marginal disutility of the last dollar taken, would be the same for all individuals. . . . Today's holding, and those in the other so-called "equal protection" decisions . . . offer no pretense to actually providing such equal treatment. It cannot be argued that the requirement of counsel on appeal is the right to the most skilled advocate who is theoretically at the call of the defendant of means. However desirable and enlightened a theory of social and economic equality may be, it is not a theory that has the blessing of the Fourteenth Amendment. Not "every major social ill in this country can find its cure in some constitutional 'principle'; and . . . this Court [is not equipped to] 'take the lead' in promoting reform when other branches of government fail to act. The Constitution is not a panacea for every blot upon the public welfare, nor should this Court, ordained as a judicial body, be thought of as a general haven for reform movements."

On the basis of the standards that he suggested were applicable, Mr. Justice Harlan reached the same conclusion as did the Court:[165]

The State by this statute, or any other statute fixing a penalty of a fine, has declared its penological interest—deterrence, retribution and rehabilitation—satisfied by a monetary payment, and disclaimed, as serving any penological purpose in such cases, a term in jail. While there can be no question that the State has a legitimate concern with punishing an individual who cannot pay the fine, there is serious question in my mind whether having declared itself indifferent to fine and jail, it can consistently with due process refrain from offering some alternative for payment on the installment plan.

However much Mr. Justice Harlan may have history and reason on his side, it is obvious that he is bucking a very strong tide. In today's Age of Aquarius, reason has little appeal and history has none. The new American *Zeitgeist* is defined by the equation: "equal = good." And equal is anything that is felt to be equal or felt to be good. The strength of the movement is exemplified by the readiness with which the new Chief Justice adopted the rhetoric even in the face of his other commitments to "strict interpretation" and to "original meaning." Certainly neither the one nor the other is satisfied by the opinion for the Court in *Williams*.

Moreover, the difficulty of application of the narrow holding was quickly revealed in another case of last Term, *Morris v. Schoonfield*.[166] The case was, by per curiam order, remanded to the lower court "for reconsideration in the light of the intervening legislation and our holding in *Williams* v. *Illinois*." Four Justices joined in a concurring opinion that read *Williams* differently than as an expression of its narrow holding. Speaking for himself and Justices Douglas, Brennan, and Marshall, Mr. Justice White said:[167]

I deem it appropriate to state my view that the same constitutional defect condemned in *Williams* also inheres in jailing

---

[165] *Id.* at 264.   [166] 399 U.S. 508 (1970).   [167] *Id.* at 509.

an indigent for failing to make immediate payment of any fine, whether or not the fine is accompanied by a jail term and whether or not the jail term of the indigent extends beyond the maximum term that may be imposed on a person willing and able to pay a fine. In each case, the Constitution prohibits the State from imposing a fine as a sentence and then automatically converting it into a jail term solely because the defendant is indigent and cannot forthwith pay the fine in full.

The Chief Justice, in some extrajudicial remarks, has asserted that law reform is more needed in the area of sentencing and penology than in those areas of criminal procedures for which the Warren Court became famous. It seems that he will have the active cooperation of most of his brethren, at least in adding this realm to, if not substituting it for, their already extensive domain.[168] Whether the doctrine of the lowest common denominator will prove a useful tool remains to be seen.

10. *Speedy trial.* A comparatively dormant provision of the Sixth Amendment, that which guarantees a speedy trial, is also beginning to show new life. Certainly one of the most distressing features of the American system of criminal justice is to be found in the inordinate delay between arrest and ultimate disposition of a criminal case. In part, of course, this has been due to the postulate of defense counsel that all delays work to the benefit of the defendant. In part, it is due to the inadequate staffing of both prosecution and defense counsel offices. In part, it is due to the Supreme Court's own decisions creating ever more bases for appeals and postconviction remedies. And a major responsibility rests on the shoulders of the trial judges who don't spend enough time at their business and lack the courage to force the parties to quick and expeditious procedures.

The Court's decisions on speedy trial tend to deal with esoterica rather than the central problem. *Dickey v. Florida*[169] represents one of the cases at the fringes.

Dickey was tried in 1968 for a crime committed in 1960. The reason for the delay was that Dickey was, in the interim, confined in a federal penitentiary on conviction of another crime. The state of

---

168 An attack upon the California indeterminate sentence system failed when the Court belatedly realized that the alleged facts on which the case was brought were untrue. The Court unanimously dismissed the writ of certiorari as improvidently granted in Conway v. Adult Authority, 396 U.S. 107 (1969).

169 398 U.S. 30 (1970). See also United States v. Sweet, 399 U.S. 517 (1970), where the central question was bypassed because of procedural defects.

Florida had filed a formal detainer with the Chief United States
Marshal to assure Dickey's availability when he was released from
federal prison. After he completed his federal sentence, he was convicted in the state courts of robbery and sentenced to ten years'
imprisonment.

Dickey's claim to denial of a speedy trial was based on his yeoman
efforts during his federal incarceration to secure a trial in the Florida
courts. The Supreme Court agreed with his contentions. The opinion for the Court, by the Chief Justice, after reciting the facts, was
short.[170]

> The right to a speedy trial is not a theoretical or abstract
> right but one rooted in hard reality on the need to have charges
> promptly exposed. If the case for the prosecution calls on the
> accused to meet the charges rather than rest on the infirmities
> of the prosecution's case, as is the defendant's right, the time
> to meet them is when the case is fresh. Stale claims have never
> been favored by the law, and far less so in criminal cases.
> Although a great many accused persons seek to put off the
> confrontation as long as possible, the right to a prompt inquiry
> into criminal charges is fundamental and the duty of the charg-
> ing authority is to provide a prompt trial. This is brought
> sharply into focus when, as here, the accused presses for an
> early confrontation with his accusers and with the State.
> Crowded dockets, the lack of judges or lawyers, and other
> factors no doubt make some delays inevitable. Here, however,
> no valid reason for the delay existed; it was exclusively for
> the convenience of the State. On this record the delay with its
> consequent prejudice is intolerable as a matter of fact and im-
> permissible as a matter of law.

There were no dissents. Mr. Justice Harlan filed a short concurring opinion resting on the Fourteenth Amendment's Due Process
Clause rather than the Sixth Amendment. Mr. Justice Brennan,
however, joined by Mr. Justice Marshall, wrote a lengthy essay on
the general subject of the defendant's right to a speedy trial, with
some emphasis on the fact that the right is the defendant's and only
incidentally that of the state. He asked and answered a series of his
own questions about the meaning of the constitutional guarantee, all
to his own obvious satisfaction. His conclusions were modestly

---

[170] 398 U.S. at 37–38. Some of the problems that can result from a speedy trial
in the second jurisdiction of a prisoner incarcerated by the first are suggested
in another case of last Term, Nelson v. George, 399 U.S. 224 (1970).

stated as not "definitive," and equally modestly characterized as only "arguments of some force." The conclusions were these:[171]

> These comments provide no definitive answers. I make them only to indicate that many—if not most—of the basic questions about the scope and context of the speedy-trial guarantee remain to be resolved. Arguments of some force can be made that the guarantee attaches as soon as the government decides to prosecute and has sufficient evidence for arrest or indictment; similar arguments exist that an accused does not lose his right to speedy trial by silence or inaction, that governmental delay which might reasonably have been avoided is unjustifiable, and that prejudice ceases to be an issue in speedy-trial cases once the delay has been sufficiently long to raise a probability of substantial prejudice. Insofar as these arguments are meritorious, they suggest that the speedy-trial guarantee should receive a more hospitable interpretation than it has yet been accorded.

It cannot be gainsaid that "many—if not most—of the basic questions about the scope and context of the speedy-trial guarantee remain to be resolved." Perhaps it is not inappropriate to note that the federal law is more remiss in this regard than that of most of the states. And it also seems that this is an appropriate subject for legislative action, lest the long-drawn-out process of case-by-case adjudication attenuate even further the long delays between arrest and ultimate disposition.

Despite the new vigor displayed in *Dickey*, the Court seemed agreed that a fugitive was not entitled to judicial process so long as he was a fugitive. In a per curiam opinion, the Court in *Molinaro v. New Jersey*[172] dismissed an appeal on being informed that the appellant was a fugitive. "While such an escape does not strip the case of its character as an adjudicable case or controversy, we believe it disentitles the defendant to call upon the resources of the Court for determination of his claims."[173] For reasons best known only to himself, Mr. Justice Douglas concurred only in the judgment. It is hard, indeed, to discern what it was in the per curiam statement with which he was not ready to agree.

11. *Trial transcripts.* *Griffin v. Illinois*,[174] compelling states to supply transcripts or their equivalent to indigent appellants in criminal cases, was a watershed opinion in the development of the equal-

---

171 398 U.S. at 56–57.

172 396 U.S. 365 (1970).

173 *Id.* at 366.

174 351 U.S. 12 (1956).

ity doctrine. Last Term's opinion on the subject, *Wade v. Wilson*,[175] holds no such promise. Mr. Justice Brennan's opinion for the Court rejected the claim that where there were multiple defendants each must be supplied with a transcript of his own. State rules did require that in the event of a death sentence, each codefendant was entitled to a separate transcript. And the defendant, here convicted of murder and sentenced to life imprisonment, argued that equality demanded the same treatment for him. He had had access to a copy for purposes of his appeal, but wanted one now for purposes of preparing post-conviction proceedings.

The Court suggested that, since petitioner had not exhausted his possibilities of borrowing a copy for use, he had no constitutional right to have a copy of his own supplied to him. Mr. Justice Black would have dismissed the writ as improvidently granted.[176]

> This case is but another of the multitudinous instances in which courts are asked interminably to hash and rehash points that have already been determined after full deliberation and review. One considered appeal is enough, in the absence of factors which show a possibility that a substantial injustice has been inflicted on the defendant.

Apparently, at least one Justice is prepared to call a halt to the expansion of post-conviction remedies, for which the Supreme Court itself must bear primary responsibility.

12. *Statutory presumptions and inferences.* Congress has, from time to time, assumed to tell the courts when, in the application of a statute, proof of one fact shall be considered sufficient proof of a different fact. And the Supreme Court has determined, from time to time, that some of these statutory presumptions went beyond the realm of reasonableness and were, therefore, invalid. *Turner v. United States*[177] presented the problem again in most familiar circumstances.

When the car in which the petitioner was a passenger was stopped by narcotics agents, the agents recovered a package thrown away by petitioner which contained cocaine. Search of the car revealed another package containing heroin. Petitioner was convicted of four narcotics violations. The charges were (1) receiving, concealing, and facilitating the transportation and concealment of heroin,

---

[175] 396 U.S. 282 (1970).

[176] *Id.* at 289.   [177] 396 U.S. 398 (1970).

knowing the heroin to have been illegally imported; (2) purchasing, possessing, and distributing heroin that was not in the original stamped package; (3) and (4) were the same except that the subject matter was cocaine.

No evidence was offered by the Government as to the origin of the drugs. But the trial court instructed the jury that on the importation counts, (1) and (3), it could infer from proof of possession that the drugs were imported. These instructions rested on 21 U.S.C. § 174: ". . . possession shall be deemed sufficient evidence to authorize conviction unless the defendant explains the possession to the satisfaction of the jury." On the stamped package charges, the judge read to the jury the provisions of 26 U.S.C. § 4704(a): " . . . the absence of appropriate tax paid stamps from narcotic drugs shall be prima facie evidence of a violation of this subsection."

In an opinion by Mr. Justice White, the Court held: The § 174 presumption was valid with regard to heroin possession because almost all heroin is imported in this country. The § 174 presumption was invalid with regard to the cocaine because some is domestically produced and there is much of it available from legal sources. The § 4704(a) prima facie evidence rule is sustainable as to the heroin count, but not as to the cocaine. The moral of the case for dope peddlers is to stick to cocaine and eschew heroin.

There is a little irony in the fact that the arrests here occurred just after petitioner's car had emerged from the Lincoln Tunnel on the New Jersey side so that violation of a straightforward statutory ban on transportation of drugs in interstate commerce would have been easy to prove. But corkscrew laws make for corkscrew problems and corkscrew judicial opinions.

Mr. Justice Marshall concurred, but would distinguish between the purchase and distribution charges. He thought that the evidence supported proof of illegal distribution but not of illegal purchase.

Mr. Justice Black dissented and was joined by Mr. Justice Douglas in one of the senior Justice's less restrained opinions. After a tirade against the "activist" philosophy of some of his brethren, he went on to tell Congress to mind its own business and not try to instruct the courts on presumptions and inferences which were strictly judicial business. He concluded by telling Congress to mend its ways and, if it chose, to make possession of drugs illegal, since it could constitutionally do so in a straightforward manner. He rejected the notion that the Court rewrite the statute to give it a meaning that its words did not warrant.

In the field of criminal procedure, it was Mr. Justice White who was most often the spokesman for the Court, writing nine of the nineteen signed majority or plurality opinions. Moreover, he registered not a single dissent in any of the nineteen cases. The next most consistent majoritarian was Mr. Justice Stewart. Between them they made the pole around which a majority coalesced. The two who most frequently dissented were Justices Black and Douglas. But the Chief Justice, usually in the cases in which the other two were with the Court, was also a major dissenter from the Court's opinions in this area. It is obvious that the Chief Justice and his two senior associates are pulling in opposite directions. Whether, with or without additional changes in judicial personnel, the Chief Justice will be able to move the Court away from the tendencies of the Warren Court is doubtful. But his position is clear and not unreflective of his work in this field while he was a judge of the Court of Appeals for the District of Columbia Circuit. Thus, some predictions about his behavior have been vindicated.

D. FREEDOM OF SPEECH AND ASSOCIATION

1. *Freedom to dissent.* Just as the current phenomenon of widespread drug addiction gives rise to so many of the Court's criminal cases, so too does the equally widespread phenomenon of the "street revolution" present the Court with many of its First Amendment problems. Again it was the Warren Court that first encountered the issues, originally with regard to the desegregation problem. And so it was the Warren Court that established the major guidelines for the attempted accommodation of the law to peaceful dissent.

The label of nonviolence has been appropriate to many recent expressions of dissent, but that label is becoming more a catchword than a description. The essence of the Court's problem derives from the fact that if it cannot condone illegal acts because they are politically motivated, neither can it condone suppression of legal activity because of its political motivation. Violence remains the antithesis of law, whether indulged by individuals or by the state. And the courts can offer neither an adequate avenue to revolution nor an adequate means for preventing it.

In a way, the thin line that the Court must walk is reflected in its decision in *Bachellar v. Maryland*.[178] Petitioners in that case had been convicted of "acting in a disorderly manner to the disturbance of the peace." The events leading to the convictions are the daily fare of American newspapers. Some fifteen protesters, under the watchful eyes of the Baltimore police and United States marshals, picketed a United States army recruiting center in Baltimore. The picket signs were, certainly by contemporary standards, decorous. The number of protesters grew through the early afternoon to thirty or forty. And they attracted attention and the appearance of others unaffiliated with their group or their ideas. The protesters engaged in leaflet distribution and discussion with members of their audience, in addition to picketing. About 3:30 P.M. the petitioners entered the station and requested that their antiwar materials be displayed in the windows of the station. Not surprisingly, the request was refused and, not surprisingly, the petitioners staged a "sit-in."

Just before 5:00 P.M., the petitioners were requested to leave so that the recruiting station could be closed. They refused to go and were removed by the marshals and the police. There is disputed evidence as to the force that was used and about whether petitioners' subsequent occupation of the sidewalk was voluntary or, as they said, forced upon them by the police. The police testimony was that the petitioners were told to desist from blocking the sidewalk but that they chose to remain. The petitioners alleged that, having been thrown to the sidewalk in the course of their removal from the station, they were forced to remain there by the police until they were thrown into a patrol wagon. The crowd that collected could be described as unfriendly but not unruly.

The trial judge's instructions to the jury set out the alternative factual bases on which a conviction of guilty could be rested. One of them was clearly unconstitutional. Since the general verdict of guilty did not reveal whether it rested on valid or invalid grounds, the Supreme Court upset the conviction. Mr. Justice Brennan spoke for a unanimous Court in stating his conclusion:[179]

> On this record, if the jury believed the State's evidence, petitioners' conviction could constitutionally have rested on a finding that they sat or lay across a public sidewalk with the intent of fully blocking passage along it, or that they refused

---

[178] 397 U.S. 564 (1970).   [179] *Id.* at 571.

to obey police commands to stop obstructing the sidewalk in this manner and move on. . . . It is impossible to say, however, that either of these grounds was the basis for the verdict. On the contrary, so far as we can tell, it is equally likely that the verdict resulted "merely because [petitioners' views about Vietnam were] themselves offensive to some of their hearers." . . . Thus, since petitioners' convictions may have rested on an unconstitutional ground, they must be set aside.

In another case of protest, *Stotland v. Pennsylvania*,[180] the Court was presented with a more difficult problem. Its disposition was somewhat strange. *Stotland* raised the seemingly important question of the validity of the exercise of "emergency powers" by a municipality that prohibited the gathering of groups of more than twelve people. The powers were invoked by the mayor of Philadelphia following the assassination of Martin Luther King. "Appellants were arrested for peaceful, nonviolent participation in outdoor gatherings of 12 or more persons in violation of the proclamation."[181] The Court dismissed the appeals from convictions on the ground that they presented "no substantial federal question." Mr. Justice Douglas dissented from the denial of review. Justices Brennan and Marshall did not participate in the disposition of the case.

There may have been good reasons why the Court chose not to accept this case as the vehicle for disposing of this issue. Because the case was on appeal and not on certiorari, however, the Court's discretion to refuse review was theoretically limited to cases affording no substantial federal question. And so the proper words were intoned, but they lacked sincerity. Mr. Justice Douglas' dissenting opinion made out the case for the importance of the question. No prior decisions of the Court could be cited to show that the question had been previously resolved.

The Court ought not to be forced to such a show of hypocrisy. If the Court's appellate jurisdiction should be totally discretionary— as it should—the jurisdictional statutes should be amended to that effect. So long as the congressional mandate makes the jurisdiction compulsory unless the case is frivolous or insubstantial, the Court ought to be sufficiently law-abiding to entertain the case on the merits and not to retreat to an empty verbal formula for its disposition. One can be sure that the issue will be back, that the Court will find it both substantial and difficult of resolution, and that it

---

[180] 398 U.S. 916 (1970).   [181] *Id.* at 917.

will ignore the precedent it has purportedly established in *Stotland*.

The attack on the utilization of disturbing-the-peace statutes to prosecute dissenters was again mounted in *Gunn v. University Committee to End War in Vietnam.*[182] Again it failed for procedural reasons. The case arose from events surrounding President Johnson's December, 1967, speech in Texas, where his audience of 25,000 included a substantial number of soldiers from nearby Fort Hood. Appellees arrived at the edge of the crowd carrying picket signs "signifying their strong opposition to our country's military presence in Vietnam."[183] They were immediately set upon and assaulted by members of the crowd and were removed by military police who turned them over to civilian authorities. They were charged in the Texas courts with disturbing the peace.

Appellees then brought suit in the federal district court to enjoin their prosecution on the ground that the statute was invalid on its face and as applied to them. The Texas statute is not typical. It provides:[184]

> "Whoever shall go into or near any public place, or into or near any private house, and shall use loud and vociferous, or obscene, vulgar or indecent language or swear or curse, or yell or shriek or expose his or her person to another person of the age of sixteen (16) years or over, or rudely display any pistol or deadly weapon, in a manner calculated to disturb the persons present at such place or house shall be punished by a fine not exceeding Two Hundred Dollars ($200)."

Shortly after the commencement of the federal suit, the state prosecution was dismissed on the ground that the alleged crime had taken place on a military enclave over which the state had no jurisdiction. The defendants in the federal action unsuccessfully moved to dismiss. The federal three-judge court ruled that the statute was invalid on its face because it was "impermissibly and unconstitutionally broad."[185]

An appeal was taken directly to the Supreme Court of the United States. There no concern was shown about the standing of plaintiffs to maintain the action and no doubts were raised about the propriety of enjoining the state criminal cases already commenced. But, in an opinion by Mr. Justice Stewart, the Court dismissed the appeal for

---

182 399 U.S. 383 (1970).

183 *Id.* at 384.

184 *Id.* at 385.

185 *Id.* at 386.

want of jurisdiction in the absence of any injunction issued by the lower court:[186]

> That requirement is essential in cases where private conduct is sought to be enjoined. . . . It is absolutely vital in a case where a federal court is asked to nullify a law duly enacted by a sovereign State.

Mr. Justice White concurred, expressing the view, on a question that the Court specifically refused to consider,[187] that appeal would lie to the court of appeals. In this he was joined by Mr. Justice Brennan.

Perhaps the surprising element in the case is the amount of time that it took for the Court to reach this conclusion. The case was first argued before the Court at the 1968 Term. It was reargued on April 29 and 30, 1970, and decided on June 29, 1970. It was not a good example to set for courts that were being exhorted to enforce the requirements of speedy trial.

Unlike *Gunn* and *Stotland*, however, *Schacht v. United States*[188] was a case in which the Court specifically overrode a procedural defect in order to declare a federal statute unconstitutional in part. This case arose out of what has come to be called "guerrilla theater." The defendant performed in a "skit" in front of an army induction center. In the uniform—or part of one—of an American soldier, he went through the motions of "shooting" a person dressed as a Vietnamese peasant and then announced that he had "killed a pregnant woman."

Section 702 of the Criminal Code makes it a crime to wear the uniform or a part thereof without authority. Section 772(f), however, permits the wearing of a uniform of the United States military forces as an actor in a theatrical or motion picture production, but only "if the portrayal does not tend to discredit that armed force." Defendant was convicted of violating § 702 and was sentenced to the maximum penalty of six months in prison and a fine of $250.

The Court sustained the validity of § 702 standing by itself. But it ruled that defendant's actions were in the course of a theatrical performance and that the qualification on the exemption in terms

---

[186] *Id*. at 389. See also Goldstein v. Cox, 396 U.S. 471 (1970); Rockefeller v. Catholic Medical Center, 397 U.S. 820 (1970); Mitchell v. Donovan, 398 U.S. 427 (1970).

[187] 399 U.S. at 390 n. 6.   [188] 398 U.S. 58 (1970).

of not discrediting the armed force whose uniform was used was an invalid qualification. The opinion for the Court was written by Mr. Justice Black. The Court said:[189]

> In the present case Schacht was free to participate in any skit at the demonstration that praised the Army, but under the final clause of § 772(f) he could be convicted of a federal offense if his portrayal attacked the Army instead of praising it. In light of our earlier finding that the skit in which Schacht participated was a "theatrical production" within the meaning of § 772(f), it follows that his conviction can be sustained only if he can be punished for speaking out against the role of our Army and our country in Vietnam. Clearly punishment for this reason would be an unconstitutional abridgment of freedom of speech. The final clause of § 772(f), which leaves Americans free to praise the war in Vietnam but can send persons like Schacht to prison for opposing it, cannot survive in a country which has the First Amendment. To preserve the constitutionality of § 772(f) that final clause must be stricken from the section.

The Government had contended that the case should be dismissed because the petition for certiorari was not filed within the time specified by Rule 22(2) of the Rules of the Court. The thirty-day period had clearly been exceeded; petitioner's filing came one hundred and one days after that period had expired. The Court held the delay excusable and the thirty-day requirement not to be a jurisdictional one but rather one subject to waiver by the Court.

Mr. Justice Harlan concurred with the opinion on the merits and with the conclusion on the procedural issue. After examination of the precedents and the origins of Rule 22(2) he asserted that while the Court was not free to waive time requirements imposed by legislation, Congress had given it the needed discretion with regard to time requirements imposed by its own rules.

Three Justices, the Chief Justice and Justices White and Stewart, in an opinion by Mr. Justice White, concurred in the result of reversal but were of the view that the question whether the "skit" was a "theatrical production" was a matter for jury resolution under proper instructions by the Court.

The ruling on the merits is likely to have less of an effect than the ruling on the flexibility of the time requirements for bringing a case to the Court. The view expressed in *Schacht* has been taken before by the Court, but hidden in footnotes. The declaration in this

---

[189] *Id.* at 63.

case, supported by all nine Justices, that the time requirement is not jurisdictional will contribute measurably to the Court's business.

Times being what they are, the problems of dissent will continue to come to the Court for resolution. Perhaps one should not be discontent with this prospect. Litigants, at least, are operating within the system. And, if the courts cannot resolve the difficult social problems that give rise to this litigation, they can provide both a safety valve and a model for the peaceable resolution of controversy.

2. *Defamation.* The law of defamation was raised to constitutional stature by the Warren Court's opinion in *New York Times Co. v. Sullivan.*[190] If the Court there did not accept Mr. Justice Black's proposition that even defamation is protected by the First Amendment, it came close to it. It and the cases that have followed have held that, at least with reference to the public press, a libel is not actionable in the absence of a demonstration of malice. And while the *New York Times* case purported to make some requirement that the person defamed be a public official or at least engaged in public activities in order to invoke the protection of the First Amendment, that requirement, too, seems more formal than real. Almost by definition, a person worthy of newspaper comment is a public figure. The Supreme Court had developed its theme in a long series of cases.[191] And the 1969 Term saw the addition of two more.

One of them was disposed of by per curiam order.[192] Senator Goldwater had successfully secured a judgment against *Fact* magazine and Ralph Ginzburg for libeling him in the course of the 1964 presidential campaign. The Court of Appeals for the Second Circuit sustained a jury verdict that found actual malice in the publication of articles that in effect asserted Goldwater's insanity. The jury had brought in a verdict of $1.00 in actual damages and punitive damages of $25,000 against Ginzburg and $50,000 against *Fact* magazine. The Supreme Court denied certiorari. Justices Black and Douglas dissented. They did not suggest that the jury did not properly find malice, in the form of "reckless disregard of the truth." But they adhered to their consistent position that even malicious libel is protected against damage actions by the First Amendment.

---

[190] 376 U.S. 254 (1964).

[191] See, *e.g.*, Beckley Newspaper Corp. v. Hanks, 389 U.S. 81 (1967); St. Amant v. Thompson, 390 U.S. 727 (1968); Pickering v. Board of Education, 391 U.S. 563 (1968).

[192] Ginzburg v. Goldwater, 396 U.S. 1049 (1970).

Of course, the denial of certiorari is not to be taken as an affirmance. But it cannot help encouraging the lower courts to understand that the Black-Douglas position remains a minority view. And, difficult as it may be to show malice, the possibility continues to exist.[193]

The other case, *Greenbelt Pub. Ass'n v. Bresler*,[194] followed the more usual course for progeny of the *New York Times* case by upsetting a judgment against the newspaper. Petitioner, publisher of a local weekly, had reported meetings at which the respondent, "a prominent local real estate developer," was engaged in negotiations with the town council to obtain zoning variances. The newspaper reported that at the public meetings some persons present had characterized the respondent's conduct of the negotiations as "blackmail." Respondent sued in the state court and recovered a judgment of $5,000 in actual damages and $12,500 in punitive damages, as awarded by the jury.

In an opinion for the Court, Mr. Justice Stewart bypassed the question whether respondent was a "public figure." The Court found sufficient error in the instructions to the jury to command reversal, because on the instructions the jury might have predicated liability "merely on the basis of a combination of falsehood and general hostility."[195] Since the general verdict did not reveal whether the jury verdict rested on improper instructions, the judgment had to be reversed.

The Court was not satisfied, however, to rest its judgment on this point of constitutional law. It chose to examine the entire record to determine whether the suit threatened to interfere with the freedom of the press. It concluded that "the reports were accurate and full."[196] Moreover, it concluded that "even the most careless readers must have perceived that the word was no more than rhetorical hyperbole [hyperbolic rhetoric?]."[197] Thus, assuming the role of the jury, the Court brought in a verdict for petitioner.

Mr. Justice White, concurring, agreed that the charge could have misled the jury. But he took exception to the Court's determination of the facts:[198]

---

[193] Cf. Time, Inc. v. Bon Air Hotel, 393 U.S. 859 (1968).

[194] 398 U.S. 6 (1970).   [196] *Id*. at 13.

[195] *Id*. at 10.   [197] *Id*. at 14.   [198] *Id*. at 22.

> What the Court does hold on the cold record is that the trial judge, the jury, and the Maryland Court of Appeals were quite wrong in concluding that "ordinary readers" could have understood that a crime had been charged. If this conclusion rests on the proposition that there was no evidence to support a judgment that the charge of blackmail would be understood by the average reader to import criminal conduct, I cannot agree. The very fact that the word is conceived to have a double meaning in normal usage is itself some evidence; and without challenging the reading of the jury's verdict by the Maryland Court of Appeals, I cannot join the majority claim of superior insight with respect to how the word "blackmail" would be understood by the ordinary reader in Greenbelt, Maryland.

One is tempted to ask what if a reading of the record had convinced the Court that an accusation of crime had been falsely and knowingly made? Would the Court then order judgment for the respondent? The literalists among the Court's members might also take another look at the Seventh Amendment, which says that "no fact tried by a jury, shall be otherwise reexamined in any Court of the United States, than according to the rules of the common law."

3. *Postal regulations.* The Court's antipathy to postal censorship did not carry over to censorship exercised by the postmaster at the behest of the recipient of unwanted mail. Most recipients of mail advertising will applaud the judgment in *Rowan v. Post Office Dept.*[199] And if many of them take advantage of the opportunities implicit in the Court's decision, a serious inroad can be made in the avalanche of junk mail that is polluting the postal service.

The case results from some legislation passed by Congress in its concern for the recipient of advertising for pornographic materials. A narrow reading of the statute by a three-judge district court was rejected by the high court in favor of an expansive protection of the consumer.

In 1967, Congress enacted § 4009 of Title 39; it is entitled "Prohibition of pandering advertisements in the mails." The statutory scheme was described by the Chief Justice, speaking for a unanimous Court, in this way:[200]

> It provides a procedure whereby any householder may insulate himself from advertisements that offer for sale "matter which the addressee in his sole discretion believes to be erotically arousing or sexually provocative." . . .

---

[199] 397 U.S. 728 (1970).   [200] *Id.* at 729–30.

Subsection (b) mandates the Postmaster General upon receipt of a notice from the addressee specifying that he has received advertisements found by him to be within the statutory category, to issue on the addressee's request an order directing the sender and his agents or assigns to refrain from further mailings to the named addressees.

In addition the statute provides for the removal of the addressee's name from all mailing lists controlled by the sender. In the event of failure to comply, the Postmaster General will hold a hearing and, if appropriate, seek enforcement of the order through the Attorney General in the federal courts.

Appellants brought a suit for a declaratory judgment that the statute was invalid as an infringement of their First Amendment rights and their right not to have property taken without due process of law. They also contended that the statute was unconstitutionally vague.

The trial court sustained the statute but construed it to mean that the mailer was prohibited only from sending "advertisements" similar to those sent earlier and that an objective standard would be applied on the question of similarity. The Supreme Court agreed that the statute was valid but rejected the narrow construction.

After an examination of the legislative history, the Court concluded: [201]

The legislative history of subsection (a) thus supports an interpretation that prohibits all future mailings independent of any objective test. . . .

It would be anomalous to read the statute to affect only similar material or advertisements and yet require the Postmaster General to order the sender to remove the addressee's name from all mailing lists in his actual or constructive possession. The section was intended to allow the addressee complete and unfettered discretion in electing whether or not he desired to receive further material from a particular sender.

If the recipient of any advertising is free to determine the meaning of "pandering" or what is "erotically arousing or sexually provocative," mail advertising may well be substantially reduced beyond those areas at which Congress was aiming. But the constitutional argument made by the Court in support of the validity of the statute is in no way dependent upon the erotic nature of the

---

[201] *Id.* at 734.

literature thus banned. The Court specifically recognized that the ban may well extend to a "dry goods catalog":[202]

> In today's complex society we are inescapably captive audiences for many purposes, but a sufficient measure of individual autonomy must survive to permit every householder to exercise control over unwanted mail. To make the householder the exclusive and final judge of what will cross his threshold undoubtedly has the effect of impeding the flow of ideas, information, and arguments that, ideally, he should receive and consider. Today's merchandising methods, the plethora of mass mailing subsidized by low postal rates, and the growth of the sale of large mailing lists as an industry in itself have changed the mailman from a carrier of primarily private communications, as he was in a more leisurely day, and have made him the adjunct of the mass mailer who sends unsolicited and unwanted mail into every home. It places no strain on the doctrine of judicial notice to observe that whether measured by pieces or pounds, Everyman's mail today is made up overwhelmingly of material he did not seek from persons he does not know. And all too often it is matter he finds offensive.
>
> . . . Nothing in the Constitution compels us to listen or to view any unwanted communication, whatever its merit; we see no basis for according the printed word or pictures a different or more preferred status because they are sent by mail.

The Court quickly disposed of the due process and vagueness arguments. Mr. Justice Brennan, joined by Mr. Justice Douglas, wrote a concurring opinion indicating that they would not allow the householder to cut off mail directed to older children. The statute allows control for mail directed to all under the age of nineteen. But that question was not in issue in this case.

It is a little surprising that Mr. Justice Black joined the opinion in light of the Chief Justice's proposition that "the right of every person 'to be let alone' must be placed in the scales with the right of others to communicate."[203] The senior Justice has heretofore seemed allergic to any suggestion of balancing where freedom of speech or press has been involved.

The opinion is heartening if it is really a forerunner of others that will afford protection to audiences as well as speakers. Whether it is or not will probably be dependent on further legislative action. But it may prove to be that the judgment in *Rowan* will not extend beyond areas of commercial communications.

---

[202] *Id*. at 736–37.   [203] *Id*. at 736.

4. *Obscenity.* One of the staples of the Warren Court era was missing from the opinions of the Court in the 1969 Term. Invalidating anti-obscenity legislation had been commonplace. The omission may merely be a lull between storms. Both the executive and legislative branches of the national government have turned their attention to the subject.[204] The product that results from these activities may well provide grist for the Supreme Court mill. Certainly some of the Justices will continue to press for control over obscenity censorship even if a majority do not.[205]

The First Amendment cases of the 1969 Term afforded no decisions likely to be seminal in the development of the law. None afforded new doctrine. There was no indication of any hasty retreat from the frontiers so recently established by the Warren Court.

E. JURY TRIAL

The jury and the expansion of its use was another notable achievement of the Warren era. This attitude continues to be reflected in the cases dealing with criminal procedure, as the materials already discussed so clearly demonstrate.[206] The same inclination existed with regard to civil matters.

In *Ross v. Bernhard*,[207] the Court extended the right to jury trial to stockholder's derivative actions with regard to those claims as to which the corporation would have had a right to jury trial if it had itself been the plaintiff. The majority opinion by Mr. Justice White acknowledged the history of the derivative suit, a creature of equity originated to provide relief for corporate stockholders against corporate officers because no remedy at law existed. And he conceded that: "What can be gleaned from this Court's opinions is not inconsistent with the general understanding, reflected by the

---

[204] See, *e.g.*, REPORT OF PRESIDENTIAL COMMISSION ON OBSCENITY AND PORNOGRAPHY (1970); *Antiobscenity Legislation, Hearings before Subcommittee No. 3 of the Committee on the Judiciary, House of Representatives*, 91st Cong., 2d Sess., Ser. 21 (1970).

[205] See, *e.g.*, Byrne v. Karalexis, 396 U.S. 976 (1969), where Justices Douglas, Black, and Stewart filed separate opinions on a motion to stay enforcement of an injunction against showing of the motion picture "I Am Curious (Yellow)." The merits will be reached in the 1970 Term. 397 U.S. 985 (1970).

[206] See text *supra*, at notes 93–106.   [207] 396 U.S. 531 (1970).

state court decisions and secondary sources, that equity could resolve corporate claims of any kind without a jury when properly
pleaded in derivative suits complying with the equity rules."[208]
Furthermore, as he noted, "until the action of the District Court
below *DePinto*[209] was alone in holding that a right to a jury trial
existed in diversity actions."[210]

Nevertheless, an amalgam of differing factors was read to mean
that the Seventh Amendment commanded jury trial in those derivative suits that involved legal issues. The first factor was the division
of the suit into the assertion of the claim by stockholders rather
than the corporation, which was equitable in nature, and the substantive claim itself, which might be legal in nature. The second
was the merger of law and equity in the federal courts by reason
of the promulgation of the Federal Rules of Procedure in 1938.
Then there were the recent decisions of the Court which, in cases
where both legal and equitable issues were present, commanded
precedence to jury trial of the legal issues.[211] Finally, there was a
recognition that the derivative suit is a paramount form of the class
action which, like the derivative suit, originated in equity and in
which legal issues are triable to a jury. By the application of this
mixture, the history of nonjury trials for derivative actions was
wiped out:[212]

> Given the availability in a derivative action of both legal and
> equitable remedies, we think the Seventh Amendment pre-
> serves to the parties in a stockholder's suit the same right to
> a jury trial which historically belonged to the corporation and
> to those against whom the corporation pressed its legal claims.

As Mr. Justice Stewart said, in dissent, speaking for the Chief
Justice and Mr. Justice Harlan as well:[213]

> The Court's decision today can perhaps be explained as a
> reflection of an unarticulated but apparently overpowering
> bias in favor of jury trials in civil actions. It certainly cannot
> be explained in terms of either the Federal Rules or the Consti-
> tution.

---

[208] *Id.* at 536–37.

[209] DePinto v. Provident Security Life Ins. Co., 323 F.2d 826 (9th Cir. 1963).

[210] *Id.* at 537 n. 9.

[211] Beacon Theatres, Inc. v. Westover, 359 U.S. 500 (1959); Dairy Queen, Inc.
v. Wood, 369 U.S. 469 (1962).

[212] 396 U.S. at 542.   [213] *Id.* at 551.

On the other hand, it must be conceded that this predilection did not carry the day in *United States v. Reynolds*.[214] That was a condemnation case in which the Government took respondent's land adjacent to a federal reservoir for use as recreation facilities. If the land taken had been "within the original scope of the project," "then its compensable value is to be measured in terms of agricultural use. If, on the other hand, the acreage was outside the original scope of the project, its compensable value is properly measurable in terms of its economic potential as lakeside residential or recreational property."[215] The lower courts had held that that issue of "proper scope of the project" was one for the jury to resolve, thereby creating a conflict with the decisions of another circuit.

The question was not of constitutional stature, for no argument was made that in condemnation actions there is a right to jury trial. But F.R.C.P. Rule 71A(h) provides that, with certain irrelevant exceptions, a party to a condemnation proceeding "may have a trial by jury of the issue of just compensation." The issue, therefore, was whether determining the original scope of the project is an integral part of the problem of fixing just compensation.

The majority of the Court, speaking through Mr. Justice Stewart this time, admitted that "the matter could be decided either way without doing violence to the language of Rule 71A(h)."[216] But the Court thought that it was intended for the jury to fulfill a narrow function in valuing the property taken and the question whether the property fell within the original scope of the project was better decided by the judge.

The dissent here might have resorted to Mr. Justice Stewart's statement about personal predilections in *Ross v. Bernhard*. But Mr. Justice Douglas, speaking for himself and Mr. Justice Black, argued that the issue the Court took away from the jury was bound up in the question that the jury was asked to decide. He concluded, however, by castigating mildly those who do not like juries:[217]

> There are powerful forces loose in this country that deprecate the use of juries. The Department of Justice and other federal agencies often seem to dislike juries in condemnation cases. . . . Juries in these condemnation cases perform . . . an historic restraint on both executive and judicial power. See *Bushell's Case*. 6 How. St. Tr. 999, decided in 1670.

---

[214] 397 U.S. 14 (1970).

[215] *Id*. at 18.

[216] *Id*. at 20.

[217] *Id*. at 23–24.

It might be noted that in his dissent, Mr. Justice Douglas refers to the Federal Rules as providing a congressional mandate. The fact is, of course, that the Rules are framed by committees selected by the Court, the Court adopts them, and unless Congress takes action to reject them they become effective. Not once in the history of the Rules has Congress ever interfered with their formulation or, indeed, given any indication that the Rules were entitled to any legislative consideration whatsoever. The dereliction of duty is Congress'. But this nonfeasance ought not to be a sufficient basis for attributing the content of the Rules to that legislative body.

F. THE COMMERCE CLAUSE

An old-fashioned Commerce Clause case found its way to the Court's docket last year. The state of Arizona attempted to impose on an Arizona grower an obligation to package its Arizona-grown cantaloupes in Arizona. The grower had been transporting them to its packaging plant in California. The Court affirmed a three-judge district court ruling that the regulation was invalid as an undue burden on interstate commerce. The opinion in *Pike v. Bruce Church, Inc.*[218] by Mr. Justice Stewart was for a unanimous Court. There was none to naysay the negative implications of the Commerce Clause or even the Court's admitted engagement in the legislative process of balancing the interests. The Court said:[219]

> Although the criteria for determining the validity of state statutes affecting interstate commerce have been variously stated, the general rule that emerges can be phrased as follows: Where the statute regulates evenhandedly to effectuate a legitimate public interest and its effects on interstate commerce are only incidental, it will be upheld unless the burden imposed on such commerce is clearly excessive in relation to the putative local benefits. . . . If a legitimate local purpose is found, then the question becomes one of degree. And the extent of the burden that will be tolerated will of course depend on the nature of the local interest involved, and on whether it could be promoted as well with a lesser impact on interstate activities. Occasionally the Court has candidly undertaken a balancing approach in resolving these issues, . . . but more frequently it has spoken in terms of "direct" and "indirect" effects and burdens.

---

[218] 397 U.S. 137 (1970).

[219] *Id.* at 142.

Mr. Justice Stewart then proceeded to balance the interests of the state of Arizona against those of the nation at large in applying the relevant standard. He found that the only interest that Arizona was asserting was the right to have what was admittedly a superior product carry an Arizona label. This was not enough to overcome the demands of freedom of interstate commerce:[220]

> While the order issued under the Arizona statute does not impose such rigidity [as was condemned in *Toomer v. Witsell*, 334 U.S. 385 (1948)] on an entire industry, it does impose just such a straitjacket on the appellee company with respect to the allocation of its interstate resources. Such an incidental consequence of a regulatory scheme could perhaps be tolerated if a more compelling state interest were involved. But here the State's interest is minimal at best—certainly less substantial than a State's interest in securing employment for its people. If the Commerce Clause forbids a State to require work to be done within its jurisdiction to promote local employment, then surely it cannot permit a State to require a person to go into a local packing business solely for the sake of enhancing the reputation of other producers within its borders.

The fact that this case was not affirmed by per curiam order without opinion is testimony to the advocate's skills of appellant's counsel and little more.

G. ABSTENTION DOCTRINE

In a Court as activist as the Warren Court, it was not surprising that the abstention doctrine became moribund. No self-denying ordinance could be appropriate to a jurisprudence that regarded the federal courts as the curer of all ills of American society. One of the surprising decisions rendered during the 1969 Term was *Reetz v. Bozanich*,[221] surprising not only because it revived the abstention doctrine but because the opinion was by Mr. Justice Douglas, one of the doctrine's most stalwart opponents. Contributing to the unusual circumstances was that the right asserted was one under the Equal Protection Clause.

Appellees contested the validity of an Alaskan statute that provided that licenses for salmon net gear should be restricted to those who had previously had such licenses or who had commercial fishing licenses for three years and actively engaged in that occupation during that time. Appellees were nonresidents who had been denied

---

220 *Id.* at 146.   221 397 U.S. 82 (1970).

a license because they could not qualify under the statute. They secured a judgment from the three-judge federal court that the statute was unconstitutional, in violation both of the Equal Protection Clause and the Alaskan constitutional provisions calling for common use of waters and fisheries. In a unanimous opinion, the Court held that the federal court should have stayed its hand:[222]

> The *Pullman* doctrine[223] was based on the "avoidance of needless friction" between federal pronouncements and state policies. . . . The instant case is the classic case in that tradition, for here the nub of the whole controversy may be the state constitution. The constitutional provisions relate to fish resources, an asset unique in its abundance in Alaska. The statute and regulations relate to the same unique resource, the management of which is a matter of great state concern. We appreciate why the District Court felt concern over the effect of further delay on these plaintiffs, the appellees here; but we have concluded that the first judicial application of these constitutional provisions should properly be by an Alaska court.

Other decisions during the Term suggested that *Reetz* should probably be regarded as a sport, that self-restraint is not yet reinstated as the governing principle. For in two cases, the Court expanded the scope of standing to sue in the federal courts far in excess of that tolerated by earlier Courts. In both *Data Processing Service v. Camp*[224] and *Barlow v. Collins*[225] the opinion for the Court was written by Mr. Justice Douglas and the only dissent came from Mr. Justice Brennan, joined by Mr. Justice White, because the expansion of the right to sue was not great enough. The allegedly narrow rationale of *Flast v. Cohen*[226] disappeared just as surely as it was predicted to do both by those who supported it and those who condemned it. These two cases were far more readily predictable than was *Reetz*. The only common element of surprise was the unanimity of the Court in all three cases.

III. THE SHAPE OF THINGS TO COME

It is readily apparent that the areas of the Warren Court's concern will continue to be those of the Burger Court, with variations in degree rather than kind. It is equally clear, however, that

---

[222] *Id*. at 87.

[223] Railroad Comm'n v. Pullman Co., 312 U.S. 496 (1941).

[224] 397 U.S. 150 (1970).

[225] 397 U.S. 159 (1970).   [226] 392 U.S. 83 (1968).

the constitutional business of the Burger Court will have attributes of its own.

The 1969 Term saw the decision of one issue that the Warren Court and its predecessors had steadfastly refused to take up. In *Walz v. Tax Comm'n*,[227] the Justices wrote over sixty pages of opinions on the question whether state tax exemptions for properties on which were buildings used for religious services, essentially churches, violated either the religion clauses of the First Amendment or the Equal Protection Clause of the Fourteenth. Professor Wilber G. Katz has treated both the opinions and the problems to keen analysis in other pages of this REVIEW.[228] The Court's opinion was written by the Chief Justice, and it embraced all rationales of the religion clauses and, therefore, none, in sustaining the exemption. It is clear that the judgment of the Court has opened rather than closed a door on new church-state problems. Exemptions from taxation for activities and persons more or less religious in their nature abound in the law. The differences among them will undoubtedly call for different treatment. And the Court will have the opportunity, which it will certainly take advantage of from time to time, to pass judgment on the more important of the resulting judicial decisions.

Moreover, the consequences of the *Walz* case will have to be added to a multitude of decisions already reached by lower courts on various schemes for state and federal financial assistance for parochial schools. Decisions of these cases, too, will help shape the image of the Burger Court. There is not likely to be the unified response against the Court as in the case of school prayers. Tax exemption for churches satisfied the fundamentalists no less than the Catholics. But assistance to parochial schools, where the prime beneficiary will be the Catholic church, necessarily arouses large public reaction that is likely to be reflected in congressional attitudes toward the Court.

Two other subjects of constitutional dimensions promise to carry even more clearly the stamp of the Burger Court in their development. At the 1969 Term the Court disposed of most of these cases on grounds of statutory construction. But some required considera-

---

227 397 U.S. 664 (1970).

228 See Katz, *Radiations from Church Tax Exemption, infra.*

tion, if not application, of constitutional standards.[229] It is to be hoped that compulsory military service will soon be sufficiently diminished to remove it from the basic issues confronting American society. Until it is, however, it is certain to create legal and constitutional problems for the solution of which the Court will be responsible.[230]

The other subject, clearly one of constitutional scope, to which the Burger Court will have to address itself derives from the welfare law cases. No less fundamental an issue is involved than the constitutional rationalization of what can politely be called "the service state." To what extent, to what degree, and under what conditions does the Constitution now compel the various governments of this nation to supply food, clothing, and shelter, health and legal services, police and fire protection, education and recreational facilities, to those of its citizens and inhabitants who do not purchase these for themselves? Some of the cases of last Term are dealt with in Professor O'Neil's article set out hereafter.[231] That these cases are but the beginning of the legal accommodations to moving the American state toward a more socialized order can readily be seen.[232]

The rights of rebelling students are also likely to provide bases for judicial pronouncements by the Court. At the 1969 Term, the issue was narrowly avoided by the dismissal of the writ of certiorari as improvidently granted in *Jones v. Board of Education*.[233] The Court there found the issue of dismissal of a student for pamphleteering to incite a strike and "takeover" by students was beclouded

---

[229] The *Welsh* case, note 230 *infra*, raised First Amendment questions.

[230] The draft law cases, disposed of one way or another by the Court in the 1969 Term, included: Gutknecht v. United States, 396 U.S. 295 (1970); Breen v. Selective Service Board, 396 U.S. 460 (1970); Toussie v. United States, 397 U.S. 112 (1970); Welsh v. United States, 398 U.S. 333 (1970); Mulloy v. United States, 398 U.S. 410 (1970); United States v. Sisson, 399 U.S. 267 (1970).

[231] See O'Neil, *Of Justice Delayed and Justice Denied: The Welfare Prior Hearing Cases, infra.*

[232] Last Term's cases falling in this category include: Goldberg v. Kelly, 397 U.S. 254 (1970); Wheeler v. Montgomery, 397 U.S. 280 (1970); Rosado v. Wyman, 397 U.S. 397 (1970); Dandridge v. Williams, 397 U.S. 471 (1970); Lewis v. Martin, 397 U.S. 552 (1970); Daniel v. Goliday, 398 U.S. 73 (1970); Wyman v. Rothstein, 398 U.S. 275 (1970).

[233] 397 U.S. 31 (1970). The problems of due process for rebelling students are discussed in O'Neil, note 231 *supra*.

by the possibility that the dismissal properly rested on the ground of lying to the administration in the course of the hearings. The lines in the Court have begun to be drawn on the question of student revolt. Mr. Justice Black objected to the dismissal because he would have affirmed the judgment below, which went against the student, on the basis of his dissenting opinion in *Tinker v. Des Moines School District*.[234] Justices Douglas and Brennan dissented and would have reversed: "The circulation [of the pamphlets] did not disrupt a classroom or any other university function. It would seem, therefore, that it is immune from punishment, censorship, and any form of retaliatory action."[235] Obviously *Jones* is but the first of many cases of this kind that will come before the Court, with each decision spawning its own cases in turn.

That consumer protection problems will also find their way to the Court's dockets is equally predictable, if the date of their arrival is still shrouded in mystery. Assuming that the institution of the Supreme Court does not undergo radical change as a result of the actions of the radical right or the radical left, it will continue to bear a heavy burden in the interpretation of the Constitution and its application to new and difficult problems of our society. And this will be the case whatever the change in personnel that may occur during the new Chief Justice's tenure.

Finally on the subject of "things to come," note should be taken of an ominous decision regarding the independence of the lower federal judiciary. As in *Walz*, the opinion was written for the *Court* by the Chief Justice. As in *Walz*, the Court's opinion in *Chandler v. Judicial Council*[236] answers few questions about future applications of the results reached.

On December 13, 1965, without hearing or record, and on the most dubious statutory authority, the judicial council of the Tenth Judicial Circuit found the chief judge of the Western District of Oklahoma "unable, or unwilling to discharge efficiently the duties of his office,"[237] and purported to remove all cases theretofore assigned to him and to prevent any further cases being assigned to him. In effect, the Tenth Judicial Council did what neither the American electorate, the Congress, the President, nor the Supreme Court, separately or in combination, could do. It removed a federal

---

[234] 393 U.S. 503, 515 (1969).

[235] 397 U.S. at 35.

[236] 398 U.S. 74 (1970).

[237] *Id.* at 77.

judge from office without the impeachment process provided by
the Constitution. The judge then petitioned the Supreme Court for
a writ of mandamus or prohibition and a stay of the order. The
stay was denied on the strange ground "that the Order was 'entirely
interlocutory in character pending prompt further proceedings
. . . and that at such proceedings Judge Chandler will be permitted to appear before the Council, with counsel. . . .' 382 U.S.
1003."[238]

Judge Chandler then addressed a letter to his fellow district
court judges saying that he objected to the removal of cases already
on his docket but would be agreeable to no further assignments.
The other district court judges then agreed as to the manner for
assigning new cases among themselves, but would not accept the
cases already assigned to Judge Chandler. The council then issued
a new order, precluding new assignments to Chandler, but leaving
with him the cases already assigned to him.

Thereupon the Solicitor General moved to dismiss the Supreme
Court case as moot, but withdrew the motion when Chandler objected that his acquiescence in assignment of new cases was for
purposes of keeping the assignment power within the ambit of the
district court rather than the judicial council. A later letter to the
council, signed by all the district court judges including Chandler,
stated that "the current order for the division of business in this
district *is agreeable* under the circumstances."[239]

When the case came to the Supreme Court for argument in
December, 1969, on the motion filed there in January, 1966, the
council argued that the Court lacked jurisdiction to issue the writs
because the order of the council was administrative in nature and
the Court could not exercise original jurisdiction. The shades of
Marbury v. Madison[240] were in evidence throughout this case.

The Solicitor General argued that the Supreme Court had jurisdiction because the Tenth Circuit Judicial Council is really nothing
other than the Tenth Circuit Court of Appeals sitting en banc and
that the proceedings should be analogized to a disbarment procedure. The Supreme Court, in a footnote, rejected the equation
between the court of appeals and the judicial council.[241] The Solicitor argued that the Court should, nevertheless, refuse jurisdic-

---

238 *Id.* at 79.

239 *Id.* at 82.

240 1 Cranch 137 (1803).

241 398 U.S. at 83 n. 5.

tion, because Chandler's acquiescence in the order made it inappropriate to invoke the extraordinary writ sought.

The Chief Justice's opinion refused jurisdiction on grounds of Chandler's acquiescence and what sounded like a proposition of failure to exhaust administrative remedies:[242]

> Whatever the merits of this apparent attempt to have it both ways [acquiescence in the order and attack upon it], one thing is clear: except for the effort to seek the aid of this Court, Judge Chandler has never once since giving his written acquiescence in the division of business sought any relief from either the Council or some other tribunal. . . .
>
> Instead, Judge Chandler . . . expressly refused to attend the hearing called by the Council for February 10, 1966, in response to this Court's order; in his brief he gives as a reason that he was unwilling to "attend a hearing conducted by a body whose jurisdiction he challenged. . . ." As a result of that refusal we have no record, no petition for relief addressed to any agency, court or tribunal of any kind other than this Court, and a very knotty jurisdictional problem as well. Parenthetically, it might be noted that Chandler could have appeared, in person or by counsel, and challenged the jurisdiction of the Council without impairing his claim that it had no power in the matter. . . .
>
> Whether the Council's action was administrative action not reviewable in this Court, or whether it is reviewable here, plainly petitioner has not made a case for the extraordinary relief of mandamus or prohibition.

All this was pronounced against a background of loud expression of belief in the importance of the independence of the judiciary. There was no suggestion that on this issue Chandler could not acquiesce in the exercise of a power that was not his to grant by acquiescence. The independence of the judiciary is for the protection of the people, not for the protection of individual judges. In thus denying relief, the Court did give sanction to the authority—even if only a temporary authority—to exercise the power that the judicial council asserted here.

Mr. Justice Harlan, in a long concurring opinion addressed to the issues, found that the Supreme Court did have jurisdiction and that the council was given the removal power by Congress, a power, however, that was not Congress' to give. The latter ruling was accomplished by the *ipse dixit* that the removal of all cases

---

242 *Id.* at 87–89.

from the judge's ken was only an exercise of judicial administration over judicial business and not one of "removal."

Mr. Justice Douglas, joined by Mr. Justice Black, wrote a dissenting opinion. He agreed with Mr. Justice Harlan that the Court had jurisdiction, but not that the council did. His opinion attacked not only the order of the Tenth Circuit Judicial Council at issue in the case, but the more recent attempt by the Judicial Conference, over which the Chief Justice presides, to control the extrajudicial activities of federal judges. In the course of his opinion he said:[243]

> An independent judiciary is one of this Nation's outstanding characteristics. Once a federal judge is confirmed by the Senate and takes his oath, he is independent of every other judge. He commonly works with other federal judges who are likewise sovereign. But neither one alone nor any number banded together can act as censor and place sanctions on him. Under the Constitution the only leverage that can be asserted against him is impeachment, where pursuant to a resolution passed by the House, he is tried by the Senate, sitting as a jury....
>
> The problem is not resolved by saying that only judicial administrative matters are involved....
>
> It is time that an end be put to these efforts of federal judges to ride herd on other federal judges. This is a form of "hazing" having no place under the Constitution. Federal judges are entitled, like other people, to the full freedom of the First Amendment. If they break a law, they can be prosecuted. If they become corrupt or sit in cases in which they have a personal or family stake, they can be impeached by Congress. But I search the Constitution in vain for any power of surveillance that other federal judges have over those aberrations.

Mr. Justice Black, too, wrote a dissenting opinion, in which he was in turn joined by Mr. Justice Douglas. And he also spoke out sharply in defense of the independence of the federal trial judiciary:[244]

> I am regrettably compelled in this case to say that the Court today, in my judgment, breaks faith with this grand constitutional principle. Judge Chandler, duly appointed, duly confirmed, and never impeached by the Congress, has been barred from doing his work by other judges. The real facts of this case cannot be obscured nor the effect of the Judicial Council's decisions defended, by any technical, legalistic effort to show

---

[243] *Id.* at 136, 137, 140.   [244] *Id.* at 142–43.

that one or the other of the Council's orders issued over the years is "valid." This case must be viewed for what it is—a long history of harassment of Judge Chandler by other judges who somehow feel he is "unfit" to hold office. Their efforts have been going on for at least five years and still Judge Chandler finds no relief. What is involved here is simply a blatant effort on the part of the Council through concerted action to make Judge Chandler a "second-class judge," depriving him of the full power of his office and the right to share equally with other federal judges in the privileges and responsibilities of the Federal Judiciary. I am unable to find in our Constitution or in any statute any authority whatever for judges to arrogate to themselves and to exercise such powers. Judge Chandler, like every other federal judge including the Justices of this Court, is subject to removal from office only by the constitutionally prescribed mode of impeachment.

The wise authors of our Constitution provided for judicial independence because they were familiar with history; they knew that judges of the past—good, patriotic judges—had occasionally lost not only their offices but had also sometimes lost their freedom and their heads because of the actions and decrees of other judges. They were determined that no such things should happen here. But it appears that the language they used and the protections they thought they had created are not sufficient to protect our judges from the contrived intricacies used by the judges of the Tenth Circuit and this Court to uphold what has happened to Judge Chandler in this case.

I fear that unless the actions taken by the Judicial Council in this case are in some way repudiated, the hope for an independent judiciary will prove to have been no more than an evanescent dream.

If Congress is really concerned about judicial usurpation of powers that do not belong to it, and not merely unhappy with the results of judicial decisions, it should be so concerned here. This little-noted judgment may well have accomplished what neither Jefferson nor the Reconstruction Congress nor Franklin Roosevelt could accomplish: a means of destroying the judicial tenure that the Constitution clearly demanded. Unlike the earlier efforts, the decision does not, of course, affect the tenure of Supreme Court Justices, but the principle does. For it is to be remembered that the authority on which the judicial council purported to act was a thirty-year-old statute never theretofore construed to authorize such powers. Would it be different if the Congress were to authorize the Chief Justice or a majority of the Court to suspend the powers of a Justice who, in their opinion, was "unable or unwilling to discharge efficiently the duties of his office"? In the past, the Court has been extraordinarily jealous of the removal powers of the President;[245] it should have been expected to be at least as jealous of the removal powers of a judicial council, especially in the face of a Constitution that provides life tenure for the judiciary. Congress should make clear that it never in fact authorized what it well knew it could not authorize.

IV. NONCONSTITUTIONAL BUSINESS

The catalog of constitutional cases set out above should be recognized as but a portion of the Court's work during the 1969 Term. Much of the Court's time was necessarily devoted to other staples. Labor law bulked large again, as it has almost since the passage of the Wagner Act. If the primary source of business was the Labor Management Relations Act, the Railway Labor Act contributed more than its fair share. The Court was as divided as ever in this area. Only two of the ten opinions[246] represented a unanimous Court. The Chief Justice was the most frequent dissenter, with Mr. Justice Harlan also in large disagreement with either the results or the reasoning of the Court. Three of the eight signed opinions were by Mr. Justice Black and two by Mr. Justice Brennan. Certainly the most important of these cases was *Boys Market v. Retail Clerks Union*, discussed in detail by Professor Gould in his article in this volume.[247]

There were five tax cases decided.[248] They, too, revealed a divided Court in three of the five cases, two of them decided by 5-

[245] See Humphrey's Executor v. United States, 295 U.S. 602 (1935); Wiener v. United States, 357 U.S. 349 (1958).

[246] Line v. Transportation Union, 396 U.S. 142 (1969); NLRB v. Rutter-Rex Mfg. Co., 396 U.S. 258 (1969); Czosek v. O'Mara, 397 U.S. 25 (1970); H. K. Porter Co. v. NLRB, 397 U.S. 99 (1970); Longshoremen v. Ariadne Co., 397 U.S. 195 (1970); Taggart v. Weinacker's, Inc., 397 U.S. 223 (1970); Sears, Roebuck v. Carpet Layers, 397 U.S. 655 (1970); NLRB v. Raytheon Co., 398 U.S. 25 (1970); Boys Market, Inc. v. Retail Clerks Union, 398 U.S. 235 (1970); Atlantic Coast Line v. Engineers, 398 U.S. 281 (1970).

[247] See Gould, *On Labor Injunctions, Unions, and the Judges: The Boys Market Case, infra.*

[248] United States v. Donnelly, 397 U.S. 286 (1970); United States v. Davis, 397 U.S. 301 (1970); Woodward v. Commissioner, 397 U.S. 572 (1970); United States v. Hilton Hotels, 397 U.S. 580 (1970); Nash v. United States, 398 U.S. 1 (1970).

to-3 votes. Mr. Justice Marshall emerged as the Court's tax expert, writing the opinion for the Court in four of the five cases.

The antitrust business fell to what may be a new low. Of the three cases,[249] two of them were per curiam clarifications of earlier efforts. One case involved a bank merger, and the Justices played at being economists.

Of the other cases decided by the Court, one arose under the securities laws,[250] three were ICC cases,[251] two were patent cases,[252] three arose under the Jones Act and the Longshoremen's Act.[253] There were two bankruptcy and reorganization cases,[254] one of which involved the tangled skein of the New Haven Railroad's financial problems. A case under the national banking laws was noteworthy as the Chief Justice's first Supreme Court opinion.[255] A government contract case,[256] two Indian cases,[257] with victories going to the Indians, a case under the Social Security Act,[258] and one case construing the Department of Agriculture's milk marketing regulatory powers[259] filled out the Court's appellate business. There was one boundary dispute that came to the Court under its original jurisdiction.[260]

With one or two exceptions, it is difficult to understand why these cases should have burdened the Supreme Court, especially

---

[249] Simpson v. Union Oil Co., 396 U.S. 13 (1969); Perkins v. Standard Oil Co., 399 U.S. 222 (1970); United States v. Phillipsburg Nat'l Bank, 399 U.S. 350 (1970).

[250] Mills v. Electric Auto-Lite Co., 396 U.S. 375 (1970).

[251] City of Chicago v. United States, 396 U.S. 162 (1969); Northern Line Merger Cases, 396 U.S. 491 (1970); American Farm Lines v. Black Ball Freight, 397 U.S. 532 (1970).

[252] Anderson's–Black Rock v. Pavement Co., 396 U.S. 57 (1969); Standard Industries, Inc. v. Tigrett Industries, Inc., 397 U.S. 586 (1970).

[253] Nacirema Co. v. Johnson, 396 U.S. 212 (1969); Moragne v. States Marine Line, 398 U.S. 375 (1970); Hellenic Lines v. Rhoditis, 398 U.S. 306 (1970).

[254] United States v. Key, 397 U.S. 322 (1970); New Haven Inclusion Cases, 399 U.S. 392 (1970).

[255] First Nat'l Bank v. Dickinson, 396 U.S. 122 (1969).

[256] United States v. Seckinger, 397 U.S. 203 (1970).

[257] Tooahnippah v. Hickel, 397 U.S. 598 (1970); Choctaw Nation v. Oklahoma, 397 U.S. 620 (1970).

[258] United States v. Webb, Inc., 397 U.S. 179 (1970).

[259] Zuber v. Allen, 396 U.S. 168 (1969).

[260] Arkansas v. Tennessee, 397 U.S. 88 (1970).

those cases arriving by way of direct appeal from trial courts under outdated jurisdictional legislation. Most of the cases were of interest only to the parties involved or were necessary only to resolve conflicts among the circuits. The evidence continues to pile up in support of a revision of the Court's appellate jurisdiction with a view to conserving the Court's valuable time for issues appropriate to its position.

V. CONCLUSION

The materials set out above were intended to be essentially descriptive rather than analytical: the record of constitutional decisions in a Supreme Court Term under the chairmanship of a new Chief Justice. They certainly afford too little for the Court's expert critics and too much for the dilettante Court watcher. It is hoped that they are of interest to the great bulk of lawyers and others who fall in between these categories.

The public image of the 1969 Term, thanks largely to impressions created by the national press, is that of an uneventful year for a Court whose new Chief Justice is moving it slowly toward judicial restraint. It is hoped that the contents of this article sufficiently disprove both the notion of tranquillity and that of any clear movement toward judicial restraint. Indeed, the impression left by reading the cases is that the Court has not been substantially changed, if at all, by the appointment of a new Chief Justice. Certainly, the new Chief is, as was predicted, a "hard-liner" in criminal cases. But he is still a "new boy" on the Court and not its leader. In one or two cases where a single vote was decisive, the new Chief Justice may have brought about conclusions different from those which would have been supported by his predecessor. And the rhetoric of the two men is certainly different. Chief Justice Burger talks about adherence to "original meaning" and "judicial restraint." Warren used different labels to reach desired results. Burger is, however, closer to Chief Justice Warren's jurisprudence and talents than he is to those of a Frankfurter or a Jackson. It is possible that the new Chief Justice, like the old one, instead of molding the Court in his own image will instead be made over in the image of the Court.

The 1969 Term showed no retreat from the Warren Court's primary objective of desegregation. It moved the reapportionment formula even further along the way to logical absurdity. It continued to write a code of criminal procedure for the states. Dissenters found succor in the Court's decisions, as did the press.

The Court's major theme remained equality and its major function continued to be the centralization of power in one branch or another of the national government. Precedents were treated cavalierly; both new ones and old ones were readily overruled or distinguished to death. The domain of judicial authority, if not judicial power, was expanded.

The forthcoming 1970 Term promises to be an interesting one. The Court will once again be fully manned and a new Justice will have a voice in its decisions. For the first time since the Hughes Court, appointees of Republican Presidents will be in a majority. But this "Republican majority" is not likely to resemble that which Messrs. Agnew and Mitchell are concerned to create. Again many of the ills that plague a sick society will be brought to the Court for treatment if not for cure. Again the Court's critics will know the joy of retrospective wisdom.

WILBER G. KATZ

RADIATIONS FROM CHURCH

TAX EXEMPTION

The Supreme Court surprised no one, not even its persistent friend Madalyn Murray O'Hair—when it held in *Walz v. Tax Commission*[1] that inclusion of real property "used solely for religious worship" in a broad tax exemption category does not violate the prohibition of laws "respecting an establishment of religion." Two factors made the decision a practical certainty. The first was the consistent tax exemption practice, rooted in the eighteenth century and sustained by an unbroken line of judicial precedent. The second was a recognition of the probable consequences of an abrupt outlawing of the exemptions, including drastic cutbacks in church welfare programs.

I had been surprised when the Court noted probable jurisdiction. Appeals in similar cases had been dismissed in 1956 and 1962 "for want of a substantial federal question."[2] Such a disposition is very convenient for cases in which the result is a foregone conclusion, but for which a reasoned opinion is difficult to write. It is intriguing to speculate why the Court now found the question "substantial." Perhaps the prospect of an extended Douglas dissent made summary dismissal impolitic. Perhaps the brethren welcomed an opportunity to explore what Mr. Justice Harlan called "the radiations of the issues involved."[3] In any event, it is principally because of these

Wilber G. Katz is George I. Haight Professor of Law, University of Wisconsin.

[1] 397 U.S. 664 (1970).

[2] Heisey v. County of Alameda, 352 U.S. 921 (1956); General Finance Corp. v. Archetto, 369 U.S. 423 (1962).

[3] 397 U.S. at 694.

radiations that *Walz* is worthy of discussion in this *Review*—and because of the radioactivity of Chief Justice Burger's first church-state opinion.

My report of the radiations from *Walz* may be biased by my point of view on the religion clauses of the First Amendment. I believe that in the interpretation of both clauses the Court's responsibility, as phrased by Justice Goldberg, is "to do loyal service . . . to the ultimate First Amendment objective of religious liberty."[4] I believe, further, that this objective is best served by a policy of neutrality, in the pursuit of which legislatures are free to make many provisions with respect to religion, including provisions which neutralize what would otherwise be the restrictive effects of government action on the freedom of religious choice.

In *Walz* the record and the appellant's brief were meager, to put it mildly. The appeal was from a summary judgment entered on the basis of three affidavits covering eleven pages. Appellant's brief contained four pages of argument. The most thorough exploration of the issues was in amicus briefs filed by the United States Catholic Conference, defending the exemptions, and by the American Civil Liberties Union, in opposition.

Chief Justice Burger spoke for five of the eight Justices. Mr. Justice Harlan wrote a separate opinion expressing "basic agreement" with the Chief Justice. Mr. Justice Brennan concurred in an opinion applying the principles he had developed in the *Schempp* school prayer case. Mr. Justice Douglas dissented.

I. The "Leaning Tower of Absolutes"

.In 1956 Professor Mark DeWolfe Howe described the structure of the Supreme Court's Establishment Clause doctrine as a "leaning tower of absolutes."[5] It was a structure that the Justices had grounded upon a one-sided view of the historical setting of the First Amendment. In this comment, I interpret the Court's work in *Walz* as dismantling the leaning tower and presenting a rough sketch for a new edifice. First, however, I want to outline the principal features of the leaning tower and report the substance of Howe's historical criticism.

The three absolutes to which Howe objected were the "impreg-

---

4 Abington School Dist. v. Schempp, 374 U.S. 203, 306 (1963).

5 Howe, The Garden and the Wilderness 168 (1965).

nable wall" concept of church-state separation, the "no aid to religion" proscription, and the strict neutrality test striking down legislation where the purpose or the primary effect is either the inhibition or the advancement of religion.

Decisions in the late 1940's expressed in strongest terms an insulation doctrine of church-state separation. In 1947, in *Everson v. Board of Education*, Mr. Justice Black wrote for the majority: "The First Amendment has erected a wall between church and state. That wall must be kept high and impregnable. We could not approve the slightest breach."[6] The dissenting Justices agreed with this view but asserted that the Court's decision opened a breach in the wall by upholding bus fare reimbursement for parents of children attending parochial schools.

In 1948, in *Illinois ex rel. McCollum v. Board of Education*, Mr. Justice Black wrote again for the Court, this time invalidating a released time program of religious instruction in public schools.[7] The *Everson* dissenters concurred in an opinion by Mr. Justice Frankfurter, insisting:[8]

> Separation means separation, not something less. . . .
> We renew our conviction that "we have staked the very existence of our country on the faith that complete separation between the state and religion is best for the state and best for religion."

In both of these cases, the separationist language was supplemented with strictures against government aid to religion. The *Everson* opinion contained this sentence: "neither [a State nor the Federal Government] can pass laws which aid one religion, aid all religions, or prefer one religion over another."[9] This "no aid" language was quoted with approval in *McCollum* and in many later cases.

The neutrality concept can be traced to *Everson*, but in *Abington School Dist. v. Schempp*, the 1963 public school prayer case, neutrality became the dominant concept—neutrality in the sense of avoiding either the advancement or the inhibition of religion:[10]

> The test may be stated as follows: what are the purpose and the primary effect of the enactment? If either is the advancement or inhibition of religion then the enactment exceeds the scope

---

[6] 330 U.S. 1, 18 (1947).

[7] 333 U.S. 203 (1948).   [9] 330 U.S. at 15.

[8] 333 U.S. at 231–32.   [10] 374 U.S. 203, 222 (1963).

of legislative power as circumscribed by the Constitution. That is to say that to withstand the strictures of the Establishment Clause there must be a secular legislative purpose and a primary effect that neither advances nor inhibits religion.

This test was quoted and applied in *Board of Education v. Allen*,[11] in which loans of textbooks to pupils in parochial schools were sustained. The test was applied again in *Epperson v. Arkansas*,[12] which struck down a statute forbidding the teaching of evolution. The Court said through Justice Fortas that the prohibition of practices which "aid or oppose" any religion is an absolute prohibition.

Professor Howe's views were expressed in a series of lectures published under the title *The Garden and the Wilderness*. His criticism could scarcely have been more severe. He charged that "By superficial and purposive interpretations of the past, the Court has dishonored the arts of the historian and degraded the talents of the lawyer."[13] His principal complaint was that the Court's Establishment Clause doctrine was spun exclusively out of the Jeffersonian threads in American church-state tradition. The Court erroneously assumed that the framers of the First Amendment "spoke in a wholly Jeffersonian dialect."[14] Howe's thesis was that the American tradition of church-state separation includes not only the Jeffersonian threads, but also those running back to Roger Williams. Both Jefferson and Williams wrote metaphorically of a wall of separation, but they viewed the wall as serving quite different ends. Howe described the Jeffersonian principle of separation as rooted in deistic rationalism and anticlericalism. Church and state should be separated "as the safeguard of public and private interests against ecclesiastical depredations and excursions."[15] Following this view, the Court seemed to have assumed that "the First Amendment intended to keep alive the bias of the Enlightenment which asserted that government must not give its aid in any form to religion lest impious clerks tighten their grip upon the purses and the minds of men."[16]

The title of Howe's book was suggested by a passage from Roger Williams. As Howe explained:[17]

> When the imagination of Roger Williams built the wall of separation, it was not because he was fearful that without such

---

[11] 392 U.S. 236 (1968).

[12] 393 U.S. 97 (1968).

[13] Howe, note 5 *supra*, at 4.

[14] *Id.* at 10.

[15] *Id.* at 2.

[16] *Id.* at 7.

[17] *Id.* at 6.

a barrier the arm of the church would extend its reach. It was, rather, the dread of the worldly corruptions which might consume the churches if sturdy fences against the wilderness were not maintained.

Williams' wall protected churches not only against restraints but also against the corrupting effects of government support. Williams and his followers believed that "the spiritual freedom of churches is jeopardized when they forget the principle of separation."[18]

In Howe's judgment, the First Amendment's prohibitions:[19]

> ... at the time of their promulgation were generally understood to be more the expression of Roger Williams' philosophy than of Jefferson's. ... [T]he predominant concern at the time when the First Amendment was adopted was not the Jeffersonian fear that if it were not enacted the federal government would aid religion and thus advance the interest of impious clerks but rather the evangelical hope that private conscience and autonomous churches, working together and in freedom, would extend the rule of truth.

The Williams principle of separation does not forbid all government aids to religion, but only those incompatible with full religious freedom. Religious freedom, according to Williams, is not merely a set of external conditions, an absence of external restraints; more profoundly, it is a condition of spirit—an interior freedom that is unlikely to thrive in established churches. Many aids to religion, however, have no tendency to sap the roots of religious freedom. For example, Howe wrote: "I find it hard to believe that Williams and his heirs were so deeply concerned with the maintenance of the wall that they would condemn the tax exemption of churches."[20]

II. Demolition and Reconstruction

A. DISMANTLING THE LEANING TOWER

Chief Justice Burger dealt directly with the celebrated "no-aid" language of Mr. Justice Black's *Everson* opinion. Once again this "test" was quoted, but this time only because it "abundantly" illustrates the "hazards of placing too much weight on a few words or phrases of the Court."[21] The Chief Justice added that in *Everson* Mr. Justice Black "had no difficulty" in upholding the reimbursement of bus fares of parochial school pupils. Readers familiar with

---

[18] *Id*. at 2.
[19] *Id*. at 19.

[20] *Id*. at 152.
[21] 397 U.S. at 670.

Everson may here raise an eyebrow, for Mr. Justice Black had suggested that the statute "approaches the verge" of the state's power.[22] The Chief Justice's cavalier reporting of *Everson* makes all the more clear his intention that the quoted language is not to be considered an authoritative gloss on the First Amendment.

Equally striking is the fact that nowhere in the *Walz* opinion is the *Schempp* case cited. The neutrality test which Mr. Justice Clark labored to formulate is not quoted. There is an echo of the first half of that test: the purpose of church tax exemption is found to be "neither the advancement nor the inhibition of religion."[23] But the Court's concern for the effect of the legislation is different from the concern expressed in *Schempp*. Now the concern is lest the effect be "an excessive government entanglement with religion."[24] There is no inquiry whether the "primary" effect advances or inhibits religion. The ACLU had argued in *Walz* that the *primary* effect of church tax exemption is advancement of religion. This is a forceful argument, since the approved secular ends are secondary in the sense of resulting from the strengthening of churches. The Court seems to have adopted the argument of the Catholic Conference that the *Schempp* "test" had never been intended to have universal application.

B. OLD MATERIALS FOR NEW STRUCTURES

While undermining the authority of the *Everson* and *Schempp* "tests," the Court gave its nod of approval to the language of *Zorach v. Clauson* that we "are a religious people whose institutions presuppose a Supreme Being," and:[25]

> We make room for as wide a variety of beliefs and creeds as the spiritual needs of man deem necessary. . . . *When the state encourages religious instruction . . . it follows the best of our traditions.* For it then respects the religious nature of our people and accommodates the public service to their spiritual needs.

---

22 330 U.S. at 16.

23 397 U.S. at 672.   24 *Id*. at 674.

25 *Id*. at 672; Zorach v. Clauson, 343 U.S. 306, 313–14 (1952). (Emphasis added by Burger, C. J.)

According to Professor Howe, *Zorach* was in the tradition of Roger Williams. Howe explained that the Williams principle of separation:[26]

> endorsed a host of favoring tributes to faith—tributes so substantial that they have produced in the aggregate what may fairly be described as a *de facto* establishment of religion. . . . The Supreme Court's unwillingness to recognize that [the Roger Williams principle of separation] has ever been an element in our constitutional tradition . . . leaves quite unexplained the persistence of the *de facto* establishment. . . . The hold of [the Williams theory of separation] is so strong that it is almost inconceivable that any branch of government . . . could today acknowledge that its objective is the destruction of this establishment. Yet the Supreme Court, by pretending that the American principle of separation is predominantly Jeffersonian and by purporting to outlaw even those aids to religion which do not affect religious liberties, seems to have endorsed a governmental policy aimed at eliminating the *de facto* establishments.

While the *Walz* opinion quoted *Zorach* to the effect that "The First Amendment . . . does not say that in every and all respects there shall be a separation of Church and State," the Court repeatedly expressed concern over "excessive government entanglement with religion."[27] The Chief Justice was doubtless referring to what Mr. Justice Harlan described as the "kind and degree of government involvement in religious life that, as history teaches us, is apt to lead to strife and frequently strain a political system to the breaking point."[28] Such language warns against forgetting the fears of Jefferson.

III. Room for Tax Exemptions in the New Tower

With the absolutes cleared away, the majority of the Court had little difficulty sustaining church tax exemptions. They emphasized that such exemptions result in less involvement with religion than would the taxing of church property:[29]

> Elimination of exemption would tend to expand the involvement of government by giving rise to tax valuation of church property, tax liens, tax foreclosures, and the direct confronta-

---

[26] Howe, note 5 *supra*, at 11–12.

[27] 397 U.S. at 669.

[28] *Id.* at 694.

[29] *Id.* at 674.

tions and conflicts that follow in the train of those legal processes.

The principal thrust of Mr. Justice Douglas' dissent was that exemptions are indistinguishable from grants of public funds. The words *subsidize* and *subsidy* run through his opinion. A Brookings Institution report is quoted: "Tax exemption, no matter what its form, is essentially a government grant or subsidy."[30] For Mr. Justice Douglas, therefore, tax exemption "takes us back where Madison was in 1784 and 1785 when he battled the Assessment Bill in Virginia."[31] Indeed, he appended to his opinion this famous bill and the full text of Madison's "Memorial and Remonstrance against Religious Assessments," the same material which Justice Rutledge had annexed to his 1948 *Everson* dissent.

The majority, however, found a difference between grants of tax funds and tax exemptions. "The grant of a tax exemption is not sponsorship [of religious activity] since the government does not transfer part of its revenue to churches but simply abstains from demanding that the church support the state."[32] More substantial is the Court's contrasting of grants and exemptions in terms of the degree to which they result in church-state involvement. "Obviously a direct money subsidy would be a relationship pregnant with involvement and, as with most government grant programs, could encompass sustained and detailed administrative relationships for enforcement of statutory or administrative standards."[33] Mr. Justice Brennan's concurring opinion contrasted "the affirmative involvement characteristic of outright governmental subsidy" with "mere passive state involvement with religion" characteristic of tax exemption.[34]

Mr. Justice Harlan agreed with Mr. Justice Douglas that exemptions do not differ from subsidies as an economic matter, but he said: "Subsidies, unlike exemptions, must be passed on periodically and thus invite more political controversy than exemptions. Moreover, subsidies or direct aid, as a general rule, are granted on the basis of enumerated and more complicated qualifications and frequently involve the state in administration to a higher degree."[35]

The exemption under attack included not only church buildings

---

30 *Id.* at 709.

31 *Id.* at 704.

32 *Id.* at 675.

33 *Ibid.*

34 *Id.* at 691.

35 *Id.* at 699.

but real property owned by a broad spectrum of charitable, educational, and other nonprofit organizations, which the Chief Justice characterized as "entities that exist in a harmonious relationship to the community at large, and that foster its 'moral or mental improvement.' "[36] It was apparently agreed that a tax exemption limited to churches would violate the Establishment Clause. If this is so, does the breadth of the exemption justify the inclusion of churches? Mr. Justice Douglas gave a definite reason for his negative answer:[37]

> Government could provide or finance operas, hospitals, historical societies, and all the rest because they represent social welfare programs within the reach of the police power. In contrast, government may not provide or finance worship because of the Establishment Clause any more than it may single out "atheistic" or "agnostic" centers or groups and create or finance them.

As already noted, the Court relied on the breadth of the exemption in finding a secular purpose, but it did not deal explicitly with the difficulty that subsidy grants may be given to nonreligious groups and that tax exemption of churches requires a justification that the nonreligious exemptions do not need. Perhaps the Court's answer was in its invocation of Justice Holmes: "a page of history is worth a volume of logic."[38]

IV. Neutrality, a "Coat of Many Colors"[39]

A. THE BEAUTY OF NEUTRALITY

In the 1950's the neutrality concept seemed to me to offer the best hope for the development of church-state doctrine.[40] After *Everson* and *McCollum,* the separation doctrine carried a threat to religious liberty. I suggested that what the Establishment Clause requires is not insulation but neutrality; that the clause does not limit the freedom of religious choice to the freedom compatible with strict separation; that it requires only the separation compatible with full religious freedom. Such a statement of course needs quali-

---

[36] *Id.* at 672.

[37] *Id.* at 708–09.

[38] *Id.* at 675–76.

[39] Harlan, J., in *Allen,* 392 U.S. at 249.

[40] See Katz, *Freedom of Religion and State Neutrality,* 20 U. Chi. L. Rev. 426 (1953). See also Katz, Religion and American Constitutions (1964).

fications, but at a time when an impregnable wall of separation was being demanded, the neutrality concept seemed to offer a badly needed corrective and a valuable key for interpreting the Establishment Clause.

With a neutrality interpretation, the Establishment Clause permits special provisions for religion of a type that I have called neutralizing aids. These are provisions designed to counteract or neutralize the restrictions of religious freedom that would otherwise result from government's secular activities. A classic example consists of the special provisions for religion made by the armed services. These programs are not designed to promote religion but to protect religious freedom. Where the government separates men from ordinary opportunities for worship and pastoral care, it may properly provide substitute opportunities, notwithstanding the fact that this policy risks embarrassing involvement with religious sects. Another example is the exception frequently incorporated in Sunday closing laws for the benefit of Orthodox Jews and Seventh-Day Adventists.

B. THE STRANGE NEUTRALITY OF PROFESSOR KURLAND

Since 1961 the term "neutrality" has often been associated with the theory suggested by the editor of this *Review:*[41]

> The principle tendered is a simple one. The freedom and separation clauses should be read as stating a single precept: that government cannot utilize religion as a standard for action or inaction because these clauses, read together as they should be, prohibit classification in terms of religion either to confer a benefit or to impose a burden. This test is meant to provide a starting point for the solution to problems . . . , not a mechanical answer to them.

This principle requires that laws be written as if religion did not exist. It rules out neutralizing aids, at least presumptively. If this is neutrality, it is a "formal" or "verbal" neutrality. I question the utility of this concept even as a starting point.

I welcomed the Court's opinion in *Schempp*, since its neutrality test did not echo Kurland and did not cast doubt on the propriety of neutralizing aids. On the day *Schempp* was decided the Court

---

[41] Kurland, *Of Church and State and the Supreme Court*, 29 U. Chi. L. Rev. 1, 96 (1961).

also decided *Sherbert v. Verner*,[42] in which the majority made mandatory a special exemption for Seventh-Day Adventists in an unemployment compensation law. Mr. Justice Harlan dissented, regarding such aids as a matter for the legislature. He explained why he was unwilling to read into the Establishment Clause a prescription of the Kurland type of neutrality:[43]

> It has been suggested that such singling out of religious conduct for special treatment may violate the constitutional limitations on state action. See Kurland, Of Church and State and The Supreme Court, 29 U. of Chi. L. Rev. 1;....My own view, however, is that at least under the circumstances of this case it would be a permissible accommodation of religion for the State, if it *chose* to do so, to create an exception to its eligibility requirements for persons like the appellant. The constitutional obligation of "neutrality" . . . is not so narrow a channel that the slightest deviation from an absolutely straight course leads to condemnation. There are too many instances in which no such course can be charted, too many areas in which the pervasive activities of the State justify some special provision for religion to prevent it from being submerged by an all-embracing secularism.

C. NEUTRALITY IN WALZ

In *Walz*, Mr. Justice Harlan highlighted requirements of "neutrality" and "voluntarism" as means of avoiding excessive government involvement with religion.[44] Church tax exemption cleared the voluntarism hurdle because it "neither encourages nor discourages participation in religious life."[45] Voluntarism is thus reminiscent of neutrality à la *Schempp*. The tax exemption is "neutral," in Mr. Justice Harlan's view, because churches are not singled out but are included in a class so broad that "religious institutions could be thought to fall within the natural perimeter." In applying the neutrality test: "The Court must survey meticulously the circumstances of governmental categories to eliminate, as it were, religious gerrymanders."

Chief Justice Burger used the word *neutrality* to characterize the difficult course which the Court must steer "between the two Religion Clauses, both of which are cast in absolute terms, and either of which, if extended to a logical extreme, would tend to clash with

---

42 374 U.S. 398 (1963).

43 *Id*. at 422.

44 397 U.S. at 694.

45 *Id*. at 696.

the other."[46] The steering is to be done with a view to "an accommodation of the Establishment and Free Exercise Clauses" which produces a "benevolent" neutrality.[47]

I have some misgivings about this term. But perhaps the phrase is merely a recognition of the Roger Williams tradition. Perhaps "benevolent" neutrality is merely a "tutored" neutrality, designed to set at rest the fears expressed in *Schempp* by Justices Goldberg and Harlan that[48]

> untutored devotion to the concept of neutrality can lean to invocation or approval of results which partake not simply of that noninterference and noninvolvement with the religious which the Constitution commands, but of a brooding and pervasive devotion to the secular and a passive, or even active, hostility to the religious.

Perhaps one may trust that the Court's benevolence is directed just as warmly toward nonbelievers as it is toward believers. Mr. Justice Harlan took pains to "suppose" that New York's tax exemption category included "groups whose avowed tenets may be antitheological, atheistic, or agnostic."[49]

V. The Zone of Legislative Discretion

Discussions of the First Amendment often give the impression that the two religion clauses leave legislatures with little or no freedom of action. It often seems to be suggested that the provision in question is either required by the Free Exercise Clause or forbidden by the Establishment Clause. *Sherbert v. Verner*[50] has perhaps contributed to this impression. The Court held that a Seventh-Day Adventist could not be denied unemployment compensation because of her refusal to take a position requiring work on Saturdays. Mr. Justice Brennan had difficulty in distinguishing *Braunfeld v. Brown*,[51] in which the Court had held that Sabbatarian exemption from Sunday closing laws are a matter for legislative discretion. *Sherbert* may therefore undermine the authority of *Braunfeld*.

In *Walz* the Chief Justice pictured the Court both as struggling navigators seeking a narrow channel between the two clauses and

---

[46] *Id.* at 668–69.

[47] *Id.* at 669.

[48] 374 U.S. at 306.

[49] 397 U.S. at 697.

[50] Note 42 *supra.*

[51] 366 U.S. 599 (1961).

as aerial acrobats traversing a "tight rope."[52] But he clarified matters by incorporating the dictum from Mr. Justice Harlan's *Sherbert* dissent that the channel is not so narrow that "the slightest
deviation from a straight course leads to condemnation."[53] Furthermore, Chief Justice Burger declared:[54]

> The limits of permissible state accommodation to religion are
> by no means co-extensive with the noninterference mandated
> by the Free Exercise Clause. To equate the two would be to
> deny a national heritage with roots in the Revolution itself.

In other words, the Establishment Clause leaves legislatures free
to expand the freedom of religious choice beyond that protected
by the Free Exercise Clause.

In *Walz* the Court was confronted not only with the plaintiff's
Establishment Clause claim but also with the contention urged by
the National Council of Churches and other *amici* that the withdrawal of church tax exemption would violate the Free Exercise
Clause. The Court did not mention this contention, but it quoted
a dictum in an 1886 case involving property "owned by but not
used for the church":[55]

> In the exercise of this [taxing] power, Congress, like any State
> legislature unrestricted by constitutional provisions, may at its
> discretion wholly exempt certain classes of property from taxa-
> tion, or may tax them at a lower rate than other property.
> *Gibbon* v. *District of Columbia*, 116 U.S. 404, 408 (1886).

Mr. Justice Brennan dealt with the free exercise problem more
explicitly:[56]

> The state involvement with religion which would be occa-
> sioned by any cessation of exemptions might conflict with
> the demands of the Free Exercise Clause. . . . It is unnecessary
> to reach any questions of free exercise in the present case, how-
> ever. And while I believe that "hostility, not neutrality, would
> characterize the refusal to provide [the exemptions], . . . I do
> not say that government *must* provide [them]."

References in the *Walz* opinions to the "entanglements" which
taxation of churches would bring about may leave some doubt as

---

[52] 397 U.S. at 668, 672.   [54] *Id.* at 673.

[53] *Id.* at 669.   [55] *Id.* at 679–80.

[56] *Id.* at 692 n. 12. Here Mr. Justice Brennan was quoting from his own opinion
in *Schempp*.

to the constitutional power to tax. It should be added that the opinions contain no discussion of the power to tax business income of churches or their income producing property.

In general, *Walz* clearly recognizes a zone of discretionary power. This is a zone within which legislatures may express their benevolence toward religion or, as I should prefer to put it, within which they may adopt measures designed to protect the freedom of religious and nonreligious choice.

VI. A Charter for Religious Pluralism

A striking feature of Mr. Justice Brennan's *Walz* opinion is his treatment of the fostering of a vigorous pluralism as an independent justification of including churches in tax exemption statutes:[57]

> ... government grants exemptions to religious organizations because they uniquely contribute to the pluralism of American society by their religious activities. Government may properly include religious institutions among the variety of private, nonprofit groups that receive tax exemptions, for each group contributes to the diversity of association, viewpoint and enterprise essential to a vigorous, pluralistic society.

To sustain tax exemptions under one of his Establishment Clause tests, Mr. Justice Brennan had to find that the exemptions did not "use essentially religious means to serve governmental ends, where secular means would suffice." He held that for the purpose of fostering a vigorous pluralism, secular means would not alone suffice:[58]

> It is true that each church contributes to the pluralism of our society through its purely religious activities, but the state encourages these activities not because it champions religion *per se* but because it values religion among a variety of private, nonprofit enterprises that contribute to the diversity of the Nation. Viewed in this light, *there is no nonreligious substitute for religion as an element in our societal mosaic, just as there is no non-literary substitute for literary groups.*

Mr. Justice Harlan in an intriguing *Walz* footnote raised a question concerning pluralism. Referring in the text of his opinion to the questions which the granting of "subsidies or direct aid" would present, he noted that "The dimension of the problem would also

---

[57] 397 U.S. at 689.   [58] *Id.* at 693. Emphasis added.

require consideration of what kind of pluralistic society is compatible with the political concepts and traditions embodied in our Constitution."[59] Turning the question around, what kinds of pluralistic societies may be incompatible with our traditions? This would presumably be true of a pluralism in which equal benefits would be given to groups from which persons are excluded on grounds of race. Might it conceivably be true of a pluralism in which equal favor would be shown to groups which reject the principle of religious liberty?

A few years ago I sketched an ideal pluralist society, a society in which a prevailing attitude toward differences reinforces and contributes to social cohesiveness.[60] In such a religiously pluralistic society, the principal religious groups not only claim freedom for themselves but affirm equal freedom for others. In such a society, these groups have also an internal freedom which is reflected in tolerance of criticism and openness to new insights. Individuals are free to doubt and to believe. This freedom is affirmed because of a realization of the need for dialogue, because groups and individuals have a stake—a religious stake—in the freedom of others. The model pluralism is also one in which there is a sensitivity to the differing needs of various groups and a disposition to accommodate these needs. Such a society need not embody perfection. It may contain groups that do not believe in or practice religious freedom. But a society can approximate the model pluralism only if such groups are no great threat to freedom, if a trust in the common commitment to religious freedom prevails among the principal groups. I interpreted Supreme Court decisions of the sixties as creating a legal structure favorable to the maturing of this kind of pluralism.

I have attempted to catch some of the radiations from the opinions in *Walz*. Their power may become apparent at the Court's October Term, 1970. On the docket are *Tilton v. Richardson*,[61] concerned with grants to church-related colleges under the federal Higher Education Facilities Act of 1963, and *Lemon v. Kurtzman*,[62] involving the Pennsylvania Non-Public Elementary and Secondary School Act of 1968.

---

[59] 397 U.S. at 699 n. 2.

[60] Katz and Southerland, *Religious Pluralism and The Supreme Court*, 96 DAEDALUS 180 (1967).

[61] Probable jurisdiction noted, 399 U.S. 904 (1970).

[62] Probable jurisdiction noted, 397 U.S. 1034 (1970).

WALTER BERNS

FREEDOM OF THE PRESS AND

THE ALIEN AND SEDITION LAWS:

A REAPPRAISAL

Until a few years ago it was customary, even among scholars, to
regard the beginning of America as the beginning of free government, at least in the modern world. According to Lincoln, the
nation was "conceived in Liberty." Seventy-five years earlier Madison, who was in a position to understand the significance of the
event, said that nothing had "excited more admiration in the world,
than the manner in which free governments had been established
in America."[1] It was, he continued, "the first instance from the
creation of the world to the American revolution, that free inhabitants have been seen deliberating on a form of government."[2] The
Union, Charles Pinckney said, is "the temple of our freedom."[3]

Such sentiments, and they could be collected by the thousands,
constitute a major part of the American political legacy. From the
beginning Americans have proclaimed liberty, have fought wars
in its name, have evaluated events and institutions and policies in
its light. They have convinced themselves not only that they are
and have always been a free people, but that they were intended
to be a free people whose institutions could serve, and were intended to serve, as a model for the world. America, Lincoln said,

Walter Berns is Professor of Political Science, University of Toronto.

[1] 3 ELLIOTT, DEBATES ON THE FEDERAL CONSTITUTION 556 (1836 ed.).

[2] *Ibid.*   [3] 4 *id.* at 316.

is "the last best hope of earth." In short, Americans were, or believed they were, the beneficiaries of a legacy of liberty.

It was, therefore, a sobering experience to be told by Professor Leonard Levy that, at least to the extent that free speech and press are essential elements of free government, Americans had been bequeathed a legacy of suppression.[4] The Bill of Rights, with its cherished guarantee of free speech and press, according to Levy, did not mean to the men who wrote it what Americans had become accustomed to think it meant. In fact, they may only have been "the chance product of political expediency."[5] "A broad libertarian theory of freedom of speech and press did not emerge in the United States until the Jeffersonians, when a minority party, were forced to defend themselves against the Federalist Sedition Act of 1798."[6] According to the traditional view, the infamous Alien and Sedition Laws, certainly the latter, would have been declared unconstitutional had they ever come before the Supreme Court, assuming that the Federalist Supreme Court would succeed in putting aside its partisan prejudices. Instead, it was left to Madison and Jefferson to protest their unconstitutionality in the Virginia and Kentucky Resolutions and then to form a new political party to effect their repeal, or more precisely, their demise:[7]

> However interesting these famous Resolutions may be for the Constitutional doctrine they contain, they were intended *primarily* as a defense, practical and spirited, of civil liberties. Some of the most severe infringements upon those liberties ever to be sanctioned by an American Congress—the Alien and Sedition Laws—were therefore more than the *occasion* of the Resolutions; they were the cause.

Yet, contrary to Professor Levy, there is reason to believe that it was not really a "broad libertarian theory" that emerged during the fight against the Alien and Sedition Laws; and that, contrary to Professors Koch and Ammon, these laws were the occasion more than the cause of Madison and Jefferson's famous resolutions. The principle on which especially Jefferson and John Taylor and some

---

[4] LEVY, LEGACY OF SUPPRESSION: FREEDOM OF SPEECH AND PRESS IN EARLY AMERICAN HISTORY (1960).

[5] *Id.* at vii.   [6] *Id.* at viii–ix.

[7] Koch & Ammon, *The Virginia and Kentucky Resolutions: An Episode in Jefferson's and Madison's Defense of Civil Liberties*, 5 WM. & MARY Q. (3d ser.) 174 (April, 1948).

other Republican leaders based their opposition was not "a broad libertarian" version of civil liberties but the doctrine of states' rights, or nullification, or disunion. The men principally responsible for the development of a liberal law of free speech and press—for fashioning a remedy for the deprivation of the constitutional rights of freedom of speech and press—were the Federalists Alexander Hamilton and James Kent, who were able to do this because, unlike Jefferson and his colleagues and successors, they were not inhibited by an attachment to the institution of slavery.

I. The Alien and Sedition Laws

The political situation that gave rise to the Alien and Sedition Laws is familiar. The treaty of peace with Britain provoked the French and those Americans who were shortly to become acknowledged Republicans. The attempt to settle the differences with the French involved the ill-fated mission of Gerry, Pinckney, and Marshall. Talleyrand's request for money as a condition of a settlement in the XYZ Affair discredited the American "Francophiles" and very nearly provoked an American-French war. ("Millions for defense, but not a cent for tribute.") As a defense measure, designed to protect the country against alien opinion and the aliens themselves (whether French, "Wild Irish," or criminal English— but in any case, Republican), and with an inflated notion of both their virtue and their strength in the country, the Federalists enacted, over the intense opposition of the Republicans, the Alien and Sedition Laws, which Federalist prosecutors and Federalist judges proceeded to use in an effort to silence their opponents. Their opponents accused them of intending to silence opposition itself and to effect a revolutionary change in the regime, namely, to establish a monarchy or a "monocracy" in the place of the republic. With the exception of the Civil War and the periods immediately preceding and succeeding it—and perhaps the contemporary "fascist pig" era—America probably has not known a time when its politics were conducted with such vehemence and hatred.[8]

It is probably the case that not even the press of the late 1960's can match that of the late 1790's, with its Benjamin Franklin Bache and William Duane of the Philadelphia *Aurora* and James Callen-

---

[8] The events are recounted in MILLER, CRISIS IN FREEDOM: THE ALIEN AND SEDITION ACTS (1951).

der, on the one side, and its William Cobbett of *Porcupine's Ga-zette* and John Ward Fenno of the *Gazette of the United States,* on the other. Callender referred to Washington and Adams as "poltroons" and "venal" and Adams as a "libeller" and a "hoary headed incendiary" whose "hands are reeking with the blood of the poor, friendless Connecticut sailor," as a liar whose office was a "scene of profligacy and . . . usury," and whose purpose was to "embroil this country [in a war] with France."[9] Cobbett, in his *Porcupine's Gazette,* the most scurrilous of the Federalist journals, referred to his political opponents as, among other things, the "refuse of nations" and "frog-eating, man-eating, blood-drinking cannibals." An action was begun against him in 1797, for libeling the Spanish minister to the United States, Don Carlos Martinez d'Yrujo. Despite the efforts of Thomas McKean, a leading Penn-sylvania Republican and chief justice of that state's supreme court (and also Martinez's father-in-law), the grand jury refused to return a true bill.[10] When McKean ran for governor of Pennsylvania, John Ward Fenno wrote:[11]

> *Twenty thousand* FRENCHMEN, and *twenty thousand* UNITED IRISHMEN: What a precious horde of Sans Culotte cutthroats are these to teach what true liberty is! And Americans remember, there are men among you, your countrymen too, who declare they wish these ruffians would come into the United States to teach Americans what *true liberty is*!!!—Pennsyl-vanians, would you like to be governed by a man whose wish it is to have these villains for your political teachers [Cobbett more than once had accused McKean of making such a statement]:—If you do not wish it, look well to your election for GOVERNOR.

It would be expecting a great measure of equanimity or magnanimity to ask public men to be undisturbed by such slander and to take no action against it. Washington, surely the most magnanimous man of the age, was unwilling to ignore it. So it is not strange that the victims of it, of both parties, resorted to the law,

---

[9] WHARTON, STATE TRIALS OF THE UNITED STATES DURING THE ADMINISTRATIONS OF WASHINGTON AND ADAMS 689 (1849).

[10] *Id.* at 322–32. Cobbett was later successfully sued for libel by Benjamin Rush and was fined $5,000 plus costs, by far the heaviest fine assessed in a libel action during this period.

[11] Gazette of the United States, Aug. 16, 1799, p. 3.

as well as to duels and less organized violence. The "Francophiles" turned to the common law administered by state courts, and the "Monocrats," or Federalists, because they were uncertain as to whether the federal courts enjoyed a common law jurisdiction, invoked federal legislation and federal courts.

The Federalists' concern with aliens and sedition gave rise to four distinct but related pieces of legislation, all enacted in less than a month's time during the summer of 1798. The first was a naturalization law that increased the period of residence required of an alien to be eligible for citizenship from five to fourteen years.[12] The principal provision of the second, the so-called Alien Friends Act, authorized the President to deport all aliens whom he regarded as "dangerous to the peace and safety of the United States."[13] It was a temporary measure, to be in force for two years after its passage. The third, entitled "An Act respecting Alien Enemies," was genuinely a wartime measure operative only during a "declared war" or a real or threatened invasion, which event was to be officially proclaimed by the President.[14] It authorized him, after issuing the proclamation, to apprehend, restrain, secure, or remove any national of a country at war with the United States. The fourth was the notorious Sedition Act, consisting of four sections.[15] The first section provided for the punishment of anyone who unlawfully combined to oppose the laws of the United States. The fourth section provided that the act was to be in force until March 3, 1801, that is, until one day before the inauguration of the next President. It is the second and third sections that have come to be known as the Sedition Act.[16] Under these provisions indictments were

---

[12] 1 Stat. 566 (1798).   [14] 1 Stat. 577 (1798).

[13] 1 Stat. 570 (1798).   [15] 1 Stat. 596 (1798).

[16] "SEC. 2. *And be it further enacted,* That if any person shall write, print, utter or publish, or shall cause or procure to be written, printed, uttered or published, or shall knowingly and willingly assist or aid in writing, printing, uttering or publishing any false, scandalous and malicious writing or writings against the government of the United States, or either house of the Congress of the United States, or the President of the United States, with intent to defame the said government, or either house of the said Congress, or the said President, or to bring them, or either of them, into contempt or disrepute; or to excite against them, or either of them, the hatred of the good people of the United States, or to stir up sedition within the United States, or to excite any unlawful combinations therein, for opposing or resisting any law of the United States, or any act of the President of the United States, done in pursuance of any such law, or of the powers vested in him by the constitution of the United States, or to resist, oppose, or defeat any such law or act, or to aid, encourage

brought against fourteen persons (one of them, William Duane, was indicted twice), ten of whom were convicted and sentenced to pay fines ranging from five dollars to a thousand dollars and to be imprisoned for periods ranging from six to eighteen months.[17] No one, apparently, neither "Wild Irishman" nor "Jacobin," was deported under either of the Alien acts.

II. The Opposition to the Alien and Sedition Laws: In Congress

> Are not we, the people of the United States of America, a sovereign and independent nation? Have we not, as a nation, all the rights pertaining to that state, equally with any other nation?[18]

The first congressman to speak out in opposition to the Alien Friends bill, the estimable Albert Gallatin, subsequently to have so distinguished a career in the service of his adopted country, sounded the theme that was to dominate the Republican attack on the Alien and Sedition Laws:[19]

> . . . it must be agreed by all that every nation had a right to permit or exclude alien friends from entering within the bounds of their society. This is a right inherent in every independent nation; but that power is vested, according to the Constitutions of different countries, in one or other branch of the Government. In this country . . . the power to admit, or to exclude alien friends, does solely belong to each individual State, and . . . the General Government has no power over them, and, therefore . . . all the provisions in this bill are perfectly unconstitutional.

---

or abet any hostile designs of any foreign nation against the United States, their people or government, then such person, being thereof convicted before any court of the United States having jurisdiction thereof, shall be punished by a fine not exceeding two thousand dollars, and by imprisonment not exceeding two years.

"Sec. 3. *And be it further enacted and declared,* That if any person shall be prosecuted under this act, for the writing or publishing any libel aforesaid, it shall be lawful for the defendant, upon the trial of the cause, to give in evidence in his defence, the truth of the matter contained in the publication charged as a libel. And the jury who shall try the cause, shall have a right to determine the law and the fact, under the direction of the court, as in other cases."

[17] The most extensive coverage of the enactment of the Alien and Sedition Laws and the subsequent trials is in Smith, Freedom's Fetters: The Alien and Sedition Laws and American Civil Liberties (1956).

[18] [Evans], An Address to the People of Virginia Respecting the Alien and Sedition Laws, By a Citizen of the State (1798).

[19] Annals of Congress 1955 (1798).

In short, while every sovereign nation has an inherent right to exclude aliens, the United States has no such right because it is not a sovereign nation. This is hardly a civil liberties argument.

Indeed, with respect to the merits of such legislation there is no difference between Gallatin's principle and that subsequently adopted by the Supreme Court of the United States. In 1892 the Court said that it "is an accepted maxim of international law, that every sovereign nation has the power, as inherent in sovereignty, and essential to self-preservation, to forbid the entrance of foreigners within its dominions, or to admit them only in cases and upon such conditions as it may see fit to prescribe."[20] A year later the Court quoted this passage and added that the "right to exclude or to expel all aliens, or any class of aliens, absolutely or upon certain conditions, in war or in peace, [is] an inherent and inalienable right of every sovereign and independent nation."[21] Unlike Gallatin and his Republican associates in Congress, however, the Court by then understood the United States to be a "sovereign and independent nation."

Whether a persuasive argument could have been made against the Alien Friends Act, an argument objecting to it on principle or expediency, is not here in question. What is relevant is that the Republican leader in the House chose to begin the debate by denying the sovereignty of the national government. Gallatin was not alone. His principally was the one argument made by the Republicans. It was the argument that led Robert Goodloe Harper, one of the Federalist leaders in the House, to doubt whether his opponents were serious and to claim that they had adopted it only because the bill could not be "opposed on the ground of expediency."[22] It was not until June 21, five days later, and on the bill's third reading, that anyone voiced an objection to it on its merits. This was done by Edward Livingston of New York, who had just arrived. He protested that the bill would give the President despotic power over aliens insofar as it would allow him to decide what conduct merited expulsion from the country.

Despite Harper's doubts, however, the opponents of the Alien Friends bill were "serious" in their stand on states' rights. They were serious because they saw, or imagined, a connection between the

---

[20] Nishimura Ekiu v. United States, 142 U.S. 651, 659 (1892).

[21] Fong Yue Ting v. United States, 149 U.S. 698, 705, 711 (1893).

[22] ANNALS OF CONGRESS 1989 (1798).

principle of power being asserted here, the authority that permitted Congress to expel aliens, and the authority to affect an interest dearer to them than any other, an interest as unconcerned with civil liberties as any interest could be: slavery. Whether pro- or anti-slavery, most southerners, including Jefferson and Madison and all who were shortly to acknowledge formally a membership in the Republican party, were united behind a policy of denying to the national government any competence to deal with the question of slavery.[23] Slavery was a "domestic" matter—that is to say, a local matter—and only the states could be trusted to deal with it and, therefore, only the states possessed the constitutional authority to deal with it. From the time of the debates beginning in February, 1790, on the first of the petitions from the Pennsylvania Quakers calling for a "sincere and impartial inquiry" into the slave trade, to Taney's opinion for the Court in *Dred Scott v. Sanford*[24] in 1857, and on a host of occasions in between, whether the issue was avowedly one of slavery or, as in the case of the Alien Friends bill, only tangentially one of slavery, southerners insisted on the competence of the states and the incompetence of the national government in this matter. Certainly Gallatin was no friend to slavery (although he said he would oppose a proposal to keep slavery out of Mississippi if it threatened the property of slave owners already in the Territory).[25] But his southern colleagues were, and it was the southerners who supplied most of the votes against the Alien Friends bill. It passed by a vote of 46 to 40, and 30 of those 40 voting against the measure came from southern slave states.[26] Of the 46 voting in favor of the measure, only 10 came from slave states, and 5 of these were from Maryland. The vote in the Senate is equally instructive. The measure carried by a vote of 16 to 7; and all 7 votes in opposition were cast by slave-state senators.[27]

---

[23] Exceptions were made in the cases of fugitive slaves and the foreign slave trade.

[24] 19 How. 393 (1857).

[25] ANNALS OF CONGRESS 1310 (1798).

[26] *Id.* at 2028. Of the others, 6 came from Pennsylvania, 2 from New York, 1 from Massachusetts, and 1 from Vermont (Matthew Lyon). Lyon was to be one of those convicted under the Sedition Act.

[27] *Id.* at 575. Only 5 of the 16 favorable votes were cast by slave-state senators: 2 from Delaware and 1 each from Maryland, North Carolina, and South Carolina. I am counting northern states as nonslave states although the process of emancipation had not been completed by 1798.

This kind of sectional split is traditionally and rightly associated with the slavery issue and it is somewhat strange that the principal historians of the event have not remarked it. The Jay's Treaty dispute is seen by some commentators as largely a dispute over slavery, if only because of Jay's failure or refusal to insist on compensation from Britain for the slaves taken during the Revolutionary War. Yet in the House only three men (George Dent and Samuel Smith of Maryland and Andrew Gregg of Pennsylvania) voted for the treaty[28] but against the Alien Friends bill, and in the Senate only two men switched sides, Humphrey Marshall of Kentucky joining his southern associates on the Alien bill, having voted for the treaty, and Alexander Martin of North Carolina voting for the Alien bill having voted against the treaty. To say, as many historians have done, that both issues provoked straight, or almost straight, party votes is to beg the question, for it in a sense assumes the prior existence of well-defined parties and ignores the question of what it was that led to the formation of these parties. More precisely, it ignores the question of the extent to which slavery and the desire to have policy about slavery made at the state level led Jefferson and his friends to form a political party in order to wrest control of the national government from the men we call Federalists.[29] Even James Morton Smith, despite the detail of his study,[30] makes no reference to the expressions of concern for the institution of slavery uttered by southerners during the course of the debate on the Alien Friends bill.

The second Republican, and the first southerner, to speak against the bill in the House of Representatives was Robert Williams of North Carolina. A preceding speaker, Samuel Sewell of Massachusetts, had claimed constitutional authority for it in the Commerce Clause, and Williams replied that it was a "curious idea, that all emigrants coming to this country should be considered as articles of commerce."[31] If this were accepted, he went on, nothing would pre-

---

28 ANNALS OF CONGRESS 1291 (1795). The vote was on the resolution for carrying the treaty into effect.

29 Most studies of the question of formation of political parties in this period tend to ignore the extent to which the issue of slavery was one causative factor. *Compare*, e.g., CHAMBERS, POLITICAL PARTIES IN A NEW NATION: THE AMERICAN EXPERIENCE, 1776–1809 (1963), *with* John Quincy Adams, *Parties in the United States* 1 (1829), in ADAMS PAPERS, microfilm, Film 469, Reel #246. Adams did attribute the birth of parties to the "establishment of slavery," among other things.

30 Note 17 *supra*.　　　　　　　　31 ANNALS OF CONGRESS 1963 (1798).

vent Congress from claiming the power to send slaves out of the country. "And as ready as the Southern States are to grant slaves are a dangerous property and an evil in their country, they will not consent to Congress assuming the power of depriving their owners of them, contrary to their will."[32] And when the proponents claimed constitutional authority under the first part of Article I, § 8, Abraham Baldwin of Georgia said that this provision respecting the power to provide for the general welfare "had never been considered as a source of Legislative power. [In fact, the] first instance in which it had ever been attempted to be acted upon . . . was on the application of the Abolition Societies to Congress to act upon which was said to be derived from these words."[33] Baldwin had no doubt that "if this bill passed into a law, Congress would again be appealed to by the advocates for an abolition of slavery, with requests that the President may be authorized to send these persons out of the country, and strong arguments will be used in favor of the measure."[34] Against this danger Baldwin had an obvious safeguard, the states, and a constitutional principle that later almost destroyed the Union, states' rights: " . . . this business of admitting or banishing aliens belonged to State Governments, and not to the General Government."[35]

Gallatin and others went so far as to argue that the power to expel aliens, like the power to expel slaves, was expressly forbidden until 1808 by Article I, § 9, of the Constitution, because the prohibition on exclusion carried with it a prohibition on expulsion, and the phrase "such persons," they insisted, referred to aliens as well as to slaves.[36] As Mr. Mercer said in the course of the debate on the Virginia Resolutions in the Virginia House of Delegates, the Alien Law "virtually destroyed the right of the states under [Art. I, § 9]; for though the states might admit . . . such persons as they might think

---

[32] Ibid.

[33] Id. at 1968.

[34] Ibid.

[35] Ibid.

[36] Id. at 1979. The provision reads as follows: "The migration or importation of such persons as any of the States now existing shall think proper to admit shall not be prohibited by the Congress prior to the year [1808]." However dangerous the suggested reading could be in the future because of its concession that Congress could then expel slaves, it was convenient to southern interests because it denied congressional power over the domestic slave trade as well as the importation of slaves. See Berns, The Constitution and the Migration of Slaves, 78 YALE L.J. 198 (1968).

proper prior to a certain period, it was to little purpose, if the President . . . could send them away."[37] Like his colleagues in the House of Representatives, Mercer was concerned that in conceding a power over aliens, they were also conceding a power over slaves. Thus, the national government must be denied a power to expel aliens. And thanks to the rhetoric of the Republican editors, the bill came to be denounced as a "draconic measure."[38]

This was not the principal response of the opponents of the bill in the House. Those from Virginia especially were in no position to inveigh against the measure in such terms unless they were willing to apply the same language to a law of their own state. As George K. Taylor of Prince Georges County, Virginia, said during the debate on the Virginia Resolutions in the Virginia House of Delegates, the state had enacted an alien law in 1792, a law that "authorized the Governor to apprehend, and secure, and compel to depart out of the commonwealth, all suspicious persons etc. *from whom the President of the United States should apprehend hostile designs against the said states.*"[39] This state law made no provision for trials, even though the Virginia constitution, Taylor said, declared trial by jury to be a sacred right. " . . . the legislature of the state could have no more power by the constitution to pass such a law than Congress had by the constitution of the United States. Yet no complaint against such a law had ever been heard until the law of Congress was passed. All the clamour had been reserved for that alone."[40] The federal law, he said, merely does what the Virginia law does: permits aliens to be sent out of the country "at the instance of the President." Taylor was answered by one Ruffin with the familiar states' rights argument to the effect that the power over aliens was a right reserved to the states,[41] which is an answer—by then a familiar answer—but not, again, a stirring declaration of the rights of man. It

---

[37] Debates in the House of Delegates of Virginia, upon Certain Resolutions before the House, upon the Important Subject of the Acts of Congress Passed at Their Last Session, Commonly Called the Alien and Sedition Laws 37 (1818) (hereinafter referred to as Debates). The references herein will be to the original volume, but the debates are reprinted in Sen. Doc. No. 873, 62d Cong., 2d Sess. (1912).

[38] Smith, note 17 *supra*, at 53.   [39] Debates 20.

[40] *Id*. at 21. See A Collection of all such Acts of the General Assembly of Virginia, of a Public and Permanent Nature, etc. 65 (1794), reprinted in 1 Revised Code of the Laws of Virginia 142–43 (1819).

[41] Debates 24.

was states' rights not civil liberties that concerned the Republicans.

The debate on the Sedition bill, which began immediately after the passage of the Alien Friends bill, was interrupted the following day (July 6) in order to discuss the question whether the country was in fact already at war with France and whether Congress should formally make a declaration of this fact. Instead, the House contented itself with agreeing (after amendments) to the Senate bill abrogating various treaties with France. It was against this background of grave international problems that these bills were debated and adopted.

Edward Livingston began the debate on the Sedition bill by moving to reject it in its entirety. John Allen of Connecticut responded in such a way that the issue of free expression under the Constitution was immediately joined, or at least broached. Allen quoted a typical tirade against President Adams from the New York *Time-Piece*, and asked whether anyone seriously contended that the liberty of the press extended to such publications. "Because the Constitution guarantees . . . the freedom of the press, am I at liberty to falsely call you a thief, a murderer, an atheist? . . . The freedom of the press and opinions was never understood to give the right of publishing falsehoods and slanders, nor of exciting sedition, insurrection, and slaughter, with impunity. A man was always answerable for the malicious publication of falsehood; and what more does this bill require?"[42] Allen was followed by Harper, who, acknowledging that he had often heard in Congress and out "harangues on the liberty of the press," defined this liberty after the manner of Blackstone, which, indeed, was the accepted understanding on the subject at the time: " . . . the true meaning of [liberty of the press] is no more than that a man shall be at liberty to print what he pleases, provided he does not offend against the laws, and not that no law shall be passed to regulate this liberty of the press."[43] Such an understanding did not preclude prosecutions of seditious libels, either at the common law or under the proposed legislation, and, according to Leonard Levy, it was only under "the pressure of the Sedition Act [that] writers of the Jeffersonian party were driven to originate so broad a theory of freedom of expression that the concept of seditious libel was, at last, repudiated."[44] Such a theory did not, however emerge from

---

[42] ANNALS OF CONGRESS 2097 (1798).

[43] *Id*. at 2102. See 4 BLACKSTONE, COMMENTARIES § 151.

[44] LEVY, note 4 *supra*, at 259–60.

the debates in the House. Livingston insisted that the bill violated the
First Amendment, and Livingston was supported in this view by the
next speaker, Nathaniel Macon of North Carolina. But the debates
reveal that neither Livingston nor Macon—nor any of their Republican colleagues—adopted a broad "libertarian" understanding of
the principle of freedom of expression. The bill "directly violated
the letter of the Constitution," Macon said.[45] He regretted that
"at a time like this, when some gentlemen say we are at war, and
when all believe we must have war, that Congress are about to pass
a law which will produce more uneasiness, more irritation, than any
act which ever passed the Legislature of the Union."[46] He challenged the Federalists to show "what part of the Constitution [au-
thorizes] the passage of a law like this."[47] But he then acknowledged
that "persons might be prosecuted for a libel under the State Governments,"[48] and questioned the necessity of a federal law. In short,
he, like his colleagues during the debate on the Alien Friends bill,
objected to the Sedition bill on constitutional grounds and, more
precisely, on states' rights grounds, but he did not argue that such
legislation was objectionable in principle. He made this clear later
in the debate, on July 10, when he asserted that liberty of the press
was sacred and ought to be left where the Constitution had left it:[49]

> The States have complete power on the subject, and when
> Congress legislates, it ought to have confidence in the States.
> . . . He believed there was nowhere any complaint of a want
> of proper laws under the State Governments; and though there
> may not be remedies found for every grievance in the General
> Government, what it wants of power will be found in the State
> Governments, and there can be no doubt but that power will
> be duly exercised when necessity calls for it.

And of course there were such state laws. Harrison Otis of Massachusetts had taxed the Republicans with inconsistency by quoting
state constitutional provisions respecting the rights of free speech
and press, then quoting statutes of the same states making libel a
criminal offense and punishing licentiousness and sedition.[50] In ac-
cusing them of inconsistency, however, he was to some extent missing the thrust of their argument. They were not contending for free
speech and press; they were contending for states' rights, for the

---

[45] ANNALS OF CONGRESS 2105–06 (1798).

[46] Ibid.   [48] Ibid.

[47] Ibid.   [49] Id. at 2152.   [50] Id. at 2148–49.

right of the states to punish seditious libel. The United States for them existed as a form of words, but not as a sovereign nation.

Livingston continued the argument as soon as Macon had resumed his seat. He insisted, in words that are being echoed today by Mr. Justice Black, that Congress may pass "*no* law" abridging the liberty of speech and press (and no law establishing "a national religion"), and the proposed bill was to him clearly such a law. But Livingston as a typical member of the inchoate Republican party was not objecting to the principle of such legislation, any more than his colleagues had objected in principle to the Alien Friends bill. On the contrary, such legislation was essential to a well-ordered republic:[51]

> But, it is said, will you suffer a printer to abuse his fellow-citizens with impunity, ascribing his conduct to the very worst of motives? Is no punishment to be inflicted on such a person? Yes. There is a remedy of offenses of this kind in the laws of every State in the Union. Every man's character is protected by law, and every man who shall publish a libel on any part of the Government, is liable to punishment. Not . . . by laws which we ourselves have made, but by the laws passed by the several States.

The Sedition bill violated the Constitution, Livingston argued, because the power to punish libels—the power to enact criminal libel laws and to enforce them—was reserved by the Constitution to the states. Furthermore, he went on, the fair administration of justice required this arrangement:[52]

> Suppose a libel were written against the President, where is it most probable that such an offence would receive an impartial trial? In a court, the judges of which are appointed by the President, by a jury selected by an officer holding his office at the will of the President? or in a court independent of any influence whatever?

Whether the state courts could fairly be described as "independent of any influence whatever"—that is, whether they could have provided impartial forums for the prosecution of criminal libels against the President of the Union—is a fair question. Surely they could scarcely have proved less impartial than the federal courts were soon to prove themselves to be. One historian, Charles Warren, has written that the "proper remedy for all the flood of scurrility and cal-

---

[51] *Id.* at 2153.   [52] *Ibid.*

umny, which swelled each succeeding year of the Adams administration, was a more rigid enforcement of the laws of criminal libel
by state officials and courts,"[53] thus agreeing altogether with Livingston. But state prosecutions depended on state officials, and no Virginia official, for example, would likely have proved assiduous in the
defense of John Adams' good name. To cite another example,
whereas the officials of Republican Pennsylvania did not hesitate to
prosecute libels against Pennsylvania Republicans, there is no record
of their being equally zealous when it came to prosecuting libels
made against the Federalist officials of the national government, the
capital of which was temporarily located in the state's principal city.
"A criminal libel proceeding," Warren continued, "was a weapon
which could be employed by both parties."[54] He was probably correct when he added, as an account of the Federalists' motives, that
they "wished absolution for their own words, and punishment only
for their opponents'."[55] But he might have said the same thing of the
Republicans.[56] The difference was (and this attests to one of the
virtues of the federal system) that the Federalists with the national
law, and attributing the worst of motives to them, would have silenced their opponents throughout the length and breadth of the
land, whereas the Republicans would have silenced the Federalists
only in those states they, the Republicans, controlled. As Jefferson
was shortly to learn through his mistaken reliance on resolutions issuing from state legislatures, to be effective on a national scale requires activity on a national scale, and ultimately control of the
national government. In the summer of 1798, however, he and his
party were preaching states' rights and, soon to become apparent,
nullification and disunion. They were not defending civil liberties—
except, one must add immediately, to the extent that civil liberty,
to them, depended on their states' rights view of the Constitution
and the Union.

   Thus, while the Jefferson party in the Congress argued the bill's

---

[53] JACOBIN AND JUNTO 97 (1931).

[54] Ibid.   [55] Ibid.

[56] In answer to Gallatin during the last stages of the debate, Harper stated that
the purpose of the bill was to transfer "the trial of libels and sedition [from the]
State courts . . . to the Courts of the United States." To leave such trials in the state
courts, he said, "would be running into Scylla, in an attempt to avoid Charybdis.
There was, certainly, as much danger of partiality on one side as the other." ANNALS
OF CONGRESS 2166 (1798).

unconstitutionality, insisting that no power to enact it could be found among the powers enumerated in the Constitution and that the First Amendment expressly prohibited it, they did so in the context of defending the right of the states to enact and enforce such laws. Only in one limited respect did they "originate" a broad libertarian theory in Levy's modern sense: one Virginia Republican, John Nicholas, questioned the distinction, what Levy calls the "alleged" distinction,[57] between liberty and license,[58] thereby challenging the prevailing Blackstonian view of the right of free expression. For, to Blackstone and the Federalists, free expression meant, to state the matter simply, no previous restraints but punishment for abuses, a view that presupposes a distinction between liberty and license and the ability of a court to discern and define it. Later the same day Gallatin pursued this point, contending that the First Amendment could not (and must not) be understood as prohibiting merely previous restraints. Whereas laws could be enacted requiring a license to print, and this would be a previous restraint on the press, what, he asked, could possibly constitute a previous restraint on the liberty of speech? Since it was impossible to conceive of such a law, he contended, and because the First Amendment forbids the abridgment of the freedom of speech as well as of the press, it must be understood to forbid more than previous restraints.[59] Such an argument would certainly constitute evidence of the beginnings of a broader libertarian theory, simply by virtue of the fact that it rejects the essential principle of the Blackstonian "theory," except for the equally obvious fact that, having made the point, Gallatin undermined it by the characteristic Republican insistence that, anyway, the trial of criminal libels "belonged to the State courts"—exclusively.[60]

Harper answered Gallatin in the last speech of the debate, and, in the course of a long rebuttal, asked: Can there be "so great an absurdity, can such a political monster exist, as a Government which has no power to protect itself against sedition and libels?"[61] What-

---

[57] Levy, note 4 supra, at x.   [58] Annals of Congress 2140, 2142 (1798).

[59] Id. at 2160. In his inability to "conceive" of a law "laying such restraints upon speech," Gallatin was displaying a politically limited imagination. See, e.g., Hague v. C.I.O., 307 U.S. 496 (1939); Kunz v. New York, 340 U.S. 290 (1951); Poulos v. New Hampshire, 345 U.S. 395 (1953).

[60] Annals of Congress 2163 (1798). Smith overlooks this critical fact about Gallatin's position. Smith, note 17 supra, at 141–42.

[61] Annals of Congress 2167 (1798).

ever the true answer may be to the question, the answer of the Jefferson party was, once again, the United States is not a sovereign government. Or more precisely, it is a collection of sovereign states each of which has a government, but it is itself not an entity authorized to govern in matters respecting aliens and sedition.

The bill was then passed by a vote of 44 to 41.[62] Two men, Stephen Bullock of Massachusetts and William Matthews of Maryland, who had voted for the Alien Friends bill voted against the Sedition bill, but otherwise, if a few absentees on each occasion are ignored, the division was the same as it had been on the earlier measure. In the Senate no one changed his vote.

III. The Opposition to the Alien and Sedition Acts: The Virginia and Kentucky Resolutions

> . . . the discontent displayed in Virginia, Pennsylvania, and Kentucky, cannot convince me that the people throughout the United States were discontented with this law. The truth is, sir, that in those sections of our country where clamors have been raised against this law, everything is disliked and everything is abused which emanates from the Federal Government.[63]

Jefferson has never been an easy subject for his devoted portrayers. His resounding rhetoric, *e.g.*, "I have sworn upon the altar of God, eternal hostility against every form of tyranny over the mind of man," has long made him an object of veneration among Americans. His remarks in his First Inaugural: "If there be any among us who would wish to dissolve this Union or to change its republican form, let them stand undisturbed as monuments of the safety with which error of opinion may be tolerated where reason is left free to combat it," and his views on church and state have made him the special favorite of modern liberals. Among Democrats he has long been regarded as the patron saint of their party. Among southern Democrats he has been and still is revered as the first and greatest champion of their cause, states' rights. In each case, however, with the exception of those who see him as the champion of the cause of separating church and state—an issue on which Jefferson was, even from a modern point of view, thoroughly "liberal" and consistent—

---

62 *Id*. at 2171.

63 Annals of Congress 932 (1799) (Rutledge).

it is a somewhat uneasy affiliation. Civil libertarians have been able to attribute their cause to Jefferson only by ignoring what Leonard Levy has called his "Darker Side."[64] They and the northern Democrats generally have had to overlook his devotion to the cause of states' rights and his hatred of national power. The southerners, who extol his constitutional principles and admire the life he was able to make for himself at Monticello—with the assistance of hundreds of slaves—have difficulty accommodating themselves to his egalitarian sentiments. In these circumstances it is not strange that Jefferson lends himself readily to folklore. Among this folklore is the opinion that he drafted the Kentucky Resolutions in order to preserve "human rights" and as a "sincere champion of the highest practicable degree of human liberty in all fields."[65] To assert that this is not true is not to suggest that Jefferson was not a champion of liberty. That would be absurd. But unless one argues that a necessary condition of liberty in America is states' sovereignty in the full Jeffersonian sense, the evidence is overwhelming that Jefferson was not acting as a champion of liberty when he drafted the Kentucky Resolutions. He drafted them to advance his states' rights view of the Constitution and to set the stage for a dissolution of the Union if this should, according to his judgment, prove necessary. This would depend, in part, on the response of the other states to the Resolutions of Kentucky and Virginia circulated during the last days of 1798.

From his point of view that response was not encouraging, and in a letter to Madison of August 23, 1799, Jefferson proposed a resumption of their efforts.[66] More resolutions should be adopted, he said, resolutions expressing "in affectionate & conciliatory language our warm attachment to union with our sister-states," but also stating the condition of this attachment, that the "American people . . . rally with us round the true principles of our federal compact." If this did not occur, if he and Madison were "to be disappointed in this," the new resolutions must express the determination of Kentucky and Virginia at least, "to sever ourselves from that union we so much value, rather than give up the rights of self government which we have reserved, & in which alone we see liberty, safety & happiness."

---

[64] LEVY, JEFFERSON AND CIVIL LIBERTIES: THE DARKER SIDE (1963).

[65] 3 MALONE, JEFFERSON AND HIS TIME 396–97, see also 394 (1962).

[66] To date, the complete letter seems to have been reprinted in full only in Koch & Ammon, note 7 *supra*, at 165–66.

Shortly after receiving this letter, Madison visited Jefferson at
Monticello, and the result of that visit is reflected in a letter Jefferson wrote to Wilson Cary Nicholas on September 5. He repeated
the proposals he had made two weeks earlier to Madison, and in
identical language—except for the omission of the last sentence
quoted above concerning a willingness to sever the union.[67] Surely
Koch and Ammon are correct in seeing this sentence as the "most
extreme statement that Jefferson ever made concerning the meaning
and intent of the Kentucky Resolutions," and the circumstances,
plus a sentence in the letter to Nicholas, support their view that it
was Madison's influence that led Jefferson to exclude the culpable
sentence from the letter going to Kentucky. "Had Madison failed to
argue as he did," they write, "the contention that the Virginia and
Kentucky Resolutions contained in germinal form the later doctrines of nullification and secession would have rested upon firmer
ground."[68] What this means is that if Madison had not persuaded
his more impetuous and less politic colleague to be circumspect in
what he committed to a letter that was likely to be seen by a number
of people, Jefferson's name would have been linked with that of
Calhoun and Jefferson Davis. But why not? Even the resolutions as
they were published were sufficient to provoke the response that
Kentucky was intending to dissolve the Union,[69] and it was public
knowledge that in 1797 Kentucky was engaged in negotiations with
Spain concerning the navigation of the Mississippi.[70] Jefferson's authorship of the resolutions, rumored at the time and admitted by him
in 1821, has long since been confirmed by the publication of his
writings containing his two drafts of them. Even the second of
these, the so-called fair copy, speaks of "nullification" and the "natural right" of each state "to nullify" acts of the national government
that, in the judgment of the state, exceed the constitutional authority "delegated" to it.[71] It calls upon the states to declare the Alien
and Sedition Laws "void, and no force," and to "take measures . . .

---

[67] 7 WRITINGS OF THOMAS JEFFERSON 389–92 (Ford ed. 1896).

[68] Koch & Ammon, note 7 *supra*, at 167, 168.

[69] Anderson, *Contemporary Opinion of the Virginia and Kentucky Resolutions*,
5 AM. HIST. REV. 238 (1900).

[70] WARFIELD, THE KENTUCKY RESOLUTIONS OF 1798: AN HISTORICAL STUDY 37–38
(1887).

[71] WRITINGS, note 67 *supra*, at 306.

for providing that neither these acts, nor any others of the General Government not plainly and intentionally authorized by the Constitution, shall be exercised within their respective territories."[72] It was Breckenridge who moderated Jefferson's language on this occasion by changing this call to civil disobedience into the call upon Congress to repeal the laws with which the resolutions end. But even the resolutions as Breckenridge moved them and as they were adopted by the legislature speak of "revolution and blood": "unless arrested on the threshold," these acts and others like them "may tend to drive these States into revolution and blood." South Carolina's Ordinance of Nullification in 1832 merely did what Kentucky threatened (or resolved) to do, and what Jefferson wanted Kentucky and other states to do. And the South Carolina nullifiers recognized Jefferson as the source of their principle: " . . . we must come back to Mr. Jefferson's plain, practical and downright principle, as our 'rightful remedy'—a *nullification* by the State . . . of the 'unauthorized act.' "[73] Why, then, should he not be taxed with planting the nullification seed that germinated after his death and blossomed in civil war? Certainly he was more moderate than John Taylor to whom he wrote counseling against dissolution of the Union.[74] But this was mainly the counsel of patience. In November of the same year, 1798, just after he had finished writing the fair copy of the resolutions, he wrote Taylor again, saying: "*For the present* I should be for resolving the alien & sedition laws to be against the constitution & merely void, and for addressing the other States to obtain similar declarations; and I would not do anything *at this moment* which should commit us further, but reserve ourselves to shape our future measures, by the events which may happen."[75] It was eight months later that he wrote Madison calling for new resolutions threatening to dissolve the Union.

In the abstract there is no reason to be shocked by such sentiments. After all, Jefferson had already played the leading role in the dissolution of one union, a role for which he has been justly praised

---

[72] *Ibid.*

[73] Speech by James Hamilton at Walterborough, South Carolina, in October, 1828, as quoted in FREEHLING, PRELUDE TO CIVIL WAR: THE NULLIFICATION CONTROVERSY IN SOUTH CAROLINA, 1818–1836 152 (1965, 1966).

[74] Jefferson to Taylor, June 1, 1798, WRITINGS, note 67 *supra*, at 263–66.

[75] Nov. 26, 1798, *id.* at 289–90. (Emphasis supplied.)

by his countrymen. Certainly Koch and Ammon were not shocked
by that sentence in the letter to Madison:[76]

> By his willingness to consider the grave possibility of sepa-
> ration from the Union, Jefferson showed that he placed no
> absolute value upon "Union." Compared to the *extreme* evil of
> ruthless violation of liberty, a destruction of the compact
> which bound the states together was the *lesser* evil.

But this assumes that the cause for which he and his colleagues were
contending was liberty. It was not. Their cause was states' rights,
and liberty only as a function of states' rights. Koch and Ammon
to the contrary, the Alien and Sedition Laws were merely the occasion of the resolutions, not the cause.

The is readily demonstrated. The Kentucky Resolutions themselves complain of the Sedition Act as a violation of the Constitution
because the Constitution manifested the determination of the states
and the people thereof "to retain to themselves the right of judging
how far the licentiousness of speech and of the press may be
abridged without lessening their useful freedom, and how far those
abuses which cannot be separated from their use should be tolerated
rather than the use be destroyed."[77] And the Kentucky Resolutions
themselves say, not that aliens should not be banished, but "that alien
friends are under the jurisdiction and protection of the laws of the
State wherein they are."[78] The trouble with the Alien and Sedition
Laws was that in enacting them the United States was assuming the
powers of a sovereign nation, powers that, according to their view
of the Constitution, were reserved to the states. This, Jefferson and
his friends could not permit. Rather than submit to this exercise of
political power or concede the constitutional theory on which it was
based, they would declare the laws null and void. Failing of support
in this, they would dissolve the Union. To preserve the liberty that
was threatened by the Alien and Sedition Laws? Not so. Rather, to
preserve the right of the states to enact and enforce their own alien
and sedition laws—a right they were exercising.

The Virginia Resolutions drafted by Madison were more moderate than those of Kentucky, but the principle for which they con-

---

[76] Koch & Ammon, note 7 *supra*, at 167.

[77] COMMAGER, ed., DOCUMENTS OF AMERICAN HISTORY 179 (8th ed. 1968).

[78] *Ibid.*

tended was the same. In the address that accompanied them this principle is clearly stated: [79]

> The sedition act presents a scene, which was never expected by the early friends of the constitution. It was then admitted, that the state sovereignties were only diminished, by powers specifically enumerated, or necessary to carry the specified powers into effect. Now, federal authority is deduced from implication, and from the existence of state law, it is inferred, that congress possesses a similar power of legislation; whence congress will be endowed with a power of legislation, in all cases whatsoever, and the states will be stript of every right reserved, by the concurrent claims of a paramount legislature.

In what, then, does the evil of the Sedition Act consist? In the next and summary sentence the Virginia legislature leaves no doubt of its view: "The sedition act is the offspring of these tremendous pretentions, which inflict a death wound on the sovereignty of the states."[80]

The debates on the resolutions confirm this interpretation. In the first place, and somewhat unexpectedly for the modern reader who is accustomed to reading of the resolutions as a defense of civil liberties, the Virginia House of Delegates devoted the greater part of its time discussing the Alien Friends Act, not the Sedition Act. The arguments against it were familiar by this time. Mr. Mercer contended that "the federal government possessed no power over Aliens in time of peace; and therefore whatever power a sovereign state could exercise with respect to them, under the general law of nations, that power belonged to the state, and not to the general government."[81] Only "specifically enumerated" powers may be exercised by the federal government, said Mr. Barbour, and no power over aliens is specifically enumerated.[82] The Alien Law represented central government usurpation. Mr. Foushee defied anyone to put his finger on any clause of the Constitution "which had taken away their [the states'] sovereignty."[83] Apparently no one bothered to put his finger on the second clause of Article VI of Mr. Madison's Constitution; Madison himself, of course, had he been present instead of working behind the scene, would have been too embarrassed to

---

[79] *Address of the General Assembly to the People of the Commonwealth of Virginia*, JOURNAL OF THE HOUSE OF DELEGATES 88–89 (15 Jan. 1799).

[80] *Ibid.*

[81] DEBATES 31.

[82] *Id.* at 47.

[83] *Id.* at 74.

do so. The state, Foushee went on, "and state only, had a right to pass" an alien law.[84] States are sovereign with respect to "strangers," insisted Mr. Daniel.[85] And so it went.

Virginia had an alien friends law indistinguishable in its essential provisions from the federal law. Virginia could not, then, consistently protest against the principles of the federal law. Virginia was not acting out of a concern for aliens (for whose exclusion Jefferson had argued in his *Notes on Virginia*, first published in 1784). Virginia was contending against a reading of the Commerce Clause that permitted Congress to regulate the movement of aliens and slaves and, more generally, a reading of the Constitution that in wide areas would permit a constitutional majority in the country to govern the country. The solution was to deny that the United States was a sovereign country.

The case against the Sedition Law was stated at the outset of the debates by John Taylor of Caroline County, and, with a single exception, later speakers in favor of the resolutions were content to state their opposition to the Sedition Law by referring to Taylor's argument.[86] Taylor had made the familiar points against the law: that it was a clear violation of the First Amendment; that men tend to label speech false and licentious simply because they disagree with it; and that it prohibited the criticism of officials essential to republican government. But he made these points within the familiar context of a defense of state sovereignty. "If Congress should undertake to regulate public opinion, they would be sure to regulate it so as to detach the people from the state governments, and attach them to the General Government."[87] This law, like the Alien Friends Law, tended to concentrate power in Congress, he said, and such a concentration "would operate to the destruction of the state governments"; this would be despotism and would precipitate "revolution."[88]

As in the case of the Alien Law, the states sovereignty argument was the only one that could consistently be adopted by Taylor and his fellow Jeffersonians, for just as Virginia had an alien law, it also

---

[84] *Id.* at 76.   [85] *Id.* at 86.

[86] "Mr. Mercer said he would not take up the time of the committee in making any observations upon [the Sedition Act]. He was willing to let the proof of its unconstitutional quality rest upon the argument of the gentleman from Caroline." *Id.* at 38.

[87] *Id.* at 121.   [88] *Id.* at 134.

had a sedition law. Taylor and his fellow Jeffersonians were attacked on this ground by George K. Taylor in the course of a spirited defense of the national law:[89]

> In England . . . the laying no *previous* restraints upon publications, is *freedom of the press*. In every one of the United States the laying no *previous* restraints upon publications hath always been and still is deemed *freedom of the press*. In England notwithstanding the freedom of the press, the publication of false scandalous and malicious writings is punishable by fine and imprisonment. In every one of the United States, notwithstanding the freedom of the press, the publication of false scandalous and malicious writings is punishable in the same manner. If the freedom of the press be not therefore abridged in the government of any particular state, by the punishment of false scandalous and malicious writings, how could it be said to be abridged when the same punishment is inflicted on the same offence by the government of the whole people.

After referring to the twelfth article of the Virginia Bill of Rights ("That the freedom of the press is one of the great bulwarks of liberty, and can never be restrained but by despotic governments"), he went on to argue that the "legislature of Virginia . . . could no more pass a law *restraining* the freedom of the press, than Congress could pass a law abridging the freedom of the press! . . . Yet it had never doubted that false, scandalous and malicious writings are punishable in Virginia."[90] He referred specifically to a 1792 law punishing "divulgers of false news," but he could have cited others.[91] If Virginia could do this without violating its bill of rights, Congress, he said, could enact the Sedition Law without violating the First Amendment.

There is no reason to believe that George Taylor did not hope to persuade his colleagues with this argument, but he was not unaware of the sense in which it was irrelevant.[92] Taylor knew that the Jeffersonians were contending primarily for a state sovereignty and he knew what they intended, if necessary, to do for it. Hence, he ended with a prayer for union and a love of it among Virginians.

---

[89] *Id.* at 156–57.   [90] *Ibid.*

[91] See, *e.g.*, HENING'S LAWS OF VIRGINIA 170 (1792).

[92] John Taylor's answer to this had already been given: "It would be as just to say that a state could pass laws for raising fleets and armies, because Congress had done so, as that Congress could infringe the liberty of speech, because the states had done so." DEBATES 134.

As General Henry (Light-Horse Harry) Lee had said during the previous day's debate, the real object of the resolutions was not repeal of the Alien and Sedition Laws but rather the "Promotion of disunion and separation of the States."[93]

The Resolutions were adopted by a vote of 100 to 63 (and in the Senate, 14 to 3). In an effort to justify its conduct—and justification was certainly required—the majority drew up its "Address of the General Assembly to the People of . . . Virginia," and voted to circulate it, along with the resolutions, at public expense. This caused the minority, led in the House of Delegates by General Lee, to draw up a "counter address," which they sought to have subjoined to the other papers. Failing in this, they published it privately. It is said by his biographer to be the work of John Marshall,[94] and while there is no proof of its authorship, there is no doubt that it constitutes the best statement from the Federalist side of the issues raised by the Alien and Sedition Laws and the Virginia Resolutions.

It begins by deploring the resolutions and "the system of which they form a conspicuous feature"—that is, the plan to dissolve the Union—and speaks of "the happiness united America enjoys" and "the evils which disunited America must inevitably suffer."[95] It then recounts, at some length, the difficulties America had encountered in its relation with Britain and France, justifying the attempts of Washington and Adams to maintain peace "without dishonor." It continues by denying that an army led by "your Washington" can

---

93 *Id.* at 116.

94 2 BEVERIDGE, THE LIFE OF JOHN MARSHALL 402 (1916). Marshall was not in the legislature at the time, but this, of course, does not preclude his authorship. Madison, the acknowledged author of the Resolutions, was not in the legislature either. Beveridge's conclusion rests on three letters. In a letter from Sedgwick to Hamilton, dated Feb. 7, 1799, he said that the address "is said to have been drawn by Marshall." 6 WORKS OF ALEXANDER HAMILTON 392 (1850 ed.). In the second, Sedgwick wrote to Rufus King under date of March 20, 1799, that for this "masterly performance . . . we are indebted to the pen of General Marshall." 2 LIFE AND CORRESPONDENCE OF RUFUS KING 581 (1895). In the third, Vans Murray wrote from Holland to John Quincy Adams on April 5, 1799, that he "should think that John Marshall wrote the address," and "*I hope* that J. Marshall did write the address." *Letters of William Vans Murray to John Quincy Adams, 1797–1803*, ANN. REP. AM. HIST. Ass'N 536 (1912).

95 ADDRESS OF THE MINORITY IN THE VIRGINIA LEGISLATURE TO THE PEOPLE OF THAT STATE; CONTAINING A VINDICATION OF THE CONSTITUTIONALITY OF THE ALIEN AND SEDITION LAWS. The address is to be found in the JOURNAL OF THE [Virginia] HOUSE OF DELEGATES (December, 1798) and in the Virginia Gazette, Jan. 29, 1799, and the supplement of that newspaper of Feb. 5, 1799. A copy of the original pamphlet is in the library of Harvard University.

"be called mercenary," and then enters into a detailed defense of the Alien and Sedition Laws. Contrary to the view held by the Jeffersonians, "America is one nation," and the "power of protecting the nation from the intrigues and conspiracies of dangerous aliens who may have introduced themselves into the bosom of our country" belongs necessarily to the general government. The minority then refers to the Virginia Alien Law and concludes as follows:

> That this measure should originally have been suggested as necessary for national safety, that it should have been preserved through a long course of reflection, that it should be deemed free from the objection of uniting the powers of different departments in the executive, as also of depriving an alien from his residence without a trial by jury, and yet it should for the same causes produce a ferment in some states, as soon as the principle was adopted by Congress, might warrant reflections which we will not permit ourselves to express.

As for the Sedition Law, to "contend that there does not exist a power to punish writings coming within the description of this law, would be to assert the inability of our nation to preserve its own peace, and to protect themselves from the attempt of wicked citizens, who incapable of quiet themselves, are incessantly employed in devising means to disturb the public repose." Every state, either by statute or by the common law, claims the right to punish such utterances, and prior to the passage of the Sedition Law, the general government could have punished them in its courts, for the "judicial power of the United States . . . extended to the punishment of libels against the government, as a common law offence." Nor does the First Amendment forbid such laws, as a "punishment of the licentiousness is not . . . a restriction of the freedom of the press." "If by freedom of the press is meant a perfect exemption from all punishment for whatever may be published, that freedom never has, and most probably never will exist."

The address concludes with praise of the Union and a call for its defense against its enemies, and in this respect only did it differ from the various documents written by the Jeffersonians. For, they did not deny the necessity of alien laws; they did not contend that libels could not be punished civilly or criminally; they did not at this time insist on denying the distinction between the liberty and the licentiousness of the press. They merely denied the sovereign existence of the United States. As Jefferson himself had occasion to say later, in a letter to Abigail Adams who had criticized him for pardoning the victims of the Sedition Law: "While we deny that Congress have a right to control the freedom of the press, we have ever asserted the right of the States, and their exclusive right, to do so."[96]

It was only after their failure to provoke a favorable response to their resolutions from the other states that the Jeffersonians—but not Jefferson—began seriously to contend against the principle of a seditious libel law. Frustrated in their attempts to impose the concept of state sovereignty on the Constitution and to persuade the other states to join them in declaring the Alien and Sedition Laws null and void, and not yet determined to force the issue by seceding from the Union (the size of the opposition in Virginia itself probably had something to do with this),[97] some of Jefferson's followers began to direct their attention to the nature of free speech and press instead of the nature of the Union, and began to attack the Sedition Law rather than the government that enacted it. It was in the course of doing this that they began to question whether the Blackstonian view of free press as merely an uncensored press is compatible with republican government, whether state or national. It was in the course of doing this that they developed what Leonard Levy has called "the new theory of First Amendment freedoms." But even then they were a great deal less "libertarian" than Levy has asserted.

IV. The "Libertarian" Response

The civil liberties argument that is missing in the attacks on the promulgation of the Alien and Sedition Laws is said by Levy to emerge immediately thereafter as a result of reflections on the experience of these laws. "In speeches, tracts, and books, George Blake, Albert Gallatin, Edward Livingston, Nathaniel Macon, James Madison, George Nicholas, John Thomson, St. George Tucker, and Tunis Wortman, among others, contributed brilliantly to the new theory of First Amendment freedoms."[98]

---

[96] Sept. 11, 1804. 11 Writings of Thomas Jefferson 51 (Lipscomb ed. 1903).

[97] "There are many considerations *dehors* of the State, which will occur to you without enumeration. I should not apprehend them, if all was sound within. But there is a most respectable part of our State who have been enveloped in the X.Y.Z. delusion, and who destroy our unanimity for the present moment." Jefferson to John Taylor, Nov. 26, 1798, 10 *id.* at 64. This is the same letter as that referred to in the text at note 75 *supra*.

[98] Levy, note 64 *supra*, at 55.

Madison made his contribution to the "new theory" in 1800 in the Report on the Resolutions, submitted to the Virginia House of Delegates by a committee charged with dealing with the responses to the 1798 resolutions. He argued that a law of seditious libel and free republican government are incompatible, that the "security of the freedom of the press requires that it should be exempt not only from previous restraint by the Executive, as in Great Britain, but from legislative restraint also; as this exemption, to be effectual, must be an exemption not only from the previous inspection of licensers, but from the subsequent penalty of laws."[99] Levy's failure to note the qualifications led him to attribute to Madison and some of the others a more "libertarian" position than they adopted, even after 1798. Madison went on to say that the national government is "destitute of every authority for restraining the licentiousness of the press,"[100] but he did not say this of the state governments. On the contrary, the officers of the national government, he said, can find a remedy "for their injured reputations, under the same laws, and in the same tribunals, which protect their lives, their liberties, and their properties."[101]

Another of the new "libertarians" was St. George Tucker, a professor of law at William and Mary. According to Levy, Tucker's exposition of freedom of speech and press "was enormously important to the emergence of an American libertarianism because his absolutist theory of freedom of discussion appeared in his scholarly edition of Blackstone, for many years the standard edition used by the American bench and bar."[102] While Tucker did, undeniably, argue against Blackstone's view of free press, and for the claim that Congress had no authority to enact laws against the licentiousness of the press, he did not espouse an "absolutist theory of freedom of discussion." He did defend the "absolute and unrestrained exercise of our religious opinions." This merely reflected his Jeffersonianism. Like his mentor, he probably held that whether his neighbor says there are twenty gods or no God "neither picks

---

[99] 6 WRITINGS OF JAMES MADISON 397 (Hunt ed. 1906). On the development of "libertarianism" and the examples thereof, see LEVY, note 4 *supra*, at 249–309.

[100] WRITINGS, note 99 *supra*, at 392.

[101] *Id*. at 393. This was in accord with the Virginia Resolutions of 1798, where Madison had written that every "libellous writing or expression might receive its punishment in the State courts."

[102] LEVY, note 4 *supra*, at 283.

[his] pocket nor breaks [his] leg." But some words do pick pockets and break legs, especially southern pockets and legs. Thus, while contending for an "absolute freedom of the press, and its total exemption from all restraint, control, or jurisdiction of the federal government," Tucker made it abundantly clear in a very visible place that the states must punish such words:[103]

> Whoever makes use of the press as the vehicle of his sentiments on any subject, ought to do it in such language as to show he has a deference for the sentiments of others; that while he asserts the right of expressing and vindicating his own judgment, he acknowledges the obligation to submit to the judgment of those whose authority he cannot legally, or constitutionally dispute. In his statement of facts he is bound to adhere strictly to the truth; for every deviation from the truth is both an imposition upon the public, and an injury to the individual whom it may respect. In his restrictures on the conduct of men, in public stations, he is bound to do justice to their characters, and not to criminate them without substantial reason. The right of character is a sacred and invaluable right, and is not forfeited by accepting a public employment. Whoever knowingly departs from any of these maxims is guilty of *a crime against the community*, as well as against the person injured; and though both the letter and the spirit of our federal constitution wisely prohibit the Congress of the United States from making any law, by which the freedom of speech, or of the press, may be exposed to restraint or persecution under the authority of the federal government, yet for injuries done the reputation of any person, *as an individual*, the state-courts are always open, and may afford ample, and competent redress, as the records of the courts of this commonwealth [Virginia] abundantly testify.

Except with respect to the question of the federal government's authority over libel, including criminal libel, there is nothing in this summarizing statement with which the friends of the Sedition Law would have disagreed. Tucker was a Jeffersonian who, after the passage of the Sedition Law, reflected on the nature of free speech and press, but he was by no means a "libertarian" in the modern sense. He was also a Jeffersonian in that he was a secessionist,[104] and

---

[103] 1 BLACKSTONE'S COMMENTARIES app. 29–30 (Tucker ed. 1803). (First emphasis supplied.)

[104] "Each [State] is still a perfect State, still sovereign, still independent, and still capable, should the occasion require, to resume the exercise of its functions, in the most unlimited extent." *Id.* at 175.

there is no necessary or historical connection between civil liberties and that infamous doctrine.

The man who "contributed pre-eminently to the emergence of an American libertarianism" was, according to Levy, Tunis Wortman, a New York attorney. His book on the freedom of the press, published in 1800, "is, in a sense, the book that Jefferson did not write but should have."[105] Its outstanding characteristics, we are told, "are its philosophic approach and its absolutist theses." Its outstanding characteristics in fact are its naïve presentation of the sentiments, arguments, and hopes of the Enlightenment and its adoption of the views of Thomas Paine. We are assured that whatever "can be performed by one man, can in general be accomplished by another";[106] that government is a simple matter, for it is "founded in maxims, which are readily embraced, and comprehended by the most common understanding";[107] that the "language of justice is uniformly legible";[108] that the triumph of truth is inevitable, for liberty and science will replace ignorance and despotism; that society and government are separable, and that the "improvement of the people . . . must be entrusted to Society itself."[109] In general, Wortman, like Paine, sees government as at best a necessary evil whose job it is to suppress crimes and to protect the community and to do nothing— or, depending on the page in hand, very little—else.

Wortman is explicit as to the necessary role of a free press in bringing about this brave new world—progress is inevitable but only in the absence of despotic government. "The government that interferes with the progress of opinion, subverts the essential order of the social state."[110] "Wherever Freedom of Enquiry is established [however], Improvement is inevitable; the smallest spark of knowledge will be cherished and kindled into flame. If only a single individual shall have acquired superior attainments, he will speedily impart them to his companions, and exalt their minds to the elevated standard of his own."[111] The decent government, he went on, has no

---

[105] LEVY, note 4 *supra*, at 283.

[106] WORTMAN, A TREATISE CONCERNING POLITICAL INQUIRY AND THE LIBERTY OF THE PRESS 55 (1800).

[107] *Id*. at 61.   [109] *Id*. at 123, 130, 133.

[108] *Id*. at 66.   [110] *Id*. at 111.

[111] *Id*. at 129. Like Mill's "On Liberty," the basic assumption of this work is the complete compatibility of truth and its pursuit and political good—or of science and politics.

need to punish falsehood. Public opinion will correct licentiousness —or at least public opinion that manifests itself in civil libel suits. And in such suits truth is a proper defense, for "[t]ruth can never be a libel." "It cannot be said that any Liberty of the Press is established by law, unless the publication of Truth is expressly sanctioned." Criminal prosecutions for libel, he argues, are productive of more evil than that which "they are intended to prevent."[112]

But then the almost inevitable qualification appeared. Despite a great deal of his argument and despite his sentiments, much of what he wrote was confined to the power of the national government. Its powers, he insisted, "do not extend to the coercion of Libel"; to argue otherwise is to extend "the empire of Constructive Authority to a height which is dangerous to the existence of a Free Republic, and repugnant to the idea of a Limited Constitution."[113] But he is not here arguing that libels need not be "coerced." On the contrary:[114]

> The coercion of Libel is rather a subject of domestic super-intendence, than an object which properly relates to the general interests of the Union. Wherever such Coercion is proper or necessary, our *State legislatures and tribunals* are possessed of sufficient authority to remedy the evil. It is, therefore, to be presumed to have been intended that the States respectively should solely exercise the power of controuling the conduct of their own citizens in such cases.

To cast doubt on the extent to which these Republican writers were "libertarian" in the modern sense is not to deny Levy's main point, namely, that the passage of the Sedition Law in 1798 provoked some Americans to begin thinking about the meaning of free speech and press and their place in republican government. Prior to the introduction of the question as a political issue, Americans had no practical reason for questioning the sufficiency of the Blackstonian understanding, which they accepted, to the extent to which they thought of it, as part of their legal inheritance. Yet it is not possible in the cases of Tucker and Wortman, any more than in those of the politicians Madison, Gallatin, Livingston, Macon, and Nicholas, to isolate their free speech and press arguments from the larger issues with which they were contending: the respective powers

---

112 *Id*. at 152, 250, 252, 256, 257, and 259.

113 *Id*. at 238.　　　　　　　　　114 *Id*. at 229–30. (Emphasis supplied.)

of the national and state governments. The only two so-called libertarians of whom this may be said without qualification are George
Blake and John Thomson.

Blake was counsel for Abijah Adams in the 1799 Massachusetts
seditious libel case, and, although a Jefferson supporter, managed to
present a reasoned argument against the concept of seditious libel
free of any attack on the federal government and of any sympathy
for the idea of state sovereignty.[115] He did not argue in favor of an
"illimited, unqualified indulgence of the rights of speaking, writing
or acting." The laws of any well-governed polity must, he said, provide a remedy to the (private) individual who is victimized by
"*wanton, malicious invective*," and this remedy might take the form
of an action brought by the aggrieved party or an indictment by the
government.[116] Thus, Blake, in addition to arguing the difficulty of
distinguishing between liberty and licentiousness, and the incom-
patibility of free government and the Blackstonian understanding of
freedom of the press, attacked the very idea of seditious libel—but
not criminal libel in its entirety. Even he, then, can scarcely be
called a modern-style libertarian.

Like Blake, John Thomson, a New York lawyer, made no con-
cessions to state sovereignty. But one aspect of his argument was
unique and carried him further in the direction of modern libertarianism than any of his contemporaries. Opinions may not be punished, he argued, because man is in no way responsible for the opinions he holds. Just as one child, without any reason, or any reason
arising in himself, prefers a drum and his brother a different toy,
when they advance in age they adopt different opinions; "and this
they can no more help, than they could preferring different play
things."[117] Laws such as the Sedition Law he saw as attempts to control men's thoughts, and since men "have no controul over their
[own] thoughts," no association of men can hope to control the
thoughts of others—this is a power that does not exist: "Consequently it must follow, that men should be allowed to express those
thoughts, with the same freedom that they arise. In other words—

---

[115] Blake's argument is set out in the Boston *Independent Chronicle* for seven
consecutive issues from April 8–11, 1799, to April 29–May 2, 1799. He was, of course,
arguing against an indictment brought under state law.

[116] *Id.*, issue of April 15–18, 1799.

[117] THOMSON, AN ENQUIRY, CONCERNING THE LIBERTY AND LICENTIOUSNESS OF THE
PRESS, AND THE UNCONTROULABLE NATURE OF THE HUMAN MIND 13 (1801).

speak or publish, whatever you believe to be the *truth*."[118] But of course it does not follow. Even if it were true that thought cannot be controlled, it would not follow that either the individual or the government lacks the power to control the expression of that thought—and the Sedition Law was manifestly directed at expression. The power of law to deter expression is implicitly admitted by Thomson in various places. Nevertheless, Levy regards Thomson's "libertarian" idea as "fascinating,"[119] presumably because of its relation to the modern tendency to regard men as unresponsible for themselves and their acts. However fascinating, it is an idea destructive of law as such. For if, as Thomson argues, acts arise out of opinions, and opinions out of pleasure or pain, "the immediately determining motives," and pleasure and pain, apparently, out of biological structure, which varies from man to man, then man is not free and law as an attempt to influence his behavior is vain.[120]

One other writer at this time presented the extreme "libertarian" argument, contending in turn against Blackstone, a legal distinction between liberty and license, criminal libel, and a privilege limited to the truth. This was George Hay, but his essays are marked by their impassioned attack on the federal government and by a support of the state-sovereignty theory of his fellow Virginians, Jefferson and Madison and the others. And even Hay, in the second edition of his essay, concedes that the state may punish libels, including libels on the President of the United States.[121]

It is altogether proper that the passage of the Sedition Law, and especially the manner of the trials conducted under its authority, should have provoked Americans to initiate inquiry into the relation

---

[118] *Id.* at 11–12.   [119] Levy, note 4 *supra*, at 320.

[120] Thomson, note 117 *supra*, at 11–13. No man, he said repeatedly, has any control over his thoughts. "On the contrary, it is his thought which controuls him"; and although the mind is an active agent, "it is purely passive with regard to the final determination." *Id.* at 13. A few pages later he showed that he did not see the implications of his basic thesis, for he went on to express the familiar Enlightenment view that "if it be admitted that free discussion has been of advantage to other sciences, then why may it not be of equal advantage to the science of politics?" *Id.* at 16. Why not, indeed? But only if men are free and not enslaved by their biological structure.

[121] "Hortensius" [Hay], An Essay on the Liberty of the Press, Respectfully Inscribed to the Republican Printers Throughout the United States (1799; 1803). For the concession referred to in the text see pp. 19–20 of the 1803 edition. For a fuller discussion of Hay's writings, see Levy, note 4 *supra*, at 269–73.

of free speech and press to free government—that is to say, into the meaning of the First Amendment. After all, even Hamilton, whom Jefferson and his party regarded as the greatest enemy of the public good as they understood it, had reservations about the wisdom of employing such legislation. He, like Marshall, may have regarded the Sedition Law as constitutional, but he did not conceal his anxieties concerning such measures from his Federalist colleagues. Writing to Oliver Wolcott when the sedition bill was first introduced on the floor of the Senate, Hamilton said: [122]

> There are provisions in this bill, which . . . appear to me highly exceptionable, and such as, more than anything else, may endanger civil war. . . . I hope sincerely the thing may not be hurried through. Let us not establish a tyranny. Energy is a very different thing from violence. If we make no false step, we shall be essentially united, but if we push things to an extreme, we shall then give to faction *body* and solidity.

But it is significant that these authors should have confined themselves, or in greater part confined themselves, to a denial of the national authority to punish seditious libels, while maintaining the right of the states to do so. They were far from espousing the views of modern libertarians. Nor was it they and their mentor Jefferson who provoked the salutary reforms in the law of free press, so that by the end of the nineteenth century it could be said that this law was more compatible with republican principles than it had been during the Alien and Sedition controversy. On the contrary, the Jeffersonians were responsible for the most flagrant denials of free speech and press ever perpetrated in this country, and they did this on behalf of the institution of slavery.

V. "Incendiary Publications"

In a 1788 letter to Jefferson, James Madison said that in Virginia he had "seen the bill of rights violated in every instance where it has been opposed to a popular current."[123] Thanks partly to his acts of commission and omission, a popular current grew in Virginia that made a mockery of the Virginia constitution's guarantees of free speech and press. For by insisting that the national

---

[122] Hamilton to Wolcott, June 28, 1798, 10 Works of Alexander Hamilton 295 (Lodge ed. 1904).

[123] Oct. 17, 1788. 5 Writings of James Madison 272 (Hunt ed. 1904).

government had no authority to legislate on the slavery issue, Madison and Jefferson contributed their great names to the cause of its perpetuation. Instead of adopting policies and constitutional doctrines that would have looked upon slavery as only a temporary national evil to be kept in a place where, to use Lincoln's language, it would be "in course of ultimate extinction," they fostered a constitutional doctrine that made abolition impossible without war and, assuming a continuance of antislavery sentiment outside the South, a division of the nation inevitable. No conflict was ever more "irrepressible" than the American Civil War, because slavery is an issue on which no country can remain neutral. Slavery either had to be placed in a position that guaranteed its "ultimate extinction," or it would have to expand until it was adopted in every part of the country. Once the national government was captured by the Jeffersonian party with its notions of the respective powers of the national and state governments, the southern states were free to govern the slavery issue themselves, the northern states, presumably, were free to be antislavery, and the national government was expected to remain neutral. 'No house thus divided could long stand. It was not without logic that the South, defeated by the success of a party sworn to prevent the expansion of slavery beyond the Missouri line, chose to secede from the Union. And it was not without logic that the extreme abolitionists preferred this secession to any continuance of the divided house: the alternative was clearly war. And it was not unreasonable for the South, despite Lincoln's protestations that neither he nor his party would interfere with the institution of slavery in the states where it already existed, to see in his election to the presidency a blow to slavery that would inevitably be fatal. It was a question of slavery or the Union, but the South's 1860 decision for slavery was merely the logical consequence of decisions made by Jefferson and Madison as far back as the first decade of the Union's existence.

Consider the problem within the context not of wars with Mexico, not of Wilmot Provisos, not of Kansas-Nebraska Acts or Lecompton Constitutions or *Dred Scott* decisions, but merely of free speech and press. The southern states, and not without reason, saw in antislavery speech a very clear and a very present danger to the institution of slavery which they regarded, here in the words of South Carolina's Governor McDuffie in 1835, as "the cornerstone of our republican edifice.''[124] Given his premise that this "republican edifice" should stand, it becomes altogether reasonable to embark on a policy of suppressing antislavery speech. This is what the South did on a major scale, in which project they had the warm support of Jefferson's latter-day heir, President Andrew Jackson.

It was a relatively simple matter to deal with local agitators. The problem for the southern states arose precisely from the fact that they were parts of a larger Union, a Union containing states that did not— or did not always—suppress their local antislavery agitators. This was a Union within which communication was deliberately facilitated by a department of the national government. With the passage of time much of the mail distributed by this department was deposited by the enemies of slavery. It must not be distributed. Antislavery newspapers must never leave their places of publication or, failing that, the post offices in the communities of their destination. State after southern state began modestly by requesting the northern states to enact penal laws "prohibiting," in the words of a resolution adopted by the North Carolina legislature in December, 1835, "the printing, within their respective limits, *all* such publications as *may have a tendency* to make our slaves discontented."[125] Two months later Virginia went further and requested, "respectfully," that the "non-slave holding States . . . adopt PENAL ENACTMENTS" to suppress the abolitionist societies themselves.[126] Because they were part of a larger Union, their peculiar institution could not be preserved without the cooperation of the other parts of that Union. Hence, when the nonslaveholding states refused to comply with this request to adopt the nonrepublican policy of suppressing speech in order to preserve what the South regarded as the "cornerstone" of its "republican edifice," some southern communities, Charlestown, South Carolina, among them, adopted the simple, if illegal, expedient of persuading the local postmasters to refuse to deliver abolitionist mail and antislavery newspapers. Then, in order to gain the sanction of the law for this, they called upon the assistance of the national government. In his annual message of December 7, 1835, President Jackson responded to the best of his ability. He too called upon the nonslaveholding states to suppress abolitionist agitation, and he went on to ask the Congress to enact a law prohibit-

---

[124] Quoted in GOODELL, SLAVERY AND ANTI-SLAVERY 413 (1855).

[125] *Ibid.*   [126] *Id.* at 414.

ing, "under severe penalties, the circulation in the Southern States, through the mail, of incendiary publications intended to instigate the slaves to insurrection."[127] Upon the motion of John C. Calhoun, this proposal was referred to a select committee of the Senate, rather than to the Post Office Committee, because, as one member put it, the latter was "composed, in large proportion [four out of five], of gentlemen from non-slaveholding States." The select committee was composed of five members: Calhoun, as chairman, King of Georgia, Mangum of North Carolina, Linn of Missouri, and Davis of Massachusetts; the last was the only member to represent a non-slaveholding state.

President Jackson's message, Calhoun said, however friendly to the slave states in its intention, proposes congressional legislation that would constitute a palpable violation of the Constitution's guarantee of freedom of the press. Indeed, it was identical in principle with the odious Sedition Law of 1798, for, although the latter prohibited the publication of certain materials, and Jackson's bill would prohibit merely the circulation of certain materials, this difference is immaterial, for the purpose of publication is circulation. The object of each is the same: "the communication of sentiments and opinions to the public." Whatever difference there was between the two measures reveals Jackson's proposal to have been more invidious, because it constituted, or would constitute, a prior censorship insofar as readers in southern states were concerned:[128]

> It would indeed have been a poor triumph for the cause of liberty, in the great contest of 1799, had the sedition law been put down on principles that would have left Congress free to suppress the circulation, through the mail, of the very publications which that odious act was intended to prohibit. The authors of that memorable achievement would have had but slender claims on the gratitude of posterity, if their victory over the encroachment of power had been left so imperfect.

Because, therefore, seen in the light of the principles of the Constitution the President's proposal was at least as odious as the hated Sedition Law, Calhoun recommended to the Senate that it be rejected out of hand—but not without a ringing of the changes on the principles of free government.

---

127 4 RICHARDSON, MESSAGES AND PAPERS OF THE PRESIDENTS 1394-95 (1907).

128 *Report of the Select Committee on Incendiary Publications*, 12 REGISTER OF DEBATES pt. 4, app. 73 (1836).

Up to this point in this affair of "incendiary publications," the reader, following Koch and Ammon's appraisal of the Virginia and Kentucky Resolutions, might be tempted to see Calhoun, as Koch and Ammon see Jefferson and Madison, as a great defender of civil liberties, and specifically of the right of free speech and press. Here is the great Democrat Jackson proposing a censorship of the mails, a censorship that would have required postmasters to examine publications to ascertain whether they contain sentiments anathema to the slave states. And here is the great Democrat Calhoun, whose heroes are Jefferson and Madison, protecting free government against this onslaught and appealing to the memory of the victory over the earlier "odious" law. But Calhoun was no more willing than Jackson to permit "incendiary publications" to circulate in southern states, and like Jefferson and Madison before him, he too appealed to the right of the states to suppress them. Jackson's proposal was a violation of the First Amendment, but even more so of the very nature of the Constitution, for it assumed a national power that in fact, Calhoun insisted, was reserved to the states. On behalf of his select committee, but not, as it turned out in the ensuing debates, with the consent of a unanimous committee, Calhoun then proposed a substitute measure and urged its adoption. This substitute deserves to be quoted at length:[129]

> Sec. 1. Be it enacted, etc., That it shall not be lawful for any deputy postmaster, in any State, Territory, or District, knowingly to receive and put into the mail, any pamphlet, newspaper, handbill, or other paper, printed or written, or pictorial representation, touching the subject of slavery, addressed to any person or post office in any State, Territory, or Distict, where by the laws of the said State, Territory, or District, their circulation is prohibited. Nor shall it be lawful for any deputy postmaster in said State, Territory, or District, knowingly to deliver to any person any such pamphlet [etc.], to any person whatever, except to such person or persons as are duly authorized by the proper authority of such State, Territory, or District, to receive the same.

Where Jackson had called for the suppression of merely incendiary publications, Calhoun called for the suppression of "any paper, printed or written . . . touching the subject of slavery," a category broad enough to include private letters. From the point of view of

---

[129] *Id.*, pt. 1, 383.

freedom of expression, his bill was certainly more odious than Jackson's, yet he attacked the latter in the name of the Constitution and the principles of free government. The only possible conclusion is that the great "triumph for the cause of liberty, in the great contest of 1799," was a triumph for states' rights, not freedom of the press.

Calhoun left no doubt about this. The President's proposed bill assumed the right of the national government to determine what papers were incendiary, and to admit such a right "would be fatal to [the slaveholding] States," for the national government would then have the right to determine what was *not* incendiary. Such a power could not be lodged in the hands of officials of the national government—they, and this included the congressmen who enact laws as well as the postmasters who in this case administer them, could not be trusted. Only the slaveholding states themselves could be trusted to govern this and any other aspect of the slavery issue. A national power to determine what was and what was not an incendiary publication would have constituted "the power to abolish slavery, [for it would have given Congress] the means of breaking down all the barriers which the slaveholding states have erected for the protection of their lives and property."[130] The Sedition Law was "odious" because Congress assumed a power belonging to the states. Jackson's measure for dealing with the problem of antislavery agitation was "odious" because, once again, it assumed a power in the national government that had been reserved to the states. Calhoun's bill did not make this constitutional mistake: the states will define (and had in fact already defined) what is incendiary, and the national government, working with those definitions, would cooperate with the states by excluding from the mails what the states wished to be excluded. By doing so, the national government would help to protect the "republican edifice" in the southern states—that is to say, slavery. Thus, the definition of the First Amendment is, as Calhoun's colleague on the select committee, Senator King of Georgia, said, "the right to print and publish whatever might be permitted by the laws of the State,"[131] and, according to Calhoun, the states "may prohibit the introduction or circulation of any paper or publication which may, in their opinion, disturb or endanger the institution [of slavery]."[132]

This is certainly not a civil liberties argument, although it is

---

[130] *Id.*, pt. 4, app. 73..   [131] *Id.*, pt. 1, 1128.   [132] *Id.* at 1139.

wholly in line with what southerners had said a generation earlier in the Alien and Sedition controversy. And like Jefferson, Calhoun was unwilling to confine his resistance to protests uttered on the floor of Congress. Whether the bill passed or failed, he said, the slaveholding states would not permit antislavery publications to circulate among them. "It [was] a case of life and death with them."[133] Nor, as he and his friends read the Constitution, would this be a defiance of the law:[134]

> But I must tell the Senate, be your decision what it may, the South will never abandon the principles of this bill. If you refuse co-operation with our laws, and conflict should ensue between your and our laws, the southern States will never yield to the superiority of yours. We have a remedy in our hands, which, in such event, we shall not fail to apply. We have high authority for asserting that, in such cases, "State interposition is the rightful remedy"—a doctrine first announced by Jefferson— adopted by the patriotic and republican State of Kentucky by a solemn resolution, in 1798, and finally carried out into successful practice on a recent occasion [*i.e.*, nullification] by the gallant State which I, in part, have the honor to represent.

In the event, the Senate substituted a modified bill for Calhoun's and then rejected that modified bill by a vote of 19 to 25, a vote in which, with very few exceptions, free states were aligned against the slave. But Calhoun was as good as his word. Despite the fact that the Congress, as part of a general statute respecting the organization of the post office, shortly thereafter provided for the punishment of any postmaster who failed to deliver any "letter, package, pamphlet, or newspaper,"[135] postmasters in the South refused to deliver antislavery papers. For example, not even Horace Greeley could get his paper, the New York *Tribune*, delivered in Lynchburg, Virginia.[136]

Whatever might be said against the institution for which Calhoun and his colleagues fought, there is nothing unreasonable about the choice of weapons they used here. Abolitionist literature was indeed incendiary in the South, its circulation did indeed threaten the preservation of slavery and therewith of the very regime erected in the slave states. Or, in Holmesian terms, it did present a very clear

---

[133] *Id.*, pt. 2, 1730–31.   [134] *Id.*, pt. 1, 1148.   [135] 5 Stat. 87 (1836).

[136] WHIPPLE, THE STORY OF CIVIL LIBERTY IN THE UNITED STATES 112–13 (1927).

and a very present danger of bringing about what southern leaders regarded as an evil that they were sworn to prevent. Although we can condemn southern leaders for their failure to adopt policies designed to put an end to slavery, it would be unreasonable to expect them to do what no leaders of any regime may do, namely, remain indifferent to dangers to the regime itself. And speech—as the abolitionists knew as well as the friends of slavery—can endanger a regime. This was especially true of southern slavery, for the states that adopted and defended it were parts of a Union "dedicated to the proposition that all men are created equal," a Union that increasingly embraced men who were dedicated to the destruction of slavery—or failing that, of the Union that permitted it to exist in any of its parts. Hence, the southern states were more and more forced to promote conformity within their ranks, with test oaths that required state officers to swear "primary and paramount allegiance" to their "sovereign" states, by silencing even those who "espoused the old necessary-evil argument," by refusing to permit, what in 1832 Virginia did permit, the publication of debates on the merits of slavery.[137] To publish such debates was a policy "blended with . . . madness and fatality."[138] One South Carolina paper even refused to print an essay *attacking* the policy of permitting a public discussion of the slavery question because "it is a subject that ought not be agitated at all in this State."[139]

In time the southern leaders, as we have seen, came to realize that they could not permit free discussion of the slavery issue even in the free states—and they had a number of northern allies with them on this at one time—or finally, the cruelest irony of all, in the Congress of the United States. The first of the so-called gag rules, according to which the House resolved not to entertain any petition relating to the subject of slavery or to permit any discussion of such petitions, was adopted in 1836, and it was not until December, 1845, that the last of them was rescinded, largely through the efforts of John Quincy Adams, who from the first had declared them to be "a direct violation of the constitution of the United States, the rules of this House, and the rights of my constituents."[140] By this

---

137 Freehling, Prelude to Civil War: The Nullification Controversy in South Carolina, 1816–36 310 (1965, 1966).

138 *Id.* at 333.

139 *Id.* at 83.   140 Register of Debates 4053 (1835).

time, however, whether it knew it or not, the nation had in effect decided that there should be freedom for antislavery speech everywhere, which means that it had decided that either slavery would end in the South or the nation would be sundered. The divided house could no longer stand.

VI. THE LIBERALIZING OF THE LAW

Harry Croswell was the printer and, under a pseudonym, the editor of *The Wasp*, a Federalist newspaper published in the Republican state of New York. Shortly after Jefferson and his party had been swept into national office on their platform of save the Republic and states' rights, Croswell, in print, accused Jefferson of paying James Callender for "calling Washington a traitor, a robber, and a perjurer [and] for calling Adams a hoary-headed incendiary." He went on to say that no "democratic editor has yet dared, or ever will dare, to meet [these charges] in an open and manly discussion." He was probably right as to the editors—for Jefferson had indeed supported Callender with money—but if he expected the Republicans, who had so recently inveighed against the national Sedition Law, to remain indifferent to what was being said about them, he was quickly disabused. An indictment was brought against him in the New York courts charging him with libeling Thomas Jefferson. Croswell, the indictment ran, "being a malicious and seditious man, of a depraved mind and wicked and diabolical disposition [intended with his words] to detract from, scandalize, traduce, vilify, and to represent him, the said Thomas Jefferson, as unworthy of the confidence, respect, and attachment of the people of the said United States, and to alienate and withdraw from the said Thomas Jefferson . . . the obedience, fidelity, and allegiance of the citizens of the state of New York, and also of the said United States; and wickedly and maliciously to disturb the peace."[141]

At the trial Croswell sought the right to call witnesses on his behalf in order to prove the truth of the accusations he had made against Jefferson, but the trial judge denied him this. The truth or falsity of the words constituting the alleged libel was irrelevant,

---

[141] People v. Croswell, 3 Johns. 336, 337 (N.Y. 1804). The best history of this litigation is in 1 GOEBEL, THE LAW PRACTICE OF ALEXANDER HAMILTON: DOCUMENTS AND COMMENTARIES 775–806 (1964).

the judge ruled, as was Croswell's intent in publishing them. This left the jury with the task of determining merely whether Croswell was indeed responsible for publishing the words and, secondly, of determining the truth of the "innuendoes"—that is to say, whether the construction put upon the published words by the prosecuting attorney was fair and acceptable. Thus, the common law of libel as understood by the state of New York was in important respects less liberal than the national Sedition Law, which permitted truth as a defense and, following Fox's Libel Act in Britain, permitted the jury "to determine the law and the fact, under the direction of the court, as in other cases." Under such conditions, and with a Republican judge presiding, it is not remarkable that Croswell was convicted. But he was not content to leave the matter there, and with the assistance of two of the leading Federalists in the country, his case was to assume a significance extending far into the future.

He petitioned for a new trial and, when this was denied as a matter of course, filed an appeal with the state supreme court. His principal defense attorney was Alexander Hamilton, and the court before which Hamilton argued included James Kent, later to become famous as Chancellor Kent and, after his retirement from the chancery bench, as the author of the extremely influential *Commentaries on American Law*. Kent's opinion in the case, built squarely and solidly on the arguments provided by Hamilton, may be said to constitute the foundation on which the American law of freedom of the press was subsequently built. This despite the fact that Kent's opinion was not controlling because the court, with only four of its five judges sitting, was evenly divided and Croswell's conviction was undisturbed.

It is striking that Hamilton should have agreed to be of counsel. The matter could have been treated and disposed of as a simple case of defamatory libel, not an issue that called for the advocacy of one of the country's leading statesmen. Instead, Hamilton, and later Kent, treated it as one of seditious libel—the victim of the alleged libel was not simply "Thomas Jefferson, Esq.," but the President of the United States. It would be foolish to deny that Hamilton's passions were probably involved. As every schoolboy knows, he and Jefferson were not friends, but this fact does not suffice to explain the considerable attention he devoted to the case and what Thomas Reed Powell once called "the wide range of [his] advocacy."[142] Croswell, Jefferson's enemy and accused libeler, and therefore at least a nominal supporter of Hamilton, could have been defended without raising the larger question of the true meaning of free speech and press under a republican constitution. Criminal libel it indubitably was—the case began with a prosecution by the state—but it did not have to become seditious libel.

The precise question raised by the motion for a new trial was whether the trial judge had erred in denying Croswell the opportunity to prove the truth of his allegedly defamatory statements and in confining the jury to determining the fact of publication. Both Hamilton and Kent, of course, argued that he had, but their interpretation of the English precedents is not persuasive, and the reader is left with the impression that Chief Justice Lewis, who filed an opinion denying the motion, is on sounder legal grounds when, for example, he insisted that Fox's Libel Act, which in 1792 settled the question of the role of the jury in English trials, was not, as Hamilton said it was, declaratory of the English law (and therefore a common law rule in New York), but was instead a revision of the law. In fact, although in form declaratory, "it was in substance a momentous change in the law of libel."[143] No more compelling is Hamilton's statement that the rule that truth is no defense in a libel action derives from a "polluted source," the Court of Star Chamber. Whatever its source, it had been firmly embraced by the common law. The question could not be answered to the satisfaction of the friends of republican government by a review of the legal authorities.

The chief of these authorities, Blackstone, had recently said that freedom of the press consisted in the right to publish without a censor's imprimatur but being liable to subsequent trial and punishment for abuses of this privilege. A law embodying this understanding of freedom of the press is surely to be preferred to a licensing system, wherein nothing is publishable except that which satisfies "the hasty view of an unleisured licenser," as Milton put it. Blackstone was surely justified in looking upon the expiration in 1694

[142] POWELL, *Kent's Contributions to Constitutional Law*, 14 COLUM. ALUM. NEWS 373 (1923). Another element accounting for Hamilton's interest was that one of his outspoken antagonists, Charles Holt, editor of the *New England Bee*, who had been convicted of libeling Hamilton, was an enemy of Croswell. See Forkosch, *Freedom of the Press: Croswell's Case*, 33 FORD. L. REV. 418 (1965).

[143] PLUCKNETT, A CONCISE HISTORY OF THE COMMON LAW 470 (1948).

of the last of the English licensing acts and the subsequent development of a body of common law with respect to the matters formerly governed by these acts as a movement in the right direction.
But it was not sufficient. He published his eleventh and last edition
of his *Commentaries* in 1791, eight years after Lord Mansfield had
handed down the decision in the *Dean of St. Asaph's Case*,[144] and
not many friends of republican government (although the two
judges opposed to Kent in *Croswell* were exceptions) could be
content with the law of that case. Especially in the trial of a seditious libel, of what benefit is the privilege to publish without the
prior consent of a censor, if a judge, rather than a jury, determines
whether the words are libelous? The more so if the law, as Blackstone said, is that the essence of a libel consists in its tendency to
cause a "breach of the public peace" and, therefore, the question
of its truth or falsity and the intent with which it was published
are irrelevant in the trial. Whether Blackstone's common-law understanding of freedom of the press is, then, compatible with republican government will depend on the mode of the trial and
the understanding of an abuse, or, in Blackstone's own terms, on
what is understood to constitute an "improper, mischievous, or
illegal publication."[145]

By refusing to regard Croswell's case as a mere matter of defamatory libel, Hamilton and Kent reached the larger issue of freedom in a republican regime. By rejecting the authority of Blackstone, they themselves became the authorities in America. To both
of them—for Kent accepted Hamilton's formulation without alter-
ation or addition—the liberty of the press "consisted in publishing
with impunity, truth with good motives, and for justifiable ends,
whether it related to men or to measures."[146] This became the basis
of the law in almost every American jurisdiction.

This new law was not libertarian in the modern sense—neither
Hamilton nor Kent advocated a law that would permit everyone to
say anything at any, or almost any, time[147]—but it was surely more
consonant with republican government, both because it permitted

---

[144] 21 St.Tr. 847 (K.B. 1783). The case is discussed at length in 2 STEPHEN, HIS-
TORY OF THE CRIMINAL LAW 330–43 (1883).

[145] 4 BLACKSTONE'S COMMENTARIES *811.   [146] 3 Johns. at 352, 393–94.

[147] Hamilton "reprobated the novel, the visionary, the pestilential doctrine of
an unchecked press. . . . [This] would encourage vice, compel the virtuous to retire,
destroy confidence, and confound the innocent with the guilty." *Id*. at 352.

truth as a defense in a trial of public or seditious libels, when it was published with good motives and for justifiable ends, and because it enlarged the role of the jury in the determination of the intent and tendency of the publication. In all criminal law, Hamilton argued, the intent constitutes the crime—homicide is not, of itself, murder. Whether intent and tendency are viewed as questions of fact, as Hamilton argued, or of law, or of a "compound of law and fact," as Kent put it, what is important in the law of criminal and especially of seditious libel is that the determination of malice and tendency not be entrusted solely to the judges who, as Hamilton said and as history confirms, "might be tempted to enter into the views of government."[148]

A role for the jury does not by itself assure impartial trials—the experience under the Sedition Law was sufficient to prove this. But it would seem to be a prerequisite in criminal trials of what is alleged to be seditious behavior. The government must be able "to control the governed," as Madison said in *Federalist* No. 51, and the law, including the law limiting the freedom of the press, is one of the means, and in a republic the most appropriate means, of doing this. But the government must also be obliged "to control itself," or to be controlled, and the requirement that the "trial of all crimes except in cases of impeachment shall be by jury" is recognition of this necessity, especially in the absence of a truly

---

[148] It was precisely this, notably in those trials conducted before Judge Samuel Chase, that had made the Sedition Law cases notorious in their time and infamous in the annals of American criminal trials. Nor does the relevance of the example of Chase end with his conduct on the bench. There is evidence in Hamilton's defense of Croswell that he had Chase and the subsequent events provoked by Chase's conduct very much in mind as he reflected on the freedom of the press and the trials for its abuse. At the beginning of the year of Croswell's trial the House of Representatives had appointed a committee "to enquire into the judicial conduct of Samuel Chase," and two months later the House voted the impeachment by a strictly partisan vote of 73 to 32. He was to be acquitted in the Senate the following year, but the issue was pending and still in doubt during the Croswell appeal. Since it was common knowledge that if the Republicans succeeded in removing Chase from the federal bench they would then proceed against other Federalist judges, a fair-minded man was entitled to be apprehensive for the future of an independent judiciary in America. Hence Hamilton, in what seems an obvious reference to these events, said in his closing argument in Croswell's case that he feared that "any political tenet or indiscretion might be made a crime or pretext to impeach, convict and remove from office, the judges of the federal courts." 3 Johns. at 358. Chase was an extreme Federalist and the Sedition Law trials he conducted were travesties of justice. But it is extremely doubtful that his removal and replacement by a Republican judge would have buttressed the independence of the judiciary.

independent judiciary. Hamilton in *Federalist* No. 83 was not prepared to say whether jury trials were more to be esteemed "as a
defense against the oppressions of an hereditary monarch, than as a
barrier to the tyranny of popular magistrates in a popular government," but essential they were. It is worth our attention to notice
that while it was Jefferson who was responsible for the fact that
the trials of seditious and other criminal libels would take place in
state courts, it was Hamilton who was responsible for reforming
the procedure in those state trials to make it conform more fully
to the principles of republican government and, not accidentally,
the federal Constitution.[149]

No less essential is the other major element in the law derived
from the work of Hamilton and Kent in Croswell's case: the right
to offer in evidence the truth of the allegedly libelous words. The
rule of the greater the truth, the greater the libel, or the more mod-
est version in Chief Justice Lewis' opinion in *Croswell* that "truth
may be as dangerous to society as falsehood," is not unreasonable in
a hereditary monarchy, or in any regime that, in Burke's words,
finds its "sole authority" in the fact that "it has existed time out of
mind." Speaking truth there may indeed be destructive of law and
government, because the regime does not rest on true principles as
such, but on historical principles. The American constitutions, on
the other hand, both the national and the states', were understood
to rest on the laws of nature, on the self-evident truth that all
men are created equal with respect to the natural rights of life, liberty, and the pursuit of happiness. Government is instituted among
men to secure these rights and derives its just powers from the consent of the governed. No man is naturally exalted over another, and
public officers hold their temporarily exalted stations only at the
pleasure of their fellow citizens. The speaking of the truth concerning men and measures and, indeed, the very basis of the regime,
cannot usually be "dangerous to society." Which means that the
English law of libel, evolving in a different system, based on differ-

---

[149] Kent's conclusion on this point was stated as follows: ". . . that upon every
indictment or information for a libel, where the defendant puts himself upon the
country, by a plea of not guilty, the jury have a right to judge, not only of the fact
of the publication, and the truth of the *innuendoes*, but of the intent and tendency
of the paper, and whether it be a libel or not; and, in short, of 'the matter put in issue
upon such indictment or information.' " 3 Johns. at 376–77, quoting from Fox's Libel
Act, 32 Geo. III, c. 60 (1792).

ent principles, had to be reformed before it could be accepted in America. In Hamilton's words, "truth is [not only] a material ingredient in the evidence of intent," and must therefore be admissible on procedural grounds, but is "all-important to the liberties of the people [and] an ingredient in the eternal order of things."[150] He hoped to see the common law "applied to the United States," and his version of the common law, whatever the case with the English version, required the rule that the defendant be permitted to prove the truth of his allegedly libelous words. The common law was "principally the application of natural law to the state and condition of society," and without adherence to its principles "the constitution would be frittered away or borne down by factions, (the evil genii, the pests of republics)."[151] Thus, the natural law dictated the form of the Constitution and, through the vehicle of the common law, the manner in which government was to be administered under it: all men were to be free to publish opinions on public men and measures—the provisions respecting freedom of the press guaranteed this—but their publications were not to be maliciously false. The truth, or true principles, was to be the standard of political life.

A distinction drawn by Kent in his opinion serves to illustrate this role of truth. "There can be no doubt," he said, "that it is competent for the defendant to rebut the presumption of malice, drawn from the fact of publication; and it is consonant to the general theory of evidence, and the dictates of justice, that the defendant should be allowed to avail himself of every fact and circumstance that may serve to repel that presumption."[152]

> And what can be a more important circumstance than the truth of the charge, to determine the goodness of the motive in making it, if it be a charge against the competency or purity of a character in public trust, or of a candidate for public favor, or a charge of actions in which the community have an interest, and are deeply concerned? To shut out wholly the inquiry into the truth of the accusation, is to abridge essentially the means of defence. It is to weaken the arm of the defendant, and to convict him, by means of a presumption, which he might easily destroy by proof that the charge was true, and that, considering the nature of the accusation, the circumstances and the time under which it was made, and the situation of the person implicated, his motive could have been

---

[150] 3 Johns. at 358.   [151] *Ibid.*   [152] *Id.* at 377.

no other than a pure and disinterested regard for the public welfare.[153]

The conduct of public men must be measured by the highest standards of probity and their character by models of virtue and purity, and any published accusation of a failure on their part, measured by these standards and models, will not be punished under the law. On the contrary, it can be said that just as republican government requires public men of the highest character, it requires a press to point to the derelictions, which is to say that it requires a law that condones accusations of derelictions. But the law, being reasonable, will not presume that everyone must live according to these strict standards. Hence, the presumption of malicious intent in a libel of a *private* person cannot be rebutted by a showing of the truth of the charge—or in Kent's words, "this doctrine will not go to tolerate libels upon private character"—because no public good is served by revelations of the derelictions of private persons, the public being neither injured by these private vices nor otherwise concerned with them.[154] But that "falsehood is a material ingredient in a public libel" is a doctrine, Kent insisted, that even the English courts had occasionally admitted and that had taken firmer root in America. It is, he concluded, "the vital support of the liberty of the press."[155] Certainly it became firmly rooted after the advocacy of Hamilton and Kent.

It is important to remark, however, in order to compare what are today held to be the true principles of the liberty of the press in a democratic polity with the original understanding, that Hamilton and Kent did not advocate that truth, even in a trial of a public libel, be a complete defense. The malicious intent in a libel of a public person can be rebutted by a showing of the truth of the charges, but just as "this doctrine will not go to tolerate libels upon private character," the showing of the truth will not alone justify "the circulation of charges for seditious and wicked ends."[156] The truth, even in a republican polity, can be employed for "seditious and

---

153 *Id*. at 377–78.   154 *Id*. at 379.   155 *Ibid*.

156 *Id*. at 378. Under New York Times v. Sullivan, 376 U.S. 254, 280–81 (1964), not only is truth a defense, because recovery depends on "actual malice" defined as "knowledge that [the statement] was false" or was made "with reckless disregard of whether it was false or not," but it is unnecessary for the defendant to prove truth so long as the victim cannot show that the defamatory statement was made with "actual malice."

wicked ends." Hence the bill that was introduced in the State Assembly one year after *Croswell* by William Van Ness, who had been on the *Croswell* brief with Hamilton. It was unanimously enacted by both houses of the legislature, and in 1821 became part of the free speech and press section of the state constitution. The bill made it proper for the defendant in the trial of a criminal libel to give in evidence the truth of the matter charged as libelous, provided it be shown in the trial that the words were "published with good motives and for justifiable ends."[157]

Thus, the law of criminal libel was changed in two respects as a result of the *Croswell* case. The jury's role was enlarged significantly beyond the mere determination of the fact of publication and the truth of the innuendoes to embrace as well the determination of the criminality of the words. Second, the truth, provided good motives and justifiable ends could be shown, would be permitted in evidence to rebut the presumption of malice and, therefore, to acquit the defendant of the libel. Put differently, the law with respect to malice was changed and the jury would thereafter play a major role in the application of the law. That this requirement that even the truth be spoken with good motives and justifiable ends was not retained inadvertently is proved by an event in the legislature. In April, 1804, shortly before the opinions in the case were delivered, the legislature enacted a bill providing, in effect, that truth be a complete defense in the trial of a public libel; but the Council of Revision (which was composed of the governor and two judges of the Supreme Court and which could be overruled only by a two-thirds majority in both houses of the legislature) returned it, objecting that the proposed law "made no distinction between libels circulated from good motives and justifiable ends, and such as were circulated for seditious and wicked purposes, or to gratify individual malice or revenge."[158] Upon consideration of these objections in the

---

[157] N.Y. Sess. Laws (1805) ch. 90; New York State Constitution of 1821, Art. 7, § 8. The constitutional provision read: "Every citizen may freely speak, write, and publish his sentiments on all subjects, being responsible for the abuse of that right, and no law shall be passed to curtail, or restrain the liberty of speech, or of the press. In all prosecutions or indictments for libels, the truth may be given in evidence to the jury; and if it shall appear to the jury that the matter charged as libelous, is true, and was published with good motives and for justifiable ends, the party shall be acquitted; and the jury shall have the right to determine the law and the fact."

[158] 3 Johns. at 411.

assembly, the bill "lost by a large majority." It was only two months later that this same assembly, along with the Senate, adopted the Van Ness–Hamilton–Kent bill unanimously.

People v. Croswell began as an episode in the Alien and Sedition controversy. Croswell had accused Jefferson of paying Callender, a victim of the Sedition Law, to vilify Washington and Adams. But whereas the Sedition Law had provoked nullification and even disunion sentiments in Virginia, the indictment and trial of Croswell provoked the most thoughtful consideration of the meaning of freedom of speech and press that Americans had, to that time, ever engaged in. What began as a party matter ended in the unanimous adoption of a provision embodying the principles of the arch Federalists Alexander Hamilton and James Kent. That these principles can truly be said to have embodied the considered opinion of Americans on the meaning of the freedom of speech and press is proved by the extent to which Kent's opinion in *Croswell* was cited in the future, not only in New York, but in states throughout the Union. Speech and press were to be free, republican government required it; but not everything said or published will go unpunished—the privilege might be abused. A jury of twelve peers will determine when it is abused.[159]

---

[159] Mr. Justice Jackson, in Beauharnais v. Illinois, 343 U.S. 250, 295, 297 (1952), after reciting the history of the *Croswell* case, "the leading state case," and the influence of Hamilton and Kent, concluded that it "would not be an exaggeration to say that, basically, this provision of the New York Constitution states the common sense of American criminal libel law. Twenty-four States of the Union whose Constitutions were framed later substantially adopted it."

ROBERT M. O'NEIL

OF JUSTICE DELAYED AND JUSTICE

DENIED: THE WELFARE PRIOR

HEARING CASES

Two decades ago, Mr. Justice Frankfurter deemed essential to due process of law "the right to be heard before being condemned to suffer grievous loss of any kind, even though it may not involve the stigma and hardships of a criminal conviction."[1] This broad precept is unexceptionable. Yet its application has been far from uniform. On the very day it was announced, the Court upheld the dismissal without any formal hearing of a federal civil servant suspected of disloyalty on the basis of personal and political affiliations.[2] In other instances of denial or withdrawal of government benefits—where "grievous loss" is surely incurred—the availability of a hearing has been a matter of much doubt.[3]

The historical development of the constitutional right to a hearing is full of discontinuities, lacunae, and contradictions. Where deprivation of life or liberty is threatened, there has never been any

Robert M. O'Neil is Professor of Law, University of California at Berkeley.

This article has benefited from helpful comments by Professor Hans A. Linde and Peter Sitkin, Esq.–R. M. O'N.

[1] Joint Anti-Fascist Refugee Comm. v. McGrath, 341 U.S. 123, 168 (1951) (concurring opinion).

[2] Bailey v. Richardson, 341 U.S. 918 (1951) (equally divided Court).

[3] See generally Davis, *The Requirement of a Trial-Type Hearing*, 70 Harv. L. Rev. 193 (1956).

question about the right to be heard before sanctions are imposed.[4] Where tangible property is to be taken (directly or indirectly) the opportunity for adversary process has long been recognized.[5] When less tangible interests are at stake, however, the precedents form a curious patchwork. Nearly forty years ago, the Supreme Court held without dissent that a certified public accountant had a constitutional right to a hearing before his application for admission to practice before the Tax Court could be rejected.[6] For a decade now, the lower courts have uniformly held that a student at a state college or university[7] (and occasionally at a private institution)[8] is entitled to a full and formal hearing before being expelled or suspended for a long period. Yet as recently as 1965 Professor Charles Reich observed that "in the case of a decision removing a family from public housing, or a decision denying aid to families with dependent children, generally the matter is finally determined at some level within the appropriate agency, after investigation by the agency, and with comparatively informal procedures, if any, available to the persons affected."[9] In the sensitive realm of public employment—where only a fraction of all workers enjoy civil service or tenure protection—a constitutional right to be heard before being discharged has never been generally recognized by the courts.[10] Thus the formality of procedures found even in the regulatory and licensing sectors are notably absent from the administration of many government benefit programs.[11]

---

[4] *E.g., In re* Oliver, 333 U.S. 257 (1948).

[5] *E.g.,* Londoner v. Denver, 210 U.S. 373 (1908).

[6] Goldsmith v. Board of Tax Appeals, 270 U.S. 117 (1926).

[7] Dixon v. Alabama State Bd. of Educ., 294 F.2d 150 (5th Cir. 1961).

[8] See Coleman v. Wagner College, 429 F.2d 1120 (2d Cir. 1970).

[9] Reich, *Individual Rights and Social Welfare: The Emerging Legal Issues,* 74 YALE L.J. 1245, 1252 (1965).

[10] The situation today is substantially as described by Professor Davis over a decade ago. See 1 DAVIS, ADMINISTRATIVE LAW TREATISE 463–73 (1958). The one possible exception is the very recent decision in Olson v. Regents, 301 F. Supp. 1356 (D. Minn. 1969). Most of the scholarly writing on the constitutional aspects of public employment—*e.g.,* Van Alstyne, *The Constitutional Rights of Public Employees: A Comment on the Inappropriate Uses of an Old Analogy,* 16 U.C.L.A. L. REV. 751 (1969)—has concerned itself with the substantive protections for free expression and political activity in the public sector and not with procedural safeguards.

[11] See Reich, note 9 *supra,* at 1253.

The reluctance of the courts to extend procedural protections to government beneficiaries is not easily explained. One theory is that such safeguards are seldom sought or conferred until after judicial recognition of major substantive rights. Yet the protection of the rights of college and university students developed in just the opposite sequence: the courts began by holding that a student was entitled to a formal hearing before being dismissed or expelled[12] and then proceeded to define the substantive civil liberties a student might claim.[13]

A second possibility is that administrative regulations (or the anticipation of them) made the quest for constitutional safeguards less urgent. To some extent this has been the case in public housing, where a strong directive from the Department of Housing and Urban Development has largely mooted the due process issue.[14] But in other contexts, there would have been no protection at all if the courts had awaited agency action; clearly this is so in the student rights area, and more recently with respect to welfare.[15]

A third and more credible theory is that courts have been slow to accord procedural protection to government beneficiaries because the interests affected were so long characterized as "privileges" or gratuities.[16] In the 1951 case of the summarily discharged civil servant,[17] the court of appeals maintained that a government employee had never been entitled to a "hearing of the quasi-judicial type" because the guarantees of due process applied only when "one is being deprived of something to which he has a right."[18] Yet even the untimely persistence and the slow death of the right-privilege distinction[19] do not adequately explain the lag in developing proce-

---

[12] Dixon v. Alabama State Bd. of Educ., 294 F.2d 150 (5th Cir. 1961); Knight v. State Bd. of Educ., 200 F. Supp. 174 (M.D. Tenn. 1961).

[13] See for a thorough review of the evolution of these protections, Wright, *The Constitution on the Campus*, 22 VAND. L. REV. 1027 (1969).

[14] See Thorpe v. Housing Authority, 393 U.S. 268 (1969).

[15] On the cat-and-mouse relationship between the regulation proposed by the Department of Health, Education, and Welfare and the Court decision finally settling the issue, see text *infra*, at notes 70–73.

[16] See 1 DAVIS, note 10 *supra*, at 452–62.

[17] Bailey v. Richardson, 341 U.S. 918 (1951).

[18] Bailey v. Richardson, 182 F.2d 46, 58 (D.C. Cir. 1950).

[19] See generally Van Alstyne, *The Demise of the Right-Privilege Distinction in Constitutional Law*, 81 HARV. L. REV. 1439 (1968); Comment, *The First Amendment*

dural safeguards for the government beneficiary. The Supreme Court has held for nearly a quarter-century that labeling certain interests as "privileges" does not permit government agencies to dispense or condition them in ways that abridge freedom of speech or discriminate on racial or religious grounds.[20]

Finally, the delay may be attributable simply to the fortuities of test case litigation. In the student rights area, lawyers began by pressing for hearings, in the hope that reinstatement would typically follow even a rudimentary observance of due process.[21] In the public housing field, litigation of all sorts began much later and concentrated initially on substantive issues.[22] In the welfare area, attorneys were simply unavailable to bring test suits until the mid-1960's.[23] And their first concerns were such outrages upon client interests as man-in-the-house,[24] employable mother,[25] and one-year waiting period regulations.[26] Thus the first test suits asking that a client be heard before benefits were terminated simply did not reach

---

and Public Employees—an Emerging Constitutional Right to Be a Policeman? 37 GEO. WASH. L. REV. 409 (1968).

[20] The series of cases began with Wieman v. Updegraff, 344 U.S. 183 (1952), or perhaps even with Everson v. Bd. of Educ., 330 U. S. 1 (1947).

[21] The two earliest cases of the "modern" period of student rights, Dixon v. Alabama State Bd. of Educ., 294 F.2d 150 (5th Cir. 1961); and Knight v. State Bd. of Educ., 200 F. Supp. 174 (M.D. Tenn. 1961), were in fact much more civil rights than student rights cases. They were brought by attorneys for civil rights organizations, seeking a recognition of the compatibility of college attendance at tax-supported institutions and protest against racial segregation.

[22] For discussion of efforts to obtain recognition for tenants' substantive rights during the 1960's, see Note, *Government Housing Assistance to the Poor,* 76 YALE L.J. 508 (1967). There had been a rash of cases during the early 1950's over the constitutionality of a federally required loyalty oath imposed on public housing tenants. See, *e.g.,* Notes, 53 COLUM. L. REV. 1166 (1953); 69 HARV. L. REV. 551 (1956). Then the housing field was virtually dormant for almost a decade until substantive rights were reasserted in, *e.g.,* Holmes v. New York City Housing Auth., 398 F.2d 262 (2d Cir. 1968); Holt v. Richmond Redevelopment and Housing Auth., 266 F. Supp. 397 (E.D. Va. 1966).

[23] See, *e.g.,* U.S. DEPARTMENT OF HEALTH, EDUCATION, AND WELFARE, NEIGHBORHOOD LEGAL SERVICES—NEW DIMENSIONS IN THE LAW (1966); LAW AND POVERTY 1965: REPORT TO THE NATIONAL CONFERENCE ON LAW AND POVERTY (1965).

[24] See King v. Smith, 392 U.S. 309 (1968).

[25] See Anderson v. Burson, 300 F. Supp. 401 (N.D. Ga. 1968).

[26] See Shapiro v. Thompson, 394 U.S. 618 (1969).

the Court until the late 1960's—long after a series of substantive rights had been tested and vindicated.[27]

Now the decisions of the Supreme Court in *Goldberg v. Kelly*[28] and *Wheeler v. Montgomery*[29]—holding that a welfare recipient is constitutionally entitled to a pretermination hearing—provide the occasion for a re-examination of this whole field of law. After a brief summary of these two cases, I shall proceed to appraise and analyze the decisions—both in terms of what was decided and what was only implied. Against this welfare law background, I shall then consider analogous questions in other government benefit programs. It is necessary to look not only at the beneficiary who is terminated, expelled, or evicted but also at the one whose status is simply not renewed at the end of a term, and even the one whose initial application is denied or rejected. The issues become increasingly difficult and the cases correspondingly fewer throughout this series of questions.

I. Welfare Benefits and Prior Hearings

A. THE OPINIONS

The issues of the right to a prior hearing reached the Supreme Court in parallel cases from New York[30] and California.[31] Both states provided fair hearings to beneficiaries who sought them after termination, in accord with the federal statutory requirement for all categorical assistance programs.[32] In addition, New York and California offered prior notice of the proposed action to any recipient

---

[27] See Comment, *The Constitutional Minimum for the Termination of Welfare Benefits: The Need for and Requirements of a Prior Hearing*, 68 Mich. L. Rev. 112 (1969), for a review of the cases and the litigation strategy while the issue was pending before the Supreme Court.

[28] 397 U.S. 254 (1970).   [29] 397 U.S. 280 (1970).

[30] Kelly v. Wyman, 294 F. Supp. 893 (S.D. N.Y. 1968).

[31] Wheeler v. Montgomery, 296 F. Supp. 138 (N.D. Cal. 1968). There were many other suits pending at the time, *e.g.*, McCall v. Shapiro, 292 F. Supp. 268 (D. Conn. 1968); Camerena v. Dep't of Pub. Welfare, 9 Ariz. App. 120 (1969).

[32] 42 U.S.C. § 302(a)(4) (old-age assistance or medical assistance for the aged); 42 U.S.C. § 602(a)(4) (aid to families with dependent children). The statute specifies neither the time at which the "fair hearing" should be held nor the contents of the hearing. The law thus leaves much room for administrative interpretation and implementation. There seems to be some uncertainty about the extent of compliance with this mandate. Comment, note 27 *supra*.

threatened with loss of benefits, and at least an informal conference at which arguments could be advanced against termination. But neither state provided a formal adversary or evidentiary hearing before the cutoff took effect.

A majority of the Supreme Court found this procedure constitutionally defective.[33] The opinion of Mr. Justice Brennan began by observing that welfare benefits "are a matter of statutory entitlement for persons qualified to receive them."[34] While conceding that in certain instances government benefits might be terminated without affording a prior hearing—notably instances in which some emergency was present—the Court found especially compelling and urgent the plight of the welfare beneficiary removed from the rolls:[35]

> . . . termination of aid pending resolution of a controversy over eligibility may deprive an *eligible* recipient of the very means by which to live while he waits. Since he lacks independent resources, his situation becomes immediately desperate. His need to concentrate upon finding the means for daily subsistence, in turn, adversely affects his ability to seek redress from the welfare bureaucracy.

Thus pretermination hearings were "indispensable" to the needs of the welfare system as well as those of the individual beneficiary: "The same governmental interests that counsel the provision of welfare, counsel as well its uninterrupted provision to those eligible to receive it."[36]

Countervailing interests were unpersuasive to the majority. While the prior-hearing requirement might entail some additional expense and administrative inconvenience, the basis of the objections was really only fiscal. However worthy in the abstract, the state's interest in conserving its resources could not outweigh the claims of the destitute beneficiary. And though the state probably could not recoup from judgment-proof recipients any payments erroneously made, "much of the drain on fiscal and administrative resources can be reduced by developing procedures for prompt pre-termination hearings and by skillful use of personnel and facilities."[37] Moreover,

---

[33] Goldberg v. Kelly, 397 U.S. 254 (1970). The decision was 5 to 3, with Chief Justice Burger and Justices Black and Stewart in dissent.

[34] 397 U.S. at 262.   [36] *Id.* at 265.

[35] *Id.* at 264.   [37] *Id.* at 266.

due process need not include both pre- and post-termination procedures. If the state simply chose to continue payments until a "fair"
hearing (consistent with the federal statute) could be held, a single
hearing would suffice.[38]

The opinion of the majority concluded by defining the contours
of the hearing that must precede termination. It need not take the
form of a "judicial or quasi-judicial trial." This hearing had a single
purpose: "to produce an initial determination" of the validity of the
welfare agency's decision to stop payments in a particular case.
Thus "minimal procedural safeguards" would suffice at this stage.
These rudiments must, however, include "adequate notice detailing
the reasons for a proposed termination, and an effective opportunity
to defend by confronting any adverse witnesses and by presenting
[the recipient's] own arguments and evidence orally." Only such a
personal and formal appearance would suffice to protect the client's
constitutional rights; he must be able to "confront and cross examine
witnesses relied on by the department."[39] He must be allowed representation by retained counsel, although the agency is not obligated to appoint counsel. The decision of the hearing officer must
rest "solely on the legal rules and evidence adduced at the hearing."[40] Accordingly, reasons must be given for the decision and
references made to the pertinent evidence. Finally, an "impartial
decision-maker is essential." While prior involvement of a welfare
official in some aspect of the case would not absolutely disqualify
him from presiding at the hearing, "he should not have . . . participated in making the determination under review."[41]

There were three dissenting opinions. Mr. Justice Stewart noted
in a cryptic paragraph that, though he found the issue a close one,
he would sustain the constitutionality of the present state practices.[42]
Mr. Justice Black argued at some length that the majority had engaged in unwarranted judicial legislation. He thought the decision
was, moreover, without precedent; he could recall no previous instance "in which the person alleged to owe money to another is required by law to continue making payments to a judgment-proof
claimant without the benefit of any security or bond to insure that
these payments can be recovered if he wins his legal argument."[43]

---

38 *Id.* at 267 and n. 14.

39 *Id.* at 270.

40 *Id.* at 271.

41 *Id.* at 271.

42 *Id.* at 285 (dissenting opinion).

43 *Id.* at 277–78 (dissenting opinion).

Finally, he expressed concern that the decision might hurt indigent persons as a class more than it would help, by causing welfare agencies to tighten the procedure for determining initial eligibility. While assuring that many beneficiaries could not be removed summarily, the decision will "also have insured that many will never get on the rolls, or at least that they will remain destitute during the lengthy proceedings followed to determine initial eligibility."[44]

The Chief Justice, in an opinion which Mr. Justice Black joined, expressed two additional concerns: First, he thought the intervention of the Court both unwise and unnecessary because the Department of Health, Education, and Welfare had already proposed a regulation providing most of the protections sought by the beneficiaries in these two cases.[45] Second, he felt the logic of the majority opinion must carry well beyond its holdings, so the Court could not conscientiously refuse to extend comparable protections to, *inter alia,* "welfare reductions or denial of increases as opposed to terminations, or decisions concerning initial applications or requests for special assistance."[46] Yet the majority had said nothing about these less drastic changes in status, and this the Chief Justice thought regrettable if not disingenuous.

B. A QUESTION OF TIMING

The result seems not only sound, but almost inevitable—given the way the issue was framed. Largely through the accident of litigation, the question that really was central and basic—whether a welfare recipient has a constitutional right to a formal, adversary hearing at all—was never before the Court. All the parties assumed that a dispute over continuing eligibility had to be submitted to an evidentiary hearing at some time, the only question being at what stage of the termination process. As far as *categorical* assistance programs were involved, of course, the issue was narrowed in this way by the "fair hearing" mandate of the Social Security Act.[47] For all other welfare programs—general assistance payments deriving from state and/or local funds—the availability of a formal hearing was theoretically an open issue. But New York and California law required

---

[44] *Id.* at 279 (dissenting opinion).

[45] *Id.* at 283 (dissenting opinion).   [46] *Id.* at 285 (dissenting opinion).

[47] 42 U.S.C. § 302 (a) (4) (old-age assistance or medical assistance for the aged); 42 U.S.C. § 602 (a) (4) (aid to families with dependent children).

procedures at least as fair as did the federal statute. If this first case had come from a less enlightened state (Georgia or Mississippi, for example), the Court would not simply have assumed the major premise on the way to announcing the minor one but would have had to face squarely the underlying issue of the right to a hearing as such.

Since only the issue of timing and not that of hearing was before the Court, a different result would have been puzzling. There have been instances, as the majority opinion noted, in which a constitutional right to be heard has been postponed until after the completion of the contested action.[48] But the circumstances justifying deferral of a conceded right to notice, personal appearance, and confrontation, are highly unusual.[49] There are the classic "emergency" cases—food is about to spoil and must be kept from grocers' shelves; a fraud is about to be perpetrated on unsuspecting securities purchasers; or a professional licensee is continuing to offer his services to trusting clients after having perpetrated malpractice.[50] In these situations, the reason for acting now and hearing later are incontestable. Moreover, there is usually an adequate remedy after the fact; if the victim of summary action later prevails, he can be made whole or nearly whole through money damages.

Apart from these emergency situations, there seems almost a general presumption that one who is constitutionally entitled to be heard at all should be heard before the change in status occurs. Few cases have dealt specifically with the issue of timing. Occasionally the matter of timing is unimportant to either party; more often the dispensing or regulating agency feels its own interests as well as those of the individual are best served by dispatch and voluntarily provides for early resolution of contested claims.[51]

In at least two contexts the Court has clearly recognized the need to assure a hearing in advance of detrimental action. Just before the welfare hearing cases were docketed, a nearly unanimous Court

---

[48] *E.g.*, Ewing v. Mytinger & Casselberry, Inc., 339 U.S. 594 (1950).

[49] See generally 1 DAVIS, note 10 *supra*, at 438–44.

[50] *E.g.*, Halsey, Stuart & Co. v. Public Serv. Comm'n, 212 Wis. 184 (1933).

[51] There is, of course, a substantial body of law concerning the timing of judicial review of administrative action. In some instances review may be accelerated, in others postponed, and in still others seemingly foreclosed altogether, although the courts are most reluctant to find review completely unavailable. See generally JAFFE, JUDICIAL CONTROL OF ADMINISTRATIVE ACTION 353–76 (1965).

held Wisconsin's prejudgment wage-garnishment procedure constitutionally deficient because no provision was made for a hearing
before the attachment took effect.[52] The majority opinion stressed
the plight of the debtor who, though wholly dependent upon his
earnings, lacked any opportunity to contest the garnishment in advance of seizure. The Court concluded: "The result is that a pre-
judgment garnishment . . . may as a practical matter drive a wage-
earning family to the wall. Where the taking of one's property is so
obvious, it needs no extended argument to conclude that absent
notice and a prior hearing . . . this pre-judgment garnishment procedure violates the fundamental principles of due process."[53]

The other context in which the timing of the hearing has been
litigated—the seizure of allegedly obscene materials—suggests a parallel basis for requiring advance resolution of conflicting claims. The
leading case is *A Quantity of Copies of Books v. Kansas*.[54] Over two
dissents, the Court held violative of due process a state procedure
for seizure and destruction of salacious publications without a prior
adversary hearing to determine the central question of obscenity.
The statute did provide for a full and fair hearing *after* the seizure.
But the Court found that alternative constitutionally insufficient:
"For if seizure of books precedes an adversary determination of
their obscenity, there is danger of abridgment of the right of the
public in a free society to unobstructed circulation of nonobscene
books."[55] The risk of error was substantial. The consequences of
error were not only detrimental to basic societal interests but effectively irreversible.

The welfare cases present a claim for prior hearing at least as
strong as those just considered—and in any event far stronger than
the routine case in which the normal presumption of priority seems
to operate. Various special factors militate for pretermination notice
and confrontation. First, the New York and California procedures
before the Court were about the most benign afforded anywhere in
the country, for beneficiaries of general as well as categorical assis-

---

[52] Sniadach v. Family Finance Corp., 395 U.S. 337 (1969).

[53] *Id*. at 341–42.

[54] 378 U.S. 205 (1964). For recent reaffirmation of this principle in the context
of motion pictures, about which the *Kansas* case left some doubt, see Natali v.
Municipal Ct., 309 F. Supp. 192 (N.D. Cal. 1969).

[55] 378 U.S. at 213.

tance programs. Unlike many states, these two complied fully with federal statutory requirements at the post-termination stage.[56] Moreover, they did offer beneficiaries threatened with termination a notice which the Court found constitutionally adequate both in time and in form. The constitutional deficiency lay in the content of the hearing. Thus, if hardship could be found in California and New York proceedings, much greater injustice could be expected elsewhere.

Second, a disproportionately high rate of reversals in the few instances where figures are kept[57] suggests an unusual risk of error inherent in the welfare eligibility process. Various circumstances may make this aspect of administrative action less reliable than others: the heavy caseload burden placed upon often inexperienced caseworkers; the high rate of turnover among caseworkers; the difficulty of garnering accurate information about a population that is frequently anonymous and difficult to reach and with whom communication is severely hampered by suspicion and by barriers of language and culture; and the lack of adequate funds within the welfare budget for detailed record keeping or verification of leads, tips, and accusations about client conduct.[58] Thus the propensity for error at the factual level is understandably quite high. The danger of wholly erroneous determinations, with attendant serious injustice, is correspondingly great. These circumstances argue strongly for an independent assessment of the factual basis of an adverse administrative action before the action is taken.

Third, the consequences of termination are quite drastic indeed, for reasons hinted at but not fully developed by the *Kelly* majority. The typical recipient, of course, does not seek welfare until he has already lost the capacity and exhausted the resources to support

---

[56] For the variations in extent of state compliance with federal mandate, see Note, *Federal Judicial Review of State Welfare Practices*, 67 COLUM. L. REV. 84, 91–92 (1967).

[57] See Bell & Norvell, *Texas Welfare Appeals: The Hidden Right*, 46 TEX. L. REV. 223–24 (1967); Brief for Appellants, Wheeler v. Montgomery, 397 U.S. 280 (1970), at pp. 12–13. The latter source cites eligibility control figures of the California Department of Social Welfare showing that 8 percent of AFDC families had been found on review to have been wrongfully terminated, while in only 1 percent of all cases was aid mistakenly continued.

[58] See Note, *Eligibility Determinations in Public Assistance: Selected Problems and Proposals for Reform in Pennsylvania*, 115 U. PA. L. REV. 1307, 1326–27 (1967).

himself.[59] To remove any doubt, most states require an applicant who comes to the agency in a financially marginal condition to become destitute and dependent before payments can begin.[60] Characteristic is Connecticut's asset ceiling of $250 per welfare family, including even the cash value of life insurance.[61] Even more stringent is the Illinois rule (for recipients of Aid to Families with Dependent Children) limiting retention of cash or personal property or life insurance to the value of one month's assistance grant.[62] The mechanism by which self-sufficiency is impaired varies somewhat from state to state, but the effect is uniform. And the result is clear: the family that is erroneously stricken from the welfare rolls may be able to survive on its retained resources (if the maximum amount has in fact been retained), but not for long. The destitute condition that compels the beneficiary to seek welfare in the first place combines with the process of qualifying for payments to make the typical beneficiary totally dependent upon what he receives from month to month from the agency.[63]

Fourth, the post-termination hearing clearly does not afford an adequate alternative. While factual errors can presumably be corrected as well after administrative action as before, the incentive to seek rectification is seriously weakened by the action itself. It is hardly surprising that few beneficiaries do in fact appeal terminations or reductions after the fact. In Illinois, for example, post-termination appeals were filed in a scant one-third of 1 percent of all public assistance cases closed during a sample period several years ago.[64] Comparable experience in the District of Columbia showed a slightly more frequent resort to the formal hearing (about 1.5 percent), although about half the initial requests were withdrawn after an informal conference.[65] The few other states where appeal rates have been sampled offer similar evidence.[66]

---

[59] See Briar, *Welfare from Below: Recipients' Views of the Public Welfare System*, in Law of the Poor 46, 50 (J. ten Broek ed. 1966).

[60] Note, *Withdrawal of Public Welfare: The Right to a Prior Hearing*, 76 Yale L.J. 1234, 1242 (1967).

[61] *Ibid.*   [62] *Ibid.*

[63] See Burrus & Fessler, *Constitutional Due Process Hearing Requirements in the Administration of Public Assistance: The District of Columbia Experience*, 16 Am. U. L. Rev. 199, 215 (1967).

[64] Note, note 60 *supra*, at 1244.

[65] Burrus & Fessler, note 63 *supra*, at 213.

[66] *E.g.*, in Texas, see Bell & Norvell, note 57 *supra*, at 223, 233.

There may be many reasons, no doubt, for the passivity of terminated welfare recipients. Arguably, of course, the administrative decision goes unchallenged in most cases because it is substantially correct. Yet no one who has surveyed the situation accepts this explanation for the great majority of unappealed decisions. The operative causes undoubtedly lie deeper. In some cases, beneficiaries may simply not know they have recourse if they are wrongfully terminated. Far more often, they have the bare information but do not know how to use it. "The point is not whether they were told about these rights," observes Scott Briar (who has sampled welfare client attitudes extensively). "Our observations indicate that many, if not most, of these recipients probably were given this information by the social worker—but rather that the information probably is not particularly meaningful and useful to a person who sees himself as a suppliant, and therefore it may be ignored or soon forgotten."[67] (Briar's survey discovered, for example, appalling misconceptions about the person to whom a complaint should be made in the event of disagreement about disposition of any part of the case.)

Joel Handler and his associates have noted the same phenomenon in more recent surveys of welfare recipients in Wisconsin. Senior administrators argued that the paucity of appeals and requests for hearings reflected the fairness and the accuracy of the system. But "administrators younger and closer to the field said that there was a great deal of withholding of information from clients, that administration was highly discretionary, and that the administrative appeal system was not working because clients were either unaware of their rights or were afraid of exercising them."[68] Thus, as one commentator recently explained the wide gap between theoretical availability and actual use of post-termination hearings: "The welfare recipient may be illiterate; he may not understand how to obtain a hearing; he may regard welfare as a charity and not realize that it may be asserted as a right; he may believe that requesting a hearing would damage his interests by angering the social worker; or he may be afraid to attend the hearing."[69] In any case, the bare opportunity to appeal a termination after it has taken effect does not seem always or adequately to protect client interests.

---

[67] Briar, note 59 *supra*, at 55.

[68] Handler & Hollingsworth, *Stigma, Privacy, and Other Attitudes of Welfare Recipients*, 22 STAN. L. REV. 1, 18 (1969).

[69] Comment, note 27 *supra*, at 130–31.

Finally, there is the pendency of the new HEW regulation, which Chief Justice Burger thought more or less mooted the case. The language had been drafted and announced many months before the cases reached the Supreme Court. The new ruling provides that whenever a fair hearing is requested because of termination or suspension of payments, "assistance will be continued during the period of appeal and through the end of the month in which a final decision on the fair hearing is reached."[70] At first glance, this regulation would appear to protect recipients' rights even more broadly than the Supreme Court's decision; it requires not merely an *evidentiary* hearing before payments stop but the statutory *fair* hearing, containing safeguards not ordered by the Court for the pretermination stage.

The mere pendency of the regulation did not, however, afford a viable alternative to the constitutional recognition of a hearing right. First, there was some doubt whether the regulation would ever have taken effect had the Court not made it almost superfluous.[71] The new rule was scheduled to go into force July 1, 1969. Implementation was postponed to October 1 of the same year and further postponed to July 1, 1970, by which time the Supreme Court would surely have decided the two pending cases. HEW could easily have taken the credit for moving first had that been its desire.[72] Moreover, the Solicitor General in his amicus curiae brief expressly relied only on the old regulations and even cast doubt upon the wisdom of the proposed new policy of continuing benefits: "[C]ogent policy considerations support the Secretary's judgment that the . . . practice [of holding no prior hearing] should be followed where . . . the State initially decides to terminate or reduce benefits."[73]

Even if implementation of the new HEW policy had been assured, a constitutional decision would still have been vital. There are obvious lacunae. The federal rule applies, of course, only to categorical

---

[70] 34 FED. REG. 1144 (1969).

[71] See Christensen, *Of Prior Hearings and Welfare As "New Property,"* 3 CLEARINGHOUSE REV. 321, 336 (1970).

[72] The Department of Housing and Urban Development, by contrast, did issue a comparable regulation in advance of a binding Supreme Court decision. See Thorpe v. Housing Authority, 393 U.S. 268 (1969).

[73] Brief for the United States as Amicus Curiae, Wheeler v. Montgomery, 397 U.S. 280 (1970), at p. 23.

assistance in which federal funds are used, and has no bearing whatever on state-supported general assistance programs such as New York's home relief, involved in some of the cases of several plaintiffs in the *Kelly* case. Moreover, there is some doubt about the enforceability of a hearing right that derives solely from a regulation of this kind. To be sure, the Supreme Court took a rather hard line in the application of a parallel HUD regulation dealing with public housing evictions, even insisting that directive be given retroactive effect.[74] Yet, as one commentator has observed: "Federal welfare regulations are administrative directives addressed solely to state agencies, and do not grant substantive rights to individuals. Thus, under the new federal regulation, there is no *right* to a prior hearing, and a recipient who bases his claim solely on that regulation may be unable to obtain relief in either a state or federal court."[75] Finally, of course, an administrative ruling of this kind—particularly one drafted in the last days of the Democratic administration and greeted with little enthusiasm by Republican successors—is a rather shaky reed to which to bind such fundamental rights. Because it was always subject to modification or even revocation, the administrative directive needed the reinforcement of constitutional doctrine adequately to protect the vital interests of welfare recipients.

Thus the result that the Court reached in this pair of cases seems eminently sound. Further reflection and analysis strengthen the case in favor of a prior hearing. Not only is the general presumption operative in favor of the right to be heard in advance of a serious deprivation, but the governmental interest in postponing the hearing is rather insubstantial. In addition, the interests of the affected individual are unusually strong. So strong, in fact, that one might well say the opportunity to be heard is meaningful only if the hearing occurs while the beneficiary is still receiving subsistence payments.

C. UNRESOLVED ISSUES

There is much left unsaid in the welfare hearing cases. Most of the omissions must have been deliberate in view of the explicit and pointed references of the dissenters. Yet they may be troublesome in the future and must therefore be taken into account by anyone

---

[74] Thorpe v. Durham Housing Auth., 393 U.S. 268 (1969).

[75] Comment, note 27 *supra*, at 117.

seeking to determine the meaning of these decisions for the re-definition of due process.

1. *The initial determination of eligibility*. The only reference to procedural protections during the initial determination of eligibility for welfare came in the dissent of the Chief Justice. The reference was only a casual suggestion that the majority had raised "intriguing possibilities" about procedural claims at other stages of welfare administration, including the intake decision.[76] Yet this question obviously lurks nearby. The brief of the Solicitor General implied that a decision to grant a pretermination hearing might logically require comparable treatment before rejecting even a frivolous ap-plication.[77] The joint brief of the claimants, in reply to the United States, vigorously disputed the suggestion on two grounds. First, that settled principles of administrative law recognize "a well founded and established distinction between initial denial and re-vocation of statutory rights, entitlement or privileges . . . which is as valid and recognized in the welfare context as in all others."[78] Second, the reply brief argued that "by hypothesis the recipient of aid is far more dependent and vulnerable than the applicant."[79]

The strategy was sound. For the moment it kept the Court's mind off collateral issues. But the argument was not so sound. The issue will surely return before long. One very thoughtful analysis of the intake process argues forcefully that the rejected applicant needs and merits a hearing for the very reasons that support the incumbent beneficiary's claim to pretermination notice and confrontation.[80] The question is obviously not settled. The implications of *Kelly* for several types of initial determinations are considered below.[81]

2. *Changes in status less drastic than termination*. Chief Justice Burger also reminded his colleagues they had not dealt with the procedural interests of the beneficiary whose payments are reduced summarily or who is denied a requested increase because of the caseworker's spot judgment. There may be informal internal ave-

---

[76] Goldberg v. Kelly, 397 U.S. 254, 284–85 (1970) (dissenting opinion).

[77] Brief for the United States as Amicus Curiae, Wheeler v. Montgomery, 397 U.S. 280 (1970), at pp. 22–23.

[78] Brief in Reply to the United States as Amicus Curiae, Goldberg v. Kelly, 397 U.S. 254 (1970), at p. 6.

[79] *Id*. at n. 5.

[80] Note, note 58 *supra*, at 1327–28.   [81] See text *infra*, at notes 202–08.

nues of appeal from such decisions. But the fair hearing assured by federal law does not apply to such interim administrative acts.[82] Much less is there any guarantee of a formal hearing under state law in the dispensation of general assistance payments. Yet in some cases a sharp reduction in benefit levels, or a refusal to increase payments when the recipient's status changes materially, may affect client interests almost as severely as the complete cessation of payments.

Nor did *Kelly* deal explicitly with the recurrent problem of temporary suspension rather than final termination of payments. The welfare laws of most states do permit summary suspension of benefits "even where no specific cause for ineligibility has been found."[83] Hence the case for notice and confrontation may be even stronger here than in the termination situation with which the Court actually dealt, since there at least a formal hearing is available after payments finally cease. Maybe the Court meant to assimilate suspension and termination without quite saying so. The *Kelly* opinion speaks throughout only of "termination." But the much briefer *Wheeler* opinion characterizes *Kelly* as holding that a pretermination evidentiary hearing is required "before welfare payments may be discontinued or suspended."[84] Although this is the only reference to temporary changes in a beneficiary's status, it may suffice.[85]

3. *Beneficiary rights after the hearing.* The *Kelly* decision is quite explicit about what the recipient is entitled to and when. But it fails to take the process one step further. What happens if the pretermination decision is adverse (as it will be in most cases) and the beneficiary appeals? (If in fact an internal appeal channel is provided, though none appears to be constitutionally required.) Must benefits continue until the appeal has been decided, or may they be terminated as soon as the initial decision is rendered? The HEW regulation is also ambiguous on this point. It provides that benefits must continue through the end of the month "in which the final decision on the fair hearing is reached."

There is also an open question about the beneficiary's status during judicial review. In fact, there is even considerable doubt he will be able to litigate his claim at this stage. Mr. Justice Brennan expressly allowed that "a complete record and a comprehensive

---

[82] 42 U.S.C. §§ 302 (a) (4), 602 (a) (4).

[83] See Note, note 60 *supra*, at 1234–35.

[84] 397 U.S. at 282.   [85] See Christensen, note 71 *supra*, at 336–37.

opinion, which would serve primarily to facilitate judicial review and to guide future decisions, need not be provided at the pre-termination stage."[86] If a court does take the case and reaches the merits, the Supreme Court decision says nothing about the agency's obligation to continue payments until there is a final resolution of the controversy. Of course the great majority of cases will never go beyond the pretermination hearing.[87] But when the beneficiary does seek court review and the court either lacks power or inclina-tion to issue a status quo order pending decision, the issue left open by *Kelly* will most surely arise.

4. *Right to counsel.* Despite its insistence on limiting the holding, it seems doubtful the Court can logically stop by recognizing a right to be represented by retained counsel. By definition, no wel-fare client can afford a lawyer and must turn to legal aid and other sources of volunteer counsel. A serious equal protection problem may now be presented if welfare agencies permit representation by counsel of beneficiaries fortunate or resourceful enough to obtain the aid of an OEO Legal Services office but fail to make any pro-vision for assignment of counsel for those less fortunate or less resourceful.[88] Thus, Mr. Justice Black seems correct in assuming that the logic of the decision must require appointment of counsel, else "the right to counsel is a meaningless one since these people are too poor to hire their own advocates."[89]

5. *The basis of the due process guarantees: property, "entitle-ment," and other benefits.* The cornerstone of the *Kelly* decision is the conviction that the interest of a welfare beneficiary in not being erroneously or summarily removed from the rolls merits constitu-tional protection. The basis of that judgment requires some further study. The Constitution provides only that due process must be

---

[86] Goldberg v. Kelly, 397 U.S. 254, 267 (1970).

[87] Even the number of requests for pretermination hearings in those jurisdictions where it is available is surprisingly small. See Brief in Reply to the United States as Amicus Curiae, Goldberg v. Kelly, 397 U.S. 254 (1970), at p. 19.

[88] *Cf.* Douglas v. California, 372 U.S. 353 (1963). Ironically, the HEW regula-tion requires that counsel be provided for all beneficiaries at the "fair hearing" (which must, under that ruling, occur before payments terminate). 34 FED. REG. 1144, 1356, 1359 (1969). Moreover, the Federal Trade Commission has recently announced that attorneys will be provided for persons charged with consumer fraud or other violations by the agency and who cannot afford to retain private counsel. N.Y. Times, Jan. 10, 1970, p. 67, col. 4.

[89] 397 U.S. at 278–79. See also Christensen, note 71 *supra*, at 339.

observed in deprivations of life, liberty, and property. Most previous cases upholding claims to be heard—where a government agency planned to proceed summarily—involved actual takings of physical property.[90] Even in the 1969 wage garnishment decision, on which the Court relied in *Kelly*, nearly jurisdictional emphasis was placed upon "the taking of one's property."[91] Conversely, claims to be heard have most often been rejected because the claimant was held to have no proprietary stake in the dispute. In *Bailey v. Richardson*,[92] for example, the court of appeals had refused to order a hearing in the public employment context because "due process of law is not applicable unless one is being deprived of something to which he has a right."[93]

These distinctions revive the specter of the long-interred right-privilege dichotomy. For some years the Supreme Court has deliberately avoided these labels and their irrational effects.[94] In prior cases involving, for example, social security[95] and unemployment compensation,[96] the Court insisted it made no difference whether one called receipt of such benefits a right or a privilege, or whether a property interest could be established. "It is too late in the day," cautioned Mr. Justice Brennan seven years ago in the unemployment compensation case, "to doubt that the liberties of religion and expression may be infringed by the denial of or placing of conditions upon a benefit or privilege."[97] The Court has simply avoided or refused the temptation to classify government benefits in the process of defining and extending safeguards for their enjoyment.[98]

Much in the *Kelly* opinion is, of course, consistent with this approach. The Court did caution that "the constitutional challenge cannot be answered by an argument that public assistance benefits

---

[90] *E.g.*, Londoner v. Denver, 210 U.S. 373 (1908).

[91] Sniadach v. Family Finance Corp., 395 U.S. 337, 342 (1969).

[92] 182 F.2d 46 (D.C. Cir. 1950), *aff'd*, 341 U.S. 918 (1951).

[93] 182 F.2d at 58.

[94] See generally Van Alstyne, note 19 *supra;* and Linde, *Justice Douglas on Freedom in the Welfare State: Constitutional Rights in the Public Sector*, 39 WASH. L. REV. 4 (1964).

[95] Flemming v. Nestor, 363 U.S. 603 (1960).

[96] Sherbert v. Verner, 374 U.S. 398 (1963).

[97] *Id.* at 404.   [98] See Wieman v. Updegraff, 344 U.S. 183 (1952).

are 'a "privilege" and not a "right." ' "[99] But this caveat was preceded by the troubling observation that "such benefits are a matter of statutory entitlement for persons qualified to receive them."[100] This comment could not have been inadvertent, since it supported a lengthy footnote quoting from Professor Charles Reich's equation of many newer forms of "entitlement" with more traditional proprietary interests.[101] Thus it seems that the Court now accepts the "new property" characterization of at least some forms of government benefits and is willing to encompass many types of beneficiary claims within the "property" dimension of the Due Process Clause.

The reference to "entitlement" invoked a response to Mr. Justice Black, who chided the Court for failing to specify the proprietary quality of welfare benefits: "It somewhat strains credulity to say that a government's promise of charity to an individual is property belonging to that individual when government denies that the individual is honestly entitled to receive such payment."[102] The majority might well have dismissed this challenge as irrelevant to the issue before it, arguing, as has often been done in the past, that interests in government benefits need not be so classified to merit protection under the Due Process Clause.[103]

The fact that the Court did thus respond and did invoke the language of entitlement to delineate a quasi-property interest seems ominous in two respects. First, the very use of this terminology may indicate that some kinds of government benefits rank higher than others on a still unannounced priority list. Claims to receive them may constitute "entitlement," while claims to other benefits may not be so favored. Second, there is a lurking implication that claims to procedural due process may require a firmer basis than claims of substantive rights. The Court had previously freed welfare recipients of waiting period restrictions[104] and demeaning income attribution

---

[99] Goldberg v. Kelly, 397 U.S. 254, 262 (1970).

[100] *Id.* at 262. For pre-*Kelly* comments on the question of statutory entitlement, see Graham, *Public Assistance: The Right to Receive; the Obligation to Repay*, 43 N.Y.U. L. Rev. 451, 454–75 (1968); Note, *Social Welfare—an Emerging Doctrine of Statutory Entitlement*, 44 Notre Dame Law. 603 (1969).

[101] Reich, note 9 *supra*, at 1255; Reich, *The New Property*, 73 Yale L.J. 733 (1964).

[102] 397 U.S. at 275.

[103] *E.g.*, Wieman v. Updegraff, 344 U.S. 183 (1952).

[104] Shapiro v. Thompson, 394 U.S. 618 (1969).

rules[105] without invoking the language of "entitlement." It is of course too early to wonder whether the acceptance of Professor Reich's concept of government benefits may not jeopardize beneficiaries of other sorts whose claims fall less clearly within the category of "entitlement."

This anxiety is heightened by the Court's differentiation of welfare payments from other types of benefits. At first the opinion suggested that "relevant constitutional restraints" apply at least as much to withdrawal of public assistance payments as to "disqualification for unemployment compensation . . . or to denial of a tax exemption . . . or to discharge from public employment."[106] But in deciding the issue of the right to a prior welfare hearing, the Court drew sharp distinctions that overshadowed these analogies: "The crucial factor in this context—a factor not present in the case of the blacklisted government contractor, the discharged government employee, the taxpayer denied tax exemption, or virtually anyone else whose governmental largesse is ended—is that termination of aid pending resolution of a controversy over eligibility may deprive an *eligible* recipient of the very means by which to live while he waits."[107] Thus emerged a paradox. On the one hand, a suggestion that welfare payments are at least as much entitled to protection as other benefits for which procedural safeguards have already been prescribed. On the other hand, a clear implication that other beneficiaries do not merit the new protection being accorded welfare recipients because they have no such unique claim to a prior hearing. The lack of mutuality is puzzling and confirms the hunch that the Court has begun compiling a rank order or priority list of government benefits.[108]

In the months immediately following the *Kelly* decision, however, lower federal courts have given the holding a more generous interpretation than its language might support. One federal court of appeals found in *Kelly* the basis for a public housing tenant's

---

[105] King v. Smith, 392 U.S. 309 (1968).

[106] 397 U.S. at 262.   [107] *Id.* at 264.

[108] Some doubt is cast upon the primacy of welfare benefits—briefly implied by the *Kelly* and *Wheeler* decisions—by the Court's rejection a short time later of welfare recipients' attacks on state maximum grant provisions. Dandridge v. Williams, 397 U.S. 471 (1970). *Cf.* also Rosado v. Wyman, 397 U.S. 397 (1970), raising other doubts about the status of welfare benefits in the scale of priorities. See for an early comment, May, *Supreme Court Approves Maximum Grants: Holds § 402 (a) (23) Permits Welfare Cuts*, 3 CLEARINGHOUSE REV. 321 (1970).

constitutional claim to a pre-eviction hearing,[109] an issue the Supreme Court earlier avoided because of a nearly coextensive HUD regulation.[110] A federal district judge held on the basis of *Kelly* that a state prisoner may not be committed to punitive segregation for postconviction infractions without written notice of charges and an adversary hearing with representation by counsel.[111] And in the boldest application to date, a federal district court in Ohio held that an applicant for admission to public housing is now entitled to a prior hearing on the question of his eligibility before the application is rejected: "Since the recent decisions of the Supreme Court [in *Kelly* and *Wheeler*] . . . it seems clear . . . that those seeking to be declared eligible for public benefits may not be declared ineligible without the opportunity to have an evidentiary hearing."[112] Thus the question that *Kelly* clearly did not reach in the welfare context—the right of an applicant to be heard before being rejected—has already been resolved in the applicant's favor in a context the Court would presumably have deemed less compelling than that in *Kelly*.

These recent decisions have begun to unfold the broader set of issues, the relevance of *Kelly* to at least three types of administrative action affecting the status of government beneficiaries: first, the availability of a hearing upon dismissal, discharge, termination or eviction; second, the procedural safeguards surrounding a refusal to renew or continue a relationship at the end of a regular term; third, the rejection of an initial application. Before parsing these issues, however, some sort of general analytical framework is essential. It seems appropriate to begin by identifying more explicitly than is usually done the values and limitations of the adversary hearing.

II. A Framework for Constitutional Analysis: Government Benefits and Adversary Hearings

Because of the way the parties narrowed the issues, the Court in *Kelly* effectively subsumed the basic constitutional ques-

---

[109] Escalera v. New York City Housing Auth., 425 F.2d 853 (2d Cir. 1970). For a consistent, pre-*Kelly* decision, see Ruffin v. Housing Auth., 301 F. Supp. 251 (E.D. La. 1969).

[110] Thorpe v. Housing Authority, 393 U.S. 268 (1969).

[111] Sostre v. Rockefeller, 312 F. Supp. 863, 871–73 (S.D. N.Y. 1970).

[112] Davis v. Toledo Metropolitan Housing Auth., 311 F. Supp. 795, 796–97 (N.D. Ohio 1970).

tion. When and why does a government beneficiary merit an adversary hearing on a disputed claim of eligibility? The Court borrowed a test announced a decade earlier in determining whether a security clearance could be revoked without a hearing.[113] Under that formula, the governmental interests in taking summary action must be balanced against the interests of the individual in knowing and challenging the basis of an adverse decision. In the security clearance case the balance weighed in the Government's favor.[114] In *Kelly*, application of the same formula supported the claims of the individual recipient.[115] Since that is about all the balancing test offers—and since it mandates no inquiry into the basic functions or values of an adversary hearing—deeper analysis is clearly appropriate.

Several guidelines must be understood at the start. First, I am talking only about cases in which the dispute or controversy revolves about what Professor Kenneth Davis calls "adjudicative facts." His definition bounds the inquiry: "Adjudicative facts are facts about the parties and their activities, businesses, and properties, usually answering questions of who did what, where, when, how, why, and with what motive or intent; adjudicative facts are roughly the kinds of facts that go to a jury in a jury case."[116] I am not here concerned with legislative facts or claims to be heard on determinations of policy or adoption of administrative rules and regulations.

Second, I confine my inquiry to relatively serious administrative actions, actions having substantial consequences for the affected private party. There are easy cases at both ends of the scale, of course. When a public housing tenant is evicted, a state college student expelled, welfare payments terminated, or a government worker discharged, everyone would concede the action is sufficiently serious to merit the concern of a court, and a fortiori of an administrative tribunal.[117] A mild reprimand or admonition, a re-

---

[113] Cafeteria & Restaurant Workers Union v. McElroy, 367 U.S. 886 (1961).

[114] The decision was 5 to 4. The Chief Justice and Justices Black, Brennan, and Douglas felt the case for an adversary hearing compelling despite the Government's conceded security interests.

[115] 397 U.S. at 263–66.   [116] Davis, note 3 *supra*, at 199.

[117] A working formula has been offered in at least one context, that of university discipline. Judge Doyle of the Western District of Wisconsin—who has probably decided more student reinstatement suits than any other member of the federal bench—has limited his concern to "serious sanctions, such as expulsion or suspension

quest for information, a change in the timing or manner of distributing benefits—these may be sanctions too inconsequential to warrant the heavy artillery of due process.

The hard cases lie between. A student is suspended for several weeks; the severity of the sanction may depend critically on whether the period is at the start or the end of a semester. A public housing tenant is told he can no longer keep a dog in his apartment; if he simply wants a friendly pet, that is one thing, but it is quite another if he happens to be blind. The welfare recipient is denied an increase in payments; the sanction may be very drastic if the increase is sought to support a new member of the family, but far less so if designed to facilitate a move to more comfortable quarters. And so it goes through the whole range of government benefits. A judgment about the gravity of the case simply cannot be made in the abstract or according to any rigid rule. A careful inquiry must be made into the precise circumstances of each case when the sanction giving rise to a demand to be heard is of such an intermediate sort.

Third, I shall not, for the moment, be concerned about the timing of the hearing. Suffice it to say—and this is the essential teaching of *Kelly*—that a case for a prior hearing differs only in degree and not in kind from the case for being heard at all. The question of the right to an adversary hearing, without regard to time, is anterior in all cases. Once the right to be heard has been established, then the hearing should precede the challenged action unless the agency has strong and constitutionally valid reasons for postponement. In any event, the matter of timing is typically an ancillary question to be resolved separately.

A. INTERESTS AND VALUES SERVED BY AN ADVERSARY HEARING

Although cases recognizing a right to a hearing are legion, explicit statements of rationale are surprisingly rare. Perhaps the reasons for holding or requiring hearings are so obvious they sel-

---

for a significant period of time." Stricklin v. Regents, 297 F. Supp. 416, 419 (W.D. Wis. 1969), *appeal dismissed*, 420 F.2d 1257 (7th Cir. 1970). See also Professor Charles Wright's perceptive discussion of the difficulty of delineating clearly between "severe" and "mild" penalties. Wright, note 13 *supra*, at 1071. Although the range of available sanctions seems no narrower in other government benefits contexts, the courts do not appear even to have attempted the process of delineation elsewhere.

dom need reiteration. Yet there are many values served by hearings that are not at all obvious and deserve occasionally to be brought to light. One could not do better than begin with Mr. Justice Frankfurter's eloquent statement:[118]

> The heart of the matter is that democracy implies respect for the elementary rights of men, however suspect or unworthy; a democratic government must therefore practice fairness; and fairness can rarely be obtained by secret, one-sided determination of facts decisive of rights.

This comprehensive postulate invites a particularization of components.

1. *Accuracy and fairness.* At base, only a hearing—probably only an adversary hearing—can prevent or correct errors of fact. Mistakes of identity, distortions or fabrications, faulty memories, bare deceit—these mendacious forces can be checked only when an opportunity is afforded to pose the truth against the falsehood. Chief Justice Warren a decade ago explained the truth-seeking function of an adversary hearing: "Where governmental action seriously injures an individual, and the reasonableness of the action depends on fact findings, the evidence used to prove the Government's case must be disclosed to the individual so that he has an opportunity to show that it is untrue."[119] The need for such confrontation is especially important "where the evidence consists of the testimony of individuals whose memory might be faulty or who, in fact, might be perjurers or persons motivated by malice, vindictiveness, intolerance, prejudice or jealousy."[120]

There is an additional element in the process, explaining the need for personal participation of the affected person: "The parties," Professor Davis pointed out, "know more about the facts concerning themselves and their activities than anyone else is likely to know, and the parties are therefore in an especially good position to rebut or explain evidence that bears upon adjudicative facts."[121] Thus

---

[118] Joint Anti-Fascist Refugee Comm. v. McGrath, 341 U.S. 123, 170 (1951) (concurring opinion).

[119] Greene v. McElroy, 360 U.S. 474, 496 (1959).

[120] *Ibid.* See also 5 WIGMORE, EVIDENCE § 1367 (3d ed. 1940) (showing evolution and soundness of "the belief that no safeguard for testing the value of human statements is comparable to that furnished by cross-examination").

[121] Davis, note 3 *supra*, at 199.

mere adjudication is not enough; there must be an opportunity for direct confrontation of accuser by accused if the opportunity to seek the truth is to be meaningful.

If superficially obvious, it is nevertheless worth asking why the administrative process should concern itself so acutely with the quest for truth. Two interests are at stake. First, the credibility of the process and its entitlement to respect—both by persons subject to it and persons whose tax dollars support it—demand that a high value be placed upon accuracy. Nothing so surely shakes public confidence as revelations of unreliability or haphazard judgment in important regulatory or distributive processes.[122]

Second, the capacity of the administrative system to deal fairly and justly with particular individuals who are subject to or dependent upon it also requires a commitment to accuracy and truth. Erroneous decisions are not always unjust. Indeed, occasional errors may improperly favor one beneficiary at little or no cost to others. But most errors are bound to produce injustice, whether by deprivation or by misallocation.

Moreover, the consequences of erroneous judgment may be both tragic and permanent. The student who is wrongfully expelled without a chance to be heard may be effectively deprived of a higher education. If he cannot take one set of exams, the sequence may be so interrupted that he will never return. Or he may be drafted before he has a chance to re-enroll, and may never again be financially able to study even if he survives military service without misfortune.[123] Similar hazards mandate a hearing prior to seizure and destruction of allegedly obscene materials. Once books have been burned or tapes erased, restitution becomes impossible. Money damages can be paid to the publisher or distributor, of course, if there is a basis for civil liability against the responsible public officials. But as the Supreme Court has pointed out repeatedly in this context, the reading or viewing public can never be made whole after the seizure and destruction.[124] The risks of irreversible error

---

[122] See Professor Newman's comment: "The public interest in procedure itself . . . is . . . to ensure that correct determinations will be made (and thus only the deserving deprivations be effected), except where some margin of error seems essential to avoid ills that inhere in procedure. . . . *The problem is to set the margin of tolerable error, given the ills of too much procedure.*" Newman, *The Process of Prescribing "Due Process,"* 49 CALIF. L. REV. 215, 228 (1961).

[123] *Cf.* Murray v. Blatchford, 307 F. Supp. 1038 (D.R.I. 1969).

[124] A Quantity of Copies of Books v. Kansas, 378 U.S. 205, 211–13 (1964).

are thus too great to permit the process to operate without the intervention of an impartial tribunal to decide the issue of obscenity.

Much the same is true in the welfare context, as the Court stressed in *Kelly*. If a beneficiary is wrongfully removed from the rolls, he can of course be restored when the truth comes out. But the effects of even a relatively brief deprivation may be almost irremediable. Deaths seldom result from interruption of payments.[125] But serious cases of malnutrition and other grave physical harm are well known to welfare workers.[126] Thus erroneous decisions may indeed create a degree of injustice intolerable in the disbursement of public funds.

There is another sort of injustice—serious damage to reputation—that can be checked only through an adversary hearing. Several courts have recognized this interest in overruling summary agency action that implied disloyalty, incompetence, or bad moral character.[127] Even if no explicit charge is made against a particular applicant, the very act of rejection may create such a "badge of infamy" when it is widely understood that eligibility follows almost automatically from formal qualifications.[128] Only through an adversary hearing can the applicant clear his name of the cloud that unexplained exclusion casts. Thus the Supreme Court held seven years ago that an applicant for admission to the bar was constitutionally entitled to a hearing on adverse *ex parte* changes that led the Committee on Character and Fitness to exclude him summarily.[129]

---

125 Elizabeth Wickenden reports the case of a baby who froze to death because its parents, newly arrived in Arlington, Virginia, and completely destitute, were denied welfare because they did not meet the now invalid one-year residence test. See Dorsen, *Poverty, Civil Liberties and Civil Rights: A Symposium*, 41 N.Y.U. L. REV. 328, 339 (1966).

126 See, *e.g.*, the description of the interim plight of the very plaintiffs in the *Kelly* case. Brief for Appellees, Goldberg v. Kelly, 397 U.S. 254 (1970), Appendix A (pp. 75-91).

127 *E.g.*, Slochower v. Bd. of Educ., 350 U.S. 551, 558-59 (1956); Heckler v. Shepard, 243 F. Supp. 841 (D. Idaho 1965); *cf.* Healy v. James, 311 F. Supp. 1275 (D. Conn. 1970), holding that state college authorities could not summarily reject the application of a campus SDS group for recognition as a student organization. A hearing must be held, *inter alia*, to determine whether the campus group shares the objectives and supports the tactics of the national organization; the absence of a hearing would leave the perhaps erroneous impression that such correspondence does exist, thus imposing a kind of guilt by association on the local members.

128 See the concurring opinion of Mr. Justice Douglas, in Joint Anti-Fascist Refugee Comm. v. McGrath, 341 U.S. 123, 174 (1951).

129 Willner v. Committee on Character and Fitness, 373 U.S. 96 (1963). The risks of injustice and fundamental concepts of fairness should make clear that the basic

2. *Accountability*. Adversary hearings also promote, in several important respects, the accountability of the agency. Only when there is a record and findings based upon evidence and argument can a reviewing court really determine, for example, whether the agency is accurately interpreting and applying the legislative mandate,[130] whether the action taken by the agency reflects valid and substantial governmental interests,[131] and whether substantive constitutional interests are being adequately protected. The problem with summary action here is not so much that it necessarily imports error as that it is inevitably ambiguous. Only when the argument and the reasons are spread upon the record can the reviewing court appraise the performance of the agency and its faithfulness to its charge.

Accountability is preserved in quite another important way through adversary hearings. Substantive rights and liberties of government beneficiaries are really only as strong as the procedural safeguards available to vindicate them.[132] If a state college student can be expelled without a hearing or the giving of any reasons by the administration, there is very little point in saying he has a constitutional right to demonstrate peacefully on the campus. Even if he has cheated on an examination as well as marched quietly against the Vietnam war, there is no assurance that a proper ground of dismissal was invoked rather than an improper ground, unless he can know the charges against him and face his accusers in an adversary setting. The recent dramatic extension of the civil liberties of public housing tenants, government employees, and welfare cli-

---

need for an adversary hearing is independent of the quest for accuracy. That is, even if complete accuracy could be achieved without a hearing (as it probably can in some phases of many government benefit programs), critical determinations should not be deemed "fair" in the absence of an opportunity to be heard. For only the adversary process accords beneficiaries the dignity and respect to which they are entitled as citizens, regardless of their dependency upon some form of government subvention. The hearing thus serves a psychological need in the administration of benefit programs that may be even more basic to a civilized system of administration than the function of ascertaining the truth. Surely the development of alternative, even completely accurate, methods of truth-seeking would not moot the need for hearings.

130 See generally Professor Jaffe's comments on "the role of judicial review." JAFFE, note 51 *supra*, at 320–27.

131 *E.g.*, Knight v. State Bd. of Educ., 200 F. Supp. 174, 181 (M.D. Tenn. 1961).

132 Roth v. Board of Regents, 310 F. Supp. 972, 979–80 (W.D. Wis. 1970).

ents, as well as those of students, would have been largely in vain without the parallel expansion of procedural safeguards. Only by insisting on the right to a hearing can the courts impose the essential measure of agency accountability for the rights and liberties of those to whom benefits are dispensed.

3. *Visibility and impartiality.* Both the appearance and the reality of objectivity and the absence of bias require that the actions of any tribunal be visible. Commitment to these values in the courts is preserved by making all proceedings public save in the most extraordinary circumstances.[133] The same public access is neither as feasible nor as effective in keeping administrative agencies honest. Yet the same values are operative, and to ensure them the agency proceedings must be both accessible and visible in ways that only adversary hearings can adequately guarantee. "The validity and moral authority of a conclusion," Mr. Justice Frankfurter observed, "largely depend on the mode by which it was reached. Secrecy is not congenial to truth-seeking and self-righteousness gives too slender an assurance of rightness." No better way than the adversary hearing has been found "for generating the feeling, so important to a popular government, that justice has been done."[134]

4. *Consistency.* The adversary hearing also serves the vital function of seeing that the agency establishes and acts in accord with its own precedent as well as within its charter. Consistency and predictability are values of a high order in the administrative process, even if they do not rise to the dignity of stare decisis by which courts are bound. Summary action clearly affords no assurance of consistency. Indeed, it invites decisions and actions varying with the pressures and needs of the moment. If the agency must state its reasons, and if the reasons given earlier can be cited in support of parallel results in later parallel cases, a far higher measure of consistency and predictability can be expected.

5. *Integrity.* I have already suggested some ways in which the adversary hearing promotes the integrity of and respect for the administrative process. But there are two additional dimensions. If the beneficiary is entitled to confront his accusers before the agency can penalize him, the risk of false accusation is significantly

---

[133] See *In re* Oliver, 333 U.S. 257, 266–73 (1948).

[134] Joint Anti-Fascist Refugee Comm. v. McGrath, 341 U.S. 123, 171–72 (1951) (concurring opinion).

decreased. The accuser knows that he, along with the agency that acts on the basis of his charges, may be held accountable under cross-examination. At the same time, the beneficiary himself may be less likely to appeal frivolously—either when the sanction is relatively slight or when the basis for agency action is substantially correct—since he too realizes that the adversary hearing will discover the truth. Thus a higher measure of responsibility is imposed upon both accuser and accused by the adversary process and the expectation of a full, formal confrontation.

In summary, the overriding interest of both beneficiary and system in the adversary process is the achievement of accuracy and fairness. The requirement of notice and the opportunity for confrontation combine to deter erroneous agency action and to avert the certainly harmful, sometimes irreversible, consequences of error. Other interests also served by the adversary process are secondary though not unimportant.

B. COUNTERVAILING GOVERNMENTAL INTERESTS

The one set of governmental interests I have already reviewed—emergency conditions demanding prompt action—argue not against hearings as such but only against prior hearings.[135] In the government benefits context, other types of interests may weigh more generally against the adversary process. These interests, though seldom dispositive, deserve careful consideration.

Perhaps most persuasive is the concern that a formal hearing may destroy collegial, informal relationships, and set at arm's length people who are not truly adversaries. Thus it has been much argued recently that college student discipline is often better handled through informal conferences with the "kindly old dean" than through full-dress adversary hearings; that student personnel officers perform a vital counseling role that may be undermined if not destroyed by recent court decisions; and that a once cooperative relationship between students and administration has now become one of conflict or combat.[136] Similar arguments have been made occasionally in other contexts—against the formalization of juvenile

---

[135] The cases are discussed in 1 Davis, note 10 *supra*, at § 7.08.

[136] *E.g.*, Perkins, The University and Due Process 8 (1967); Glazer, *Campus Rights and Responsibilities: A Role for Lawyers*, 39 American Schol. 445, 447–51 (1970).

court proceedings after the *Kent*[137] and *Gault*[138] decisions, for example, and even in the welfare context, where informal counseling surely constitutes a vital aspect of the caseworker's task.[139]

There are several answers to these concerns. First, of course, not every aspect of the once informal relationship has now been formalized by recognition of the right to a hearing. Informal counseling by the dean's office still reaches vastly more students on most campuses than are ever involved in formal hearings.[140] Moreover, the formal hearing is mandatory only if the beneficiary himself requests it. On the campus, in the welfare agency, or almost anywhere else (save perhaps in the juvenile court), a preference shared on both sides for continued informal relationships need not be thwarted by the Due Process Clause.

Further, it is far from clear where a hostile relationship does develop that the courts are to blame for creating it. Radical students and punitive deans would be no more congenial in the absence of procedural safeguards, as suggested by experience on private campuses (where constitutional safeguards do not yet apply).[141] Nor would welfare mothers be any more inclined to accept passively an arbitrary termination or reduction of payments in the absence of a right to be heard and to appeal. Indeed, if anything, the opposite may be the case. Protests against the system and its policies may well be diverted into more constructive channels by creating an opportunity to confront one's accusers and vindicate one's interests in a

---

[137] Kent v. United States, 383 U.S. 541 (1966).

[138] *In re* Gault, 387 U.S. 1 (1967). Note especially in this regard the dissenting opinion of Mr. Justice Stewart, expressing concern that the formalization of procedures may seriously undermine the values of the juvenile court because "a juvenile proceeding's whole purpose and mission is the very opposite of the mission and purpose of a prosecution in a criminal court." *Id.* at 79.

[139] See Wedemeyer & Moore, *The American Welfare System*, in LAW OF THE POOR 2, 12–13 (J. ten Broek ed. 1966).

[140] Even during the troubled year 1964–65 at the University of California at Berkeley, the chairman of the Faculty Committee on Student Conduct (a member of the law faculty with considerable expertise in matters of procedure) concluded that informal procedures were still appropriate, and acceptable, for 90 percent of the cases heard—all but the highly controversial political cases. His report noted that "the bulk of cases involves cheating or stealing or general disorderly conduct. The student admits the charges in all but insignificant detail and attempts to explain or justify. There is no need for pleading or charges or cross-examination."

[141] See O'Neil, *Private Universities and Public Law*, 19 BUFFALO L. REV. 155 (1970).

presumably neutral forum. At least there is little evidence that the conceded "judicialization" of many once informal relationships between benefactor and beneficiary has exacerbated tensions created by wholly different forces.

Second, there is a valid concern that insistence on strict procedural safeguards may rigidify the dispensation of benefits and thus undermine important interests of a whole class of present and potential beneficiaries. Chief Justice Burger expressed this anxiety in his *Kelly* dissent. While those now on the rolls may indeed be harder to get off the rolls, the natural bureaucratic response will be to make it much harder for future applicants to get on these rolls.[142] Growing recognition of student rights may have caused some universities to scrutinize their admission policies more closely, although such surveillance has almost certainly been designed to spot applicants who may disrupt the campus rather than those who will demand formal adversary hearings when accused of disruption. And the predicted result would follow only to the extent the initial decision on eligibility remains unreviewable, a premise that is already in doubt.[143]

Moreover, even if better protection for those within the system does raise the barriers for those outside, it is far from clear that such a cost is excessive or unreasonable. Important differences between the respective sets of interests favor greater solicitude for the incumbent. There is a clear element of reliance within the system. The public housing tenant has given up his private apartment, the student has forgone opportunities to matriculate elsewhere, and the welfare recipient may have given away or put beyond his control assets that would initially have made him ineligible but would also have kept him alive if his application had been rejected. Thus if a preference has been expressed between insider and outsider in favor of the former and if some choice is inevitable, the choice has rightly been made.

There is a third concern about the extension of procedural rights. This tendency may well cause internal agency initiative to atrophy in vital areas. If left to its own devices, the argument runs, the administrative process would eventually do a better job than the

---

142 397 U.S. at 279.

143 See Note, note 58 *supra*, at 1327–28. And see discussion in the text *infra*, at notes 202–08.

courts, for administrators know both the needs of their beneficiaries and the resources of the system far better than do the courts.[144] The argument finds a counterpart, again, in the *Kelly* case. The dissenters argued the Court should stay its hand, since the responsible agency was about to issue a ruling that would adequately meet the needs of all parties. The proposed HEW regulation was, in fact, more generous than the Court's mandate in certain respects. It assured that payments would continue until the statutory fair hearing was held and the fair hearing included certain safeguards not demanded by the Court. Yet as we have seen, the agency dragged its feet on promulgation of the rule for some months and seemed to be in no mood to take the critical step unless the courts compelled it.[145] For the Court to have stayed its hand would thus have supported the status quo rather than stimulating agency initiative in fashioning new and especially appropriate procedures. In the student dismissal area, moreover, college and university administrators moved slowly enough in the reshaping of conduct rules and procedures even after the judicial mandate was clear.[146] Before the courts began to speak, in the early 1960's, campus regulations remained pretty much as they had been at the turn of the century. Discipline at Grayson Kirk's Columbia varied little from that of Nicholas Murray Butler's time.[147] Thus the record of recent experience belies any such optimism about the self-improving impulse of the administrative process. All too often, the only way to move

---

[144] Compare, however, Professor Newman's view that "administrators (and investigating committees, grand juries, and in fact all lesser officials with jobs to do) have demonstrated . . . that they are less trustworthy with respect to procedure than are judges." Newman, note 122 *supra*, at 230.

[145] See Christensen, note 71 *supra*.

[146] This conclusion emerges from a study conducted in the spring of 1970 by the author and three 1970 graduates (then third-year students) of the University of California Law School (Boalt Hall). The study surveyed student conduct rules at some twenty-two major universities (half public and half private, paired in eleven states). Rules and regulations were obtained for three sample years—1959–60, 1965–66, and 1969–70. Even at the large public universities, major reforms in procedural protections did not occur until late in the decade—suggesting that student protest may have been a more effective catalyst for change than litigation. For this and other conclusions from the survey, the author is particularly indebted to Mr. Ted W. Harris of the Class of 1970 for his thorough and insightful work.

[147] See, *e.g.*, Van Alstyne, *Procedural Due Process and State University Students*, 10 U.C.L.A. L. Rev. 368 (1963), reporting the rather surprising results of an earlier survey of disciplinary procedures.

agencies toward adequate procedural safeguards for beneficiaries' rights is for the courts to push from behind.

Fourth, it is argued that the agency's discretion may be impaired and the confidentiality of some of its sources jeopardized by requiring an adversary hearing. If, as one court has already held, a nontenured professor is entitled to a hearing on the nonrenewal of his term contract,[148] then academic judgment may be upset and confidentiality breached. The risks are real and grave, but not inevitable even in this most sensitive of areas. For if the administration (in the form of a dean or department chairman) gives constitutionally valid reasons for the failure to renew the contract—*i.e.*, deficient teaching, meager evidence of creative research, or inadequate progress toward a higher degree—that should be the end of the matter.[149] The right to be heard does not always encompass the right to know who made the initial evaluations on which the ultimate judgment was based. Nor need the department open all its files to the aggrieved junior member. The scope and character of the hearing must of course reflect common sense and vary with the special needs and circumstances of the parties.[150] Evidence that must be disclosed when a student is expelled for cheating—or a faculty member suspended for plagiarism, for that matter—need not be exposed to public view when the dispute concerns a nonrenewal. Yet the essential right to know the reasons for an adverse determination and to argue in one's own behalf before the judgment becomes final is not crippled by such limitations.

Finally, there is the matter of expense. Hearings are costly, both in time and money. Lawyers are expensive, as are court reporters and stenographers. Administrative efficiency may be impaired by protracted hearings. Important questions may be kept in limbo interminably by formalities. Lawyers comprehend all this, but laymen do not. Thus the concern is altogether understandable, just as it is substantial. Yet in the determination of constitutional rights, the courts have repeatedly deemed such administrative concerns irrelevant. School integration cannot be postponed because it is likely

---

[148] Roth v. Board of Regents, 310 F. Supp. 972 (W.D. Wis. 1970).

[149] See discussion of the *Roth* decision, text *infra*, at notes 199–201.

[150] *Cf.* on the need to protect confidentiality of sources even against a fairly strong claim of disclosure, McCray v. Illinois, 386 U.S. 300 (1967). Comparable limitations could undoubtedly be fashioned for the administrative process where appropriate to meet particular governmental exigencies.

to cause disorder.[151] Adequate police protection cannot be denied a controversial speaker or an unpopular parade because providing it will be costly or inconvenient for the city.[152] Similarly, a hearing cannot be withheld or even postponed simply because it may be expensive or disruptive. The agency must find ways to afford hearings within its budget and get its other work done at the same time. These are not irreconcilable goals for large bureaucratic organizations that already carry on myriad, complex, and often costly functions.

C. CONTENT OF THE HEARING: HOW MUCH PROCESS IS DUE?

When a constitutional right to some form of hearing is recognized, the most difficult part of the analysis begins. What particular safeguards—of the dozens theoretically available to the administrative process—constitute due process in the specific instance? Which of these safeguards cannot be denied if the hearing is to be meaningful? By what standards are these questions of implementation to be decided? There is surely no simple code that furnishes the answers. Every judge has his own sense of what "fairness" or "justice" includes in the realm of procedures, but there is no uniformity of judicial instinct. The question of defining or prescribing due process is—as Professors Sanford Kadish[153] and Frank Newman[154] have perceptively shown—as perplexing as it is fundamental.

In the *Kelly* case, the Supreme Court majority could agree that certain safeguards were requisite while others were dispensable. Thus the client faced with termination had a constitutional right to bring his own lawyer with him but not to have one appointed. The tribunal should be impartial, but no rigid rule of separation of functions would disqualify every member of the agency staff who had some prior involvement with the case. An opportunity to confront and cross-examine adverse witnesses was absolutely essential, yet the Constitution did not require a verbatim transcript of their answers. The seven-day notice that New York provided

---

[151] Cooper v. Aaron, 358 U.S. 1 (1958).

[152] Hurwitt v. City of Oakland, 247 F. Supp. 995 (N.D. Calif. 1965); Williams v. Wallace, 240 F. Supp. 100 (M.D. Ala. 1965).

[153] Kadish, *Methodology and Criteria in Due Process Adjudication—A Survey and Criticism*, 66 YALE L.J. 319 (1957).

[154] Newman, note 122 *supra*.

under existing procedure adequately apprised beneficiaries of impending termination, "although there may be cases where fairness would require that a longer time be given."[155]

Thus from reading the *Kelly* decision we know a great deal about what the Justices believe to be the essential elements of due process in the particular circumstances. But we know virtually nothing—save possibly with regard to the right of confrontation[156] —about the reasons why particular guarantees obtain at a given stage of the administrative process.

The lower courts have had to fend for themselves in shaping the contours of process that is due government beneficiaries. Within the past five years, for example, each of the following issues has been litigated in the context of state college student expulsion or dismissal: (1) How far in advance of the hearing must notice be given, and in what form?[157] (2) Does the student have a right to be represented at the hearing by counsel—and does it make a difference whether the university appears by an attorney?[158] (3) Must the hearing be public if the student requests it? If the university wishes a public hearing but the student desires it closed?[159] (4) Does the student or his attorney have a right to examine adverse statements on which the charges are based?[160] To cross-examine adverse witnesses at the hearing?[161] (5) Must a verbatim transcript in detailed summary of the testimony be kept?[162] (6) May the committee or hearing officer proceed in absentia if the student fails

---

[155] 397 U.S. at 268.

[156] *Id.* at 269–70.

[157] *Compare* Due v. Florida Agricultural & Mechanical Univ., 283 F. Supp. 396 (N.D. Fla. 1963), *with* Scoggin v. Lincoln Univ., 291 F. Supp. 161 (W.D. Mo. 1968).

[158] *Compare* Barker v. Hardway, 233 F. Supp. 228 (S.D. W.Va. 1968), *with* French v. Bashful, 303 F. Supp. 1333 (E.D. La. 1969).

[159] *Compare* Buttny v. Smiley, 281 F. Supp. 280 (D. Colo. 1968), *with* Moore v. Student Affairs Comm., 284 F. Supp. 725 (M.D. Ala. 1968).

[160] See Estaban v. Central Mo. State College, 277 F. Supp. 649, 651 (W.D. Mo. 1967).

[161] *Compare* Dixon v. Alabama State Bd. of Educ., 294 F.2d 150, 159 (5th Cir. 1961), *with* Estaban v. Central Mo. State College, 277 F. Supp. 649, 652 (W.D. Mo. 1967).

[162] *Compare* Due v. Florida Agricultural & Mechanical Univ., 283 F. Supp. 396, 403 (N.D. Fla. 1963), *with* Estaban v. Central Mo. State College, 277 F. Supp. 649, 652 (W.D. Mo. 1967).

to appear after receiving timely notice?[163] (7) Must the person who has the power to impose sanctions or penalties actually hear the case or study the transcript?[164] (8) Must there be a complete separation of functions and a prohibition of *ex parte* communication between those who prosecute and those who decide?[165] (9) Must the student have an opportunity to appeal internally from an adverse decision at the initial level?[166] (10) May a student be suspended on an interim basis or must the hearing precede even a temporary change in status, and in what circumstances?[167]

The wonder is not that so many specific safeguards have been sought but rather that in nearly all the ten enumerated areas the lower federal and state courts have divided sharply. Some have held there is a right to counsel in all cases, others that there is no such right of representation, and at least one other that the student may bring his lawyer whenever the university appears by counsel. Comparable divisions characterize most of the other areas, making it virtually impossible to give clear answers to university administrators who seek guidance in developing disciplinary codes consistent with due process. There is certainty only at the extremes. On the one hand, the student must be given formal notice of the specific charges. On the other hand, guilt need not be proved beyond a reasonable doubt or determined by a jury.

The task of prescribing due process thus remains at large. What guideposts might mark the path more clearly?[168] First, we could

---

163 *Compare* Wright v. Texas Southern Univ., 392 F.2d 728 (5th Cir. 1968), *with* Marzette v. McPhee, 294 F. Supp. 562 (W.D. Wis. 1968).

164 See Estaban v. Central Mo. State College, 277 F. Supp. 649, 652 (W.D. Mo. 1967).

165 *Compare* Wasson v. Trowbridge, 382 F.2d 807, 813 (2d Cir. 1968), *with* Jones v. State Bd. of Educ., 279 F. Supp. 190, 202 (M.D. Tenn. 1968).

166 *Compare* Knight v. State Bd. of Educ., 200 F. Supp. 174 (M.D. Tenn. 1961), *with* Zanders v. Louisiana State Bd. of Educ., 281 F. Supp. 747, 761 (W.D. La. 1968).

167 *Compare* Jones v. State Bd. of Educ., 279 F. Supp. 190, 202 (M.D. Tenn. 1968), *with* Stricklin v. Regents, 297 F. Supp. 416, 420–21 (W.D. Wis. 1969).

168 British and Commonwealth courts have recently found it necessary to undertake a strikingly similar inquiry in student dismissal cases. The touchstone there has been "natural justice" rather than "due process"—a phrase of comparable breadth and imprecision. In University of Ceylon v. Fernando, 61 Ceylon New L. Rep. 505 (1960), it was held that in the absence of stated rules to be followed in dismissing a student for alleged cheating on an examination, principles of natural justice did entitle the student to "be adequately informed of the case he had to

begin with a model of some sort—the criminal trial or the requirements of the Administrative Procedure Act—and then require the agency to justify any deviations from that model. Some years ago Professor Kadish suggested a formula for what he called "justification of the attenuated procedure":[169]

> Whether it be determined that the impact is equivalent to or less than the consequences of a criminal conviction, a rational decision of whether the demands of due process allow any attenuation of traditional procedures must depend upon the case made in justification for the attenuation. The relation between the two factors would appear to be direct; the greater the severity of the impact of the determinations, the greater the degree of urgency and persuasiveness that must be shown. In the area of the federal employee loyalty program, for example, the Court has indicated its conviction that the impact of findings of disloyalty *is* similar to criminal sanctions. One might expect, therefore, the requirement of a relatively strong justification for increasing the hazard of misdeterminations.

This particular choice of model or norm may not be right for government benefit cases. Professor Newman has suggested the need for "awareness that due process sometimes should give people more rights than criminal proceedings ensure. The fact that pretrial discovery may be narrow in criminal cases, for example, hardly means that it should be no broader in hearings on license applications."[170] For the same reason the Administrative Procedure Act, which already incorporates compromises between competing inter-

---

meet, and given an adequate opportunity of meeting it." The denial of cross-examination was held not to be a violation of natural justice in the absence of a timely request for confrontation.

For a much later and more elaborate inquiry into the relevant principles of natural justice, see R. v. Senate of the University of Aston, [2] 1969 All E.R. 964 (Q.B.D. 1969). The Justices concluded that natural justice had been denied when the university proceeded to expel without a formal hearing of any sort—especially since the examiners had considered issues other than the student's academic performance in reaching their decision. *Id*. at 975.

See also, for a less generous view of the scope of natural justice in student dismissal cases, King v. University of Saskatchewan, 68 W.W.R. 745 (Sup. Ct. of Canada 1969). The court held that faculty members could serve in the same case on both inferior and superior tribunals within the university.

[169] Kadish, note 153 *supra*, at 352.

[170] Newman, note 122 *supra*, at 220. The criminal model may also be inappropriate because of its emphasis on the role of the jury and the value of judgment by peers.

ests, should not be the norm. The question here is not whether further attenuation is justified, but whether any departures are warranted. This caution suggests a second approach. Rather than taking an existing model of procedure as the point of departure, one should start with a hypothetical proceeding in which all guarantees are fully enjoyed, and then require justification of any deviations from that ideal base. The hypothetical model would thus amalgamate the best of the criminal and civil procedure on the assumption that both could be practiced in a single forum. Exceptions or variations could then be authorized on a selective basis, reflecting particular governmental interests.

Certain obvious deviations from the ideal model would require no justification. No one seriously argues, for example, that a "grand jury" must "indict" the beneficiary before a hearing can occur, although the requirement of a prior hearing may serve some of the very same interests. It is not claimed that "guilt" must be proved according to the criminal standard, although it is vital to recognize that the agency or government bears the initial burden of proof on all disputed facts. In addition to these safeguards which are simply inappropriate to the administrative process, others might be positively harmful, or destructive of the flexibility and informality that should mark agency proceedings at their best. Thus the criminal or even civil trial rules of evidence are never invoked in agency hearings, and should not be. A complete separation of functions (of the sort essential to preserve judicial integrity) might undermine the agency's vital counseling function, preventing a senior professor, for example, from advising and informally reviewing the work of a junior nontenured colleague if he is later to sit in judgment on the younger man's case. Such departures as these require no justification beyond reference to the nature of administrative procedure.

A wholly different approach to the due process determination would be to start at the opposite end—assuming only the bare essentials of a hearing—and require the beneficiary or claimant to justify augmentation. The presumption, in other words, would be against representation by counsel, but the beneficiary could make a showing of special need for legal advice on the basis of the complexity of the case or his own inability to present or challenge the critical evidence, etc. But procedural safeguards should not be so jealously reserved or sparingly dispensed. Given the relative familiarity with the administrative process, it is certainly harder for the beneficiary in a single instance to show why he should have a particular protection then for the agency to demonstrate why he should not have it. Thus if there are any presumptions, they should run in the beneficiary's favor with the burden of rebuttal on the agency.

There is a third and middle ground that may best serve the interests of agency and beneficiary alike. A reviewing court should insist initially upon a rather high level of protection in all cases—including representation by counsel and probably appointed counsel for all indigents;[171] opportunity for discovery and for cross-examination; preparation of a transcript or at least the making of a complete tape of the hearing; a public hearing; and so on. If the beneficiary feels stricter safeguards are essential, he can seek them and after an adverse decision can appeal the denial of them. The court will then examine the particular balance of interests and equities and decide—as courts have frequently done in the student dismissal cases—whether a higher standard should apply on an ad hoc basis. Conversely, if the agency feels special needs warrant dilution of the regular protections—a vital source of information would be jeopardized by disclosure, or a public hearing would be unmanageable—it can make the exception and proceed subject to judicial review under the same standards. Experience with enough cases of this sort should generate a set of procedural standards sufficient to protect the interests of all parties.

D. FULL JUDICIAL REVIEW: A VIABLE ALTERNATIVE TO THE
   ADVERSARY HEARING?

When an agency fails to hold a full hearing and the matter comes before a reviewing court, it is sometimes suggested that the administrative default can be cured by de novo judicial review.[172] It is true the court can certainly perform most or all of the adjudicative tasks as well as the agency—indeed, in some respects better, because the court has compulsory process, more effective constraints against

---

[171] Not only does the new regulation of the Department of Health, Education, and Welfare provide for counsel in fair hearings, see note 88 *supra*, but the Federal Trade Commission has ordered that counsel be made available to indigents appearing before the commission to answer charges. This is apparently the first federal regulatory agency to confer such a right in civil proceedings. N.Y. Times, Jan. 10, 1970, p. 67, col. 4.

[172] For the strongest such suggestion, see Jordan v. American Eagle Fire Ins. Co., 169 F.2d 281 (D.C. Cir. 1948).

contempt, better procedures for making records, and so on. But for the typical government beneficiary, judicial review must be a supplement and not a substitute for the administrative hearing to which he is entitled.

The court cannot cure the agency's dereliction for a variety of reasons. First, the costs of litigation are incalculably greater. Even with the aid of volunteer lawyers, few welfare recipients can afford to file lawsuits every time they are threatened with termination. Other beneficiaries, notably middle-class college students and public employees, must bear the entire costs, since they seldom qualify for legal aid. Second, there are often rather serious barriers to judicial review of withdrawal of government benefits, and a fortiori to initial denial of claims. Whatever vestiges remain of the "privilege" concept of public largesse emerge as rules of standing and justiciability when agency discretion in withholding or taking away a benefit is challenged in court.[173] Third, there is of course nothing to challenge in court if the agency acts summarily and without explanation. Judicial review is possible only if there is some record either in the form of a hearing or at least a statement of reasons for the action. Fourth, the long delays created by typically overcrowded dockets make judicial review a meaningful alternative only for the beneficiary who can afford to wait. Thus the welfare recipient or public housing tenant is usually in no position to wait until his case comes to the top of the calendar in the ordinary course. There is of course, no guarantee that the administrative process acts more promptly. But if the agency must stay its hand until the question of eligibility has been determined within, there is at least a strong incentive for dispatch of a kind that finds no counterpart in the courts. Thus for many reasons court review provides no appropriate alternative to agency hearing.

Are there other alternatives? The agency does have a choice where a prior hearing is required. "Due process does not, of course, require two hearings," the Court recognized in *Kelly*. "If, for example, a state simply wishes to continue benefits until after a 'fair' hearing there will be no need for a preliminary hearing."[174] The matter of timing does afford the agency some option. But there is

---

[173] Recent relaxations of the rules of standing have, of course, made judicial review more accessible for all plaintiffs, including those seeking to vindicate a claim to government largesse. See, e.g., Barlow v. Collins, 397 U.S. 159 (1970).

[174] 397 U.S. at 267 n. 14.

no suggestion here or elsewhere that the basic functions and values of an adversary hearing can be served by any other procedure yet devised. In the absence of some hypothetical alternative model, it seems axiomatic that only a hearing can afford an aggrieved beneficiary a meaningful opportunity to be heard.

III. THE FRAMEWORK APPLIED

One task remains: To apply the abstract analysis to particular situations. Three phases in the dispensation of government benefits merit attention—the termination or dismissal, the nonrenewal, and the rejection of an initial application. One preliminary matter must, however, be disposed of: the cases involving licenses or admission to professional or occupational practice.

A. THE LICENSING CASES: SUI GENERIS

Read broadly, the cases involving the denial or granting of professional and other licenses would resolve all other problems. The Supreme Court long ago held that an accountant could not be denied admission to practice before the Board of Tax Appeals without a hearing.[175] More recently the Court took a similar view of New York's rejection of an application for admission to the bar based upon unfavorable character references.[176] It is assumed a fortiori that the withdrawal or cancellation of a license or permit to practice an occupation or profession requires some formal hearing.[177] If the licensing cases were applicable in other contexts, there would be no need for further inquiry.

The licensing cases are not, however, adequate precedent for the government benefits area. Fundamentally, a license is much more a form of regulation than a dispensation of government largesse. Were there no regulation at all, however essential that regulation might be, any person who wished could undertake the licensed activity at his own risk. The granting of the license thus involves a determination of competence and qualification within the scope of regulatory power, a selection of some among all those who seek

---

[175] Goldsmith v. Board of Tax Appeals, 270 U.S. 117, 123–24 (1926).

[176] Willner v. Committee on Character and Fitness, 373 U.S. 96, 103–06 (1963). *Cf.* Hornsby v. Allen, 326 F.2d 605 (5th Cir. 1964).

[177] See generally 1 DAVIS, note 10 *supra*, at § 7.18.

access to the regulated field or activity. In this sense the denial of a license represents a limitation or restraint upon the theoretical liberty of the citizen in an unregulated society.

Moreover, the rejection of an application automatically implies some lack of competence, moral character, or responsibility. This inference arises because in most regulated sectors—save possibly for broadcasting by radio and television—there is no quantitative reason for denying any new applicant a chance to enter the field. Whether he can practice profitably is his own business. Whether there are too many lawyers or doctors or automobile drivers or liquor dealers is no business of the licensing agency, whose sole concern should be one of quality: to protect the public, and sometimes other members of the regulated sector, from incompetent or inferior practitioners.

The denial of most applications for government benefits imports no such stigma. The number of opportunities available at any given time is limited, even perhaps in the welfare area. Public housing projects typically have many more applicants than vacancies.[178] State colleges and universities can admit only a fraction of prospective matriculants. Government agencies can hire only a limited number of employees and, except in the Post Office and menial lines of work, applications exceed openings. Thus a rejection or denial may reflect a judgment about competence or character. But that is not, as with the denial of a license, the inevitable implication of adverse action.

For both reasons, then, the case of the licensee or prospective licensee is rather different from that of the typical government beneficiary. Though the Supreme Court has never sought to distinguish the two classes of cases—indeed, in *Kelly* it rather casually assimilated them—the distinction seems clear enough to demand a separate analysis. The insistence upon granting a hearing to the licensee or applicant may thus be persuasive by analogy but hardly dispositive of the issues now before us.

B. DISCHARGE, DISMISSAL, TERMINATION, EXPULSION, AND EVICTION

I begin with the easiest of the three phases in the dispensation of government benefits. In many programs, the matter is already set-

---

178 See the figures on the ratio of applicants to vacancies in New York City— about 10:1 in recent years. PROJECT ON SOCIAL WELFARE LAW, HOUSING FOR THE POOR: RIGHTS AND REMEDIES 172, n. 41 (1967).

tled. For welfare recipients, *Kelly* clearly established both the right to a full hearing and the right to an adversary prior hearing. For public housing tenants, comparable rights have been recognized by administrative regulation, reinforced by one Supreme Court decision,[179] and more recently given constitutional underpinning by several lower federal courts.[180]

The state college or university student, too, clearly has a constitutional right to a hearing when he is expelled or suspended for a substantial period.[181] The only issue that remains is one of timing. Prior to *Kelly* the lower federal courts divided on the question whether a college could suspend the student first and then hold the hearing later, the controversial practice of interim suspension.[182] In *Kelly* the Supreme Court said nothing about students in distinguishing other types of beneficiaries. Yet equities similar to those of the welfare client could surely be invoked in the case of a student summarily suspended on the eve of examinations or at a time when he is draft-vulnerable or in a way that will forfeit a fellowship. Whenever such special circumstances are present, the case for a prior hearing seems compelling. Even when no special equities are present, the university should bear the burden of showing why it cannot hold even a preliminary hearing before imposing a suspension.[183]

This leaves public employment as the area in which, ironically, the question of the right to a hearing was earliest litigated but last to be resolved. A casual comment in *Kelly* might suggest otherwise: "Relevant constitutional restraints," observed Mr. Justice Brennan, "apply as much to the withdrawal of public assistance as to . . . discharge from public employment."[184] The citation supporting the

---

[179] Thorpe v. Housing Authority, 393 U.S. 268 (1969).

[180] Escalera v. New York City Housing Auth., 425 F.2d 853 (2d Cir. 1970); Ruffin v. Housing Auth., 301 F. Supp. 251 (E.D. La. 1969).

[181] Dixon v. Alabama State Bd. of Educ., 294 F.2d 150 (5th Cir. 1961).

[182] *Compare* Jones v. State Bd. of Educ., 279 F. Supp. 190, 202 (M.D. Tenn. 1968), *with* Stricklin v. Regents, 297 F. Supp. 416, 420–21 (W.D. Wis. 1969), *appeal dismissed*, 420 F.2d 1257 (7th Cir. 1970).

[183] Indeed, in one of the very earliest student dismissal cases of the 1960's, it was simply assumed that a prior hearing would be granted if the right to a hearing was recognized at all. Knight v. State Bd. of Educ., 200 F. Supp. 174, 178 (M.D. Tenn. 1961) (due process required "an opportunity to present [the students'] side of the case before such drastic disciplinary action was invoked by the university authorities").

[184] 397 U.S. at 262.

reference was to *Slochower v. Board of Higher Education*,[185] a 1956 decision involving a tenured professor at Brooklyn College who had been summarily dismissed for invoking the privilege of the Fifth Amendment before a congressional investigating committee. A regulation of the board made discharge mandatory and automatic under such circumstances. The Court held that a claim of constitutional right could not be made the sole basis for summary discharge of a public employee. At the close of the opinion, Mr. Justice Clark did say something about a hearing:[186]

> The State has broad powers in the selection and discharge of its employees, and it may be that proper inquiry would show Slochower's continued employment to be inconsistent with a real interest of the State. But there has been no such inquiry here. We hold that the summary dismissal of appellant violates due process of law.

This statement, while surely relevant, is very far from establishing a government employee's right to a hearing on dismissal. That is clear both from the context and from later decisions. The Court in *Slochower* really said no more than that the ground on which the dismissal was based—resort to a constitutional privilege not to incriminate one's self—clearly would not support so serious a sanction. The only way in which the state could use Slochower's conduct as the basis for dismissal was by establishing a relationship between that conduct and some valid interest of the state or the university—for example, by showing that he had perjured himself or been contemptuous of the committee. Such a nexus could be determined only by a hearing. Thus a hearing would have to be held, not before Slochower could be dismissed at all, but before he could be dismissed for a constitutionally protected act.

Later cases support this limited view of *Slochower*. The Court has gone back and forth on the matter of a public employee's right to a hearing, coming very close to recognizing such a right but avoiding the constitutional question in *Greene v. McElroy*,[187] then backing away again in *Cafeteria and Restaurant Workers Union v. McElroy*.[188] (The latter case established the balancing test used by the Court in *Kelly*, but ultimately denied the request for a hearing on cancellation of a security clearance.) One important milepost along

---

185 350 U.S. 551 (1956).

186 *Id.* at 559.

187 360 U.S. 474 (1959).

188 367 U.S. 886 (1961).

the way is the 1959 decision in *Vitarelli v. Seaton*.[189] There the Court held that a public employee is entitled to a hearing if agency procedures confer such a right. The agency cannot play fast and loose with its own rules, adhering to them when it wishes but by-passing them when it does not. The basic constitutional question was not in focus. But the Court simply assumed that Vitarelli (a professional employee of the Department of the Interior) "could have been summarily discharged ... at any time without the giving of a reason."[190] Later, the Court observed that neither an act of Congress nor an executive order (dealing with internal security matters) "alter[ed] the power of the Secretary to discharge summarily an employee in petitioner's status, without the giving of any reason."[191] The problem of the case was that the Secretary "gratuitously decided to give a reason" and because the reason given was national security, backed himself into a procedural web foreclosing summary action.

Slochower and *Vitarelli*, taken together, suggest only that when the sole reason given for a dismissal is either a constitutionally invalid one or one that requires, by statute or regulation, compliance with specific procedures, there is a right to a hearing. In both cases, moreover, the stated basis of the adverse judgment bore so heavily on the integrity or the loyalty of the employee as to create a "badge of infamy," an implication so damaging that only a full hearing could vindicate the individual's interest in reputation and make it possible for him to obtain employment in the private sector.

Absent these special equities, the public employee's claim to a hearing rests on shaky precedent. Many Supreme Court decisions have reinforced substantive rights of government workers: not to be discharged for criticizing the policies of the agency or superior officials;[192] not to be required to sign a loyalty oath that infringes freedom of expression;[193] not to be compelled to disclose constitutionally protected affiliations,[194] etc. But nothing has been said about the right to a hearing since the *Cafeteria Workers* case, in which a hearing had been denied for security reasons and the action was sustained by a sharply divided Court. Incredible as it may seem, only one

---

[189] 359 U.S. 535 (1959).

[190] *Id.* at 539.   [191] *Ibid.*

[192] Pickering v. Bd. of Educ., 391 U.S. 563 (1968).

[193] Elfbrandt v. Russell, 384 U.S. 11 (1966).

[194] Shelton v. Tucker, 364 U.S. 479 (1960).

lower federal court decision[195] appears to recognize unequivocally a constitutional right to be heard before employment is terminated, and even that judgment masquerades as generous construction of agency regulations.

Long before *Kelly*, the courts had accorded government workers a host of substantive rights that could be vindicated only through adversary hearings, the requirement of specific charges, and an opportunity to confront and cross-examine accusers.[196] Moreover, the disparity in treatment between government employees and other beneficiaries seems inexplicable. Being fired from a government job is at least as serious a sanction as being evicted from a housing project or being suspended from college. Nor are there unique interests attending the government's function as employer that find no parallels in the responsibilities of landlord, educator, and benefactor. There may, of course, be special problems in particular cases. Claims to confidentiality of sources may well be stronger in security discharge proceedings than in eviction or expulsion cases. But these interests can surely be respected without denying generally the right to an adversary hearing. And unless special circumstances intervene, the hearing should occur prior to the effective date of the discharge for all the reasons already discussed.

C. NONRENEWALS OF GOVERNMENT BENEFITS

The distinction between a termination and a nonrenewal is not always easy to define. Many benefits are technically granted for only a limited term. But the presumption of continuing eligibility is so strong that a refusal to renew or extend the relationship is properly treated as a termination. A student enrolls for only a year at a time. But if a freshman is denied, for nonacademic reasons, a chance to enroll for the sophomore year, he is really being terminated rather than denied a renewal of his student status.[197] A public housing tenant, similarly, may have a lease for a year—or even on a month-to-month basis—but a refusal to renew or extend the lease is tantamount to an eviction and so treated by the courts.[198]

---

[195] Olson v. Regents, 301 F. Supp. 1356 (D. Minn. 1969).

[196] See generally Linde, note 94 *supra;* Van Alstyne, note 10 *supra.*

[197] Saunders v. Virginia Polytechnic Inst., 417 F.2d 1127 (4th Cir. 1969).

[198] In Thorpe v. Housing Authority, 393 U.S. 268 (1969), for example, the Court treated as an "eviction" the exercise of the housing authority's option under the lease to terminate tenancy by giving notice at least fifteen days before the end

The paradigm case of true nonrenewal is, of course, the non-tenure academic appointment. There is a mild presumption that the instructor or assistant professor who does satisfactory teaching and makes adequate progress toward a higher degree will be continued, at least until the tenure decision is made. But there is nothing auto-matic about this relationship as about the others just cited. Histori-cally, therefore, it has simply been assumed that a nontenure em-ployee could be dropped at the end of a term without the giving of any reasons and with no recourse. Within recent months, however, a pair of federal district court decisions have dramatically altered this easy assumption on which academic and other public adminis-trators have operated.

In *Roth v. Board of Regents*,[199] Judge Doyle of the Western Dis-trict of Wisconsin held that a nontenure assistant professor may not be denied renewal without a statement of the reasons for the action and an opportunity at least to be heard in his own behalf. Starting with the assumption that improper reasons did not in fact underlie the action before him, Judge Doyle nonetheless concluded that the enforcement of substantive safeguards to which a public employee is now entitled would require a hearing in nonrenewal cases as much as in dismissals or discharges of tenured faculty and workers covered by civil service. For the failure to renew without giving any reasons could as well mask constitutionally improper reasons as reflect a constitutionally valid judgment about professional achievement and progress.

The decision is far less drastic than might at first appear. It does not hold that a full adversary hearing must be held on every non-renewal, or that confidential documents must be disclosed:[200]

> The burden of going forward and the burden of proof rests with the professor. Only if he makes a reasonable showing that the stated reasons are wholly inappropriate as a basis for deci-sion or that they are wholly without basis in fact would the

of any monthly term. Such action was an eviction rather than a nonrenewal because the lease also entitled the tenant to automatic renewal for successive monthly terms unless the family composition or income were altered or specific terms of the lease violated.

[199] 310 F. Supp. 972 (W.D. Wis. 1970). See also the companion case, Gouge v. Joint School Dist. No. 1, 310 F. Supp. 984 (W.D. Wis. 1970), extending similar procedural protections to public school teachers.

[200] 310 F. Supp. at 980.

university administration become obliged to show that the
stated reasons are not inappropriate or that they have a basis
in fact.

The opinion does not say how precise the stated reasons must be
to shift the burden of proof. If explanations like "unsatisfactory
teaching" or "limited evidence of distinguished scholarship" would
suffice, the duty placed upon the administration by the *Roth* decision would be rather slight. The possibility remains, moreover, that
a decision resting in fact on one ground (*i.e.*, controversial political
activities) may be justified for the record on another (*i.e.*, lack of
scholarly output), since the performance of few junior faculty
members is academically or pedagogically impeccable. Nor does the
decision insulate against largely *ad hominem* judgments reflecting
the personal likes and dislikes of elder colleagues. Nonetheless,
Judge Doyle has clearly taken a bold step toward lifting the shroud
of secrecy that has long surrounded the nonrenewal of probationary
appointments. The case seriously undermines the belief that a non-
tenure employee can be summarily terminated by giving no reasons
and may obtain judicial review only if the agency gratuitously
gives an invalid or implausible reason.

Meanwhile, parallel efforts are being made to ensure these same
safeguards. Committee A of the American Association of University Professors recently proposed a new set of procedures to guide
renewal decisions. The statement recommends, *inter alia*, that a junior teacher should be entitled to notice in writing of the reasons for
a decision not to renew his appointment, and should be able to seek
review by a "decision-making body." That body should have authority to request reconsideration by the appropriate faculty committee when it concludes that insufficient deliberation was initially
given the matter.[201]

The solution to the nonrenewal problem lies in recognizing its
intermediate character in the range of administrative actions and in
devising commensurate procedures. The decision not to extend a
contract or appointment for a further term is less drastic than a discharge or dismissal from a continuing or tenured position, but more
drastic than the typical decision not to grant the appointment ini-

---

[201] The new guidelines were first announced in Chronicle of Higher Educ.,
April 13, 1970, p. 4, cols. 3–5. See also *Report of Committee A, 1969–70*, 56
A.A.U.P. BULL. 153, 167 (1970).

tially. The *Roth* decision and the Committee A proposals attempt to reflect precisely that fact by fashioning a hearing procedure that assures adequate notice of the action and its basic rationale and which affords a chance to argue against the decision and its under-pinning. Although no cross-examination or disclosure of confidential files is contemplated, at least at the outset, administrators accustomed to announcing nonrenewals without any explanation may find the new requirements burdensome and annoying. Yet presumably they can learn to live with these new rules, designed as they are to ensure fundamental fairness at the threshold of a young man's career.

D. REJECTION OR DENIAL OF INITIAL APPLICATIONS

We come at length to what may be the hardest case of all, the one on which existing law is least helpful. There are easy situations at the two extremes. On the one end, the licensing cases in which the Supreme Court has twice unequivocally held there is a constitutional right to a hearing when the applicant meets all the formally stated criteria for admission.[202] At the other extreme, no one supposes there is a right to be heard when one candidate for a prize scholarship is chosen over many others, or when the President fails to nominate to a diplomatic post a person whose friends have eagerly recommended him. The hard cases lie across the broad middle range. The matter is not quite so simple as the district judge thought in the Toledo public housing case holding, after *Kelly*, that "those seeking to be declared eligible for public benefits may not be declared ineligible without the opportunity to have an evidentiary hearing."[203]

Nor is the issue as clear the other way as it seemed to the welfare clients' attorneys in *Kelly*, who urged the Court to respect the "well-founded and established distinction between initial denial and revocation of statutory rights, entitlements or privileges."[204] In fact, a hearing may be appropriate to some kinds of rejections and denials but inappropriate to others. What is needed is a set of standards to

---

[202] Willner v. Committee on Character and Fitness, 373 U.S. 96, 103–06 (1963); Goldsmith v. Board of Tax Appeals, 270 U.S. 117, 123–24 (1926).

[203] Davis v. Toledo Metropolitan Housing Auth., 311 F. Supp. 795, 797 (N.D. Ohio 1970).

[204] Brief in Reply to the United States as Amicus Curiae, Goldberg v. Kelly, 397 U.S. 254 (1970), at 6. *Cf.* Note, note 58 *supra*, at 1327–28.

guide the particular judgment. The following questions suggest a framework.

1. *Effect of rejection upon the applicant.* At least two sorts of consequences flowing from a denial or rejection may warrant some sort of hearing, the one to reputation, the other to subsistence. The license cases point up the importance of holding a hearing when the rejection creates an automatic inference damaging to the applicant's reputation (for competence, for moral character, for loyalty).[205] The inference arises either where such licenses are granted pro forma, or where the particular applicant clearly meets every criterion except the one that centrally involves his reputation or standing. An equally compelling case can be made for challenging the inference generated by denial of a security clearance or even perhaps the rejection of an employment application for a highly sensitive job.

Subsistence or survival is an individual interest meriting at least comparable solicitude. Generally, it is true the incumbent welfare beneficiary or tenant has a greater claim to be heard than the suppliant. But this is not always the case. The evicted tenant may well be able to live with relatives while his case is being resolved, while the applicant may have come to the gates only because all other sources of shelter have been exhausted. The seeker of welfare may sometimes be even more destitute than the receiver and thus in greater need of a prompt and equitable resolution of his claim. Even large and bureaucratic agencies should be able to examine briefly at the threshold the circumstances of the initial applicant, and in deserving cases to grant a prompt hearing or extend a form of emergency aid pending resolution.

2. *Nature of the decision-making process.* The availability of a hearing at the application stage should also vary with the nature of the particular decision. Many judgments about eligibility are too simple and obvious to warrant a hearing, as where a claimant aged sixty-two is rejected for social security or retirement benefits that do not commence until age sixty-five. Others may reflect simply the application to uncontested facts of general policies or rules. These do not come within the "adjudicative" area at all. At the other extreme, some eligibility decisions may be so complex or may necessarily involve such vast discretion—high-level administrative ap-

---

205 *E.g.*, Heckler v. Shepard, 243 F. Supp. 841, 847–52 (D. Idaho 1965).

pointments, awarding of prizes, fellowships, and the like—that no readily ascertainable standards could be brought to bear in reviewing the rejection. Between the easy cases lie many in which the process is moderately complex or involves a measure of discretion exercised within broad guidelines or regulations. For these cases a hearing would not be inappropriate or unmanageable. The ultimate decision whether to grant it must depend upon the degree of complexity of discretion, tempered by the several other factors considered here.[206]

3. *Relationship of hearing to substantive interests.* Sometimes a hearing will be deemed essential even though neither of the foregoing elements is present, simply to vindicate vital substantive interests of the class from which the particular applicant comes. If one black person is rejected for a government job, that fact does not create a justiciable claim by itself. But if several blacks are rejected and there is reason to believe less qualified whites are being hired, a hearing may be essential simply to establish whether or not the agency is practicing subtle racial discrimination and to prevent future bias.

For just this reason one court has implied that an applicant for public employment may not be rejected for refusing to sign a loyalty oath without a chance to explain his reasons for refusing. The court concluded that the basic principle of pertinent Supreme Court loyalty-security decisions simply could not be vindicated without an opportunity for the arguably loyal nonsigner to be heard.[207]

4. *Relationship of hearing to the administrative process and agency performance.* For similar reasons a court may occasionally require an agency to articulate its standards for acceptance and rejection of applicants.[208] The agency may take the hint and issue regulations on its own. But if it fails to do so, leaving prospective applicants in the dark about the criteria actually employed or the way in which conduct may be shaped to gain or retain eligibility,

---

[206] For two recent illustrations of situations in which a hearing has been required on denial of an initial application, see Healy v. James, 311 F. Supp. 1275, 1282 (D. Conn. 1970), involving eligibility of a controversial political group for recognition as a campus student organization, and Stacy v. Williams, 306 F. Supp., 963 (N.D. Miss. 1969), involving applications of controversial speakers for access to college and university campus forums.

[207] Heckler v. Shepard, 243 F. Supp. 841, 847–52 (D. Idaho 1965).

[208] *E.g.*, Holmes v. New York City Housing Auth., 398 F.2d 262 (2d Cir. 1968), in which the court of appeals strongly urged the Housing Authority to publish and define the criteria used in determining eligibility for admission to projects.

hearings on particular cases—chosen almost at random—may be the only way to force the agency to explain publicly how it manages the intake process. It may also be the only way in which other branches of government—notably the courts called upon to review agency decisions and the legislature asked to appropriate funds for its support—will be able to judge an important dimension of administrative performance. The equities of the individual applicant or even of the class from which he comes are relatively unimportant under this rubric. The essential factor is the willingness and capacity of the agency to keep the public apprised of its standards.

This discussion at least suggests the error of confining procedural safeguards at the initial stage to the licensing cases. There are few government benefit programs, perhaps none, in which an agency should not occasionally be required to explain and justify a rejection, either because the equities of a particular case are compelling or because agency responsibility can be assured only in this way. The *Kelly* decision neither affirms nor denies such a principle. Yet much of what the Court said about the plight of the beneficiary who is forced off the welfare rolls logically applies to the welfare claimant who is kept off the rolls for equally invalid or erroneous reasons. The case in which the Court will have to consider the extension of its logic may not be far in the future.

IV. Conclusion

Is the right to a hearing worth the quest, after all? How substantial a guarantor of individual rights is procedural due process? Professor Joel Handler has wisely warned that assimilation of government benefit dispensing procedures to those employed in regulatory and licensing contexts may be an unreal goal, not because it cannot be attained, but because it will not necessarily produce major reform. The range of discretion in administration of most government benefit programs is so vast, so far beyond the reach of reviewing courts, that judicialization of procedure may reach only the highest level and most visible agency actions. Thus Professor Handler cautions:[209]

> The experience of administration of business regulation and the peculiar problems of welfare administration cast doubt on the benefits to be gained from a program of rights. Its lack

---

[209] Handler, *Controlling Official Behavior in Welfare Administration*, in Law of the Poor 155, 176 (J. ten·Broek ed. 1966).

of utility in helping to fulfill the broader legislative goals—the rehabilitation of people-changing aspects of welfare programs —is manifest.

Yet it may be premature to judge the efficacy of quasi-judicial procedures in the government benefits context until we have more of them. The safeguards actually available to the beneficiary are still so far behind not only the criminal process but the business-regulatory context as well that major progress would be required even to establish a basis of comparison. Perhaps welfare beneficiaries and public housing tenants will not be greatly helped by knowing why they are being terminated or evicted. The agency will often take its course anyway, undeterred by the annoying demand of formalities. But the history and the essential premises of due process are more hopeful. Strict adherence to fair procedures is at least worth a try.[210]

---

[210] There is a final and perplexing question beyond the scope of this discussion but unavoidable in any complete analysis: How far can case-by-case constitutional adjudication really ensure the basic values claimed for due process? In a recent letter to the author, Professor Hans Linde cautions on this point: "I do not believe that the solution to the problems of fair administration of mass benefits can be found in the due process clause but only in legislative reforms that minimize the need for factual determinations and discretionary judgments. This does not do away with the need for deciding due process cases in the form in which they now arise. But . . . due process analysis cannot itself cope with the problems; it can only demonstrate, and hasten, the need for legislative restructuring of the programs."

WILLIAM B. GOULD

ON LABOR INJUNCTIONS, UNIONS,

AND THE JUDGES:

THE BOYS MARKET CASE

... whatever may be a union's ad hoc benefit in a particular case, the meaning of collective bargaining for labor does not remotely derive from reliance on the sanction of litigation in the courts. . . . But a union, like any other combatant engaged in a particular fight, is ready to make an ally of an old enemy, and so we also find unions resorting to the otherwise much excoriated labor injunction. Such intermittent yielding to expediency does not change the fact that judicial intervention is illsuited to the special characteristics of the arbitration process in labor disputes; nor are the conditions for its effective functioning thereby altered.[1]

On June 1, 1970, the Supreme Court decided *Boys Market, Inc. v. Retail Clerks Union*[2] and held, 5 to 2,[3] that federal courts were not precluded from issuing injunctions against strikes in violation of collective bargaining agreements negotiated between unions and employers. In contrast to current events in Great Britain,[4] time has

---

William B. Gould is Professor of Law, Wayne State University.

[1] Mr. Justice Frankfurter, dissenting, in Textile Workers Union v. Lincoln Mills, 353 U.S. 448, 462–63 (1957).

[2] 398 U.S. 235 (1970).

[3] Mr. Justice Marshall did not participate. Mr. Justice Blackmun was not yet a member of the Court.

[4] The British attitude was aptly summarized by Sir Winston Churchill in 1911 when he said: "It is not good for trade unions that they should be brought in con-

now nearly blurred the debate about the role of law and judges in American labor-management relations. On this side of the Atlantic the unions are no longer resentful of the courts and their potential for harmful meddling in affairs of which they know little.[5] But it is perhaps more than arguable that *Boys Market* will stir up the embers of this well-worn argument and thus revive serious questions about judicial competence in dealing with unions.

At the same time, the transformation in the labor movement's thinking is reflected in the fact that some union leaders and lawyers may greet the *Boys Market* holding as a weapon to tame an increasingful unruly and rebellious rank and file.[6] Some unions may find the task of urging members to return to work pursuant to court order less difficult than a situation in which equally meaningful sanctions are absent. But the decision's emphasis on adherence to contractual responsibility as a paramount aspect of national labor law may exaggerate the inherent tensions between industrial peace

---

tact with the courts, and it is not good for the courts." Quoted in Milne-Bailey, Trade Union Documents 380 (1929). See generally Royal Commission on Trade Unions and Employers' Associations 1965–1968, Cmnd. No. 3623 (1968) [hereinafter cited as Donovan Report]; *In Place of Strife: A Policy for Industrial Relations*, Cmnd. No. 3888 (1969); Conservative Political Centre, Fair Deal at Work: A Conservative Approach to Modern Industrial Relations (1968). See also Grunfeld, *Donovan—the Legal Aspects*, 6 Brit. J. Ind. Rel. 316 (1968); Wigham, *Tough Path to the "Fair Deal,"* The Times (London), July 7, 1970, p. 27, col. 1. *Compare* McCarthy, *The Nature of Britain's Strike Problem*, 8 Brit. J. Ind Rel. 224 (1970), *with* Turner, Is Britain Really Strike Prone? (1969). I have summarized some of the recent developments in Gould, *Book Review*, 48 Texas L. Rev. 987 (1970).

[5] See *e.g.*, Rice, *Collective Labor Agreements in American Law*, 44 Harv. L. Rev. 572 (1931); Gregory, *The Law of Collective Agreement*, 57 Mich. L. Rev. 635 (1959). For more recent handling of industrial relations problems by the Supreme Court as they relate to economic pressures, see National Woodwork Mfrs. Ass'n v. NLRB, 386 U.S. 612 (1967) (product boycotts); NLRB v. Fruit & Vegetable Packers & Warehousemen, 377 U.S. 58 (1964) (consumer picketing); American Ship Building Co. v. NLRB, 380 U.S. 300 (1965) (lockouts).

[6] See Gould, *The Status of Unauthorized and "Wildcat" Strikes under the National Labor Relations Act*, 52 Corn. L. Q. 672 (1967); Raskin, *Rumbles from the Rank and File*, The Reporter Jan. 28, 1965, at 27; Federal Mediation & Conciliation Service, 18th Annual Report 13 (1965); 21st Annual Report 13 (1968). For some of the factors that are responsible for this phenomenon in the automobile industry, see Gooding, *Blue-Collar Blues on the Assembly-Line*, Fortune Magazine 69 (July, 1970). This phenomenon is not restricted to the United States. See Farnsworth, *Europe's Militant Unions Leaving Leaders Behind*, N.Y. Times, May 4, 1970, p. 1, col. 2. Even the model of industrial peace, Sweden, seems to be no exception. See Samuelsson, The Ironminers Walkout—Signal of Change? (Jan. 28, 1970) (Swedish Information Service).

and emerging opposition to the claims of union leadership for the authority to discipline their membership.[7] Moreover, while the Court's ruling presents formidable difficulties for the unions (as well as the judges who are now moved further into the tricky business of labor contract interpretation), it is conceivable that the majority opinion's reasoning may evolve contractual rights as well as obligations for the workers' representatives.

I. THE LAW OF § 301 BEFORE BOYS MARKET

Mr. Justice Frankfurter's quoted warnings were directed against the Supreme Court's conclusions in *Textile Workers Union v. Lincoln Mills*,[8] *i.e.*, that § 301 (a) of the National Labor Relations Act (NLRA), which provides that "[s]uits for violation of [labor] contracts . . . may be brought in any district court of the United States having jurisdiction of the parties, without respect to the amount in controversy or without regard to the citizenship of the parties,"[9] authorized the federal courts to "fashion a body of federal law for the enforcement of . . . collective bargaining agreements" and that specific performance of promises to arbitrate grievances under such collective agreements was part of the federal law.[10] In essence, *Lincoln Mills* stated that § 301 articulated contract obligations for employers as well as unions. And the fear was—and one not held by Mr. Justice Frankfurter alone—that the judges would be unequipped for the task and, even less charitably, that a judicial bias against the unions which had been evidenced in the earlier part of the century could return under § 301.[11] Rebuttal to

---

[7] *Cf.* NLRB v. Allis Chalmers, 388 U.S. 175 (1967); Parks v. IBEW, Local 24, 314 F.2d 886, 905 (4th Cir. 1963); Atleson, *Union Fines and Picket Lines: The NLRA and Union Disciplinary Power*, 17 U.C.L.A. L. REV. 681 (1970); Gould, *Some Limitations upon Union Discipline: The Radiations of Allis Chalmers*, paper delivered at Seventeenth Annual Institute on Labor Law, Southwestern Legal Foundation, Oct. 15, 1970; Summers, *Legal Limitations on Union Discipline*, 64 HARV. L. REV. 1049 (1951).

[8] See note 1 *supra*.   [9] 29 U.S.C. § 185.

[10] 353 U.S. at 451. *Cf.* Kramer, *In the Wake of Lincoln Mills*, 9 LAB. L.J. 835 (1958).

[11] See Cox, *Reflections upon Labor Arbitration*, 72 HARV. L. REV. 1482 (1959); Shulman, *Reason, Contract, and the Law in Labor Relations*, 68 HARV. L. REV. 999 (1955). *Cf.* Bickel & Wellington, *Legislative Purpose and the Judicial Process: The Lincoln Mills Case*, 71 HARV. L. REV. 1 (1957).

dissenters' criticisms was provided by the *Steelworkers Trilogy*,[12] which declared that the inexpertness of judges was to be carefully circumscribed by rules that doubts about arbitrability were to be resolved in its favor by the courts and that, unless clear infidelity to the agreement was evidenced, the awards of arbitrators were to be enforced by the courts. Accordingly, the status of the arbitration process as a means to resolve labor disputes was considerably enhanced. The *Steelworkers Trilogy* reiterated a theme which had initially been articulated in *Lincoln Mills:* "Plainly the agreement to arbitrate grievance disputes is the *quid pro quo* for an agreement not to strike. [Section 301] . . . expresses a federal policy that federal courts should enforce these agreements on behalf of or against labor organizations and that industrial peace can best be obtained only in that way."[13]

Although the Court spoke more qualifiedly about the *quid pro quo* concept at a later date,[14] this approach was reiterated in *United Steelworkers v. Warrior & Gulf Navigation Co.* where Mr. Justice Douglas said:[15]

> The present federal policy is to promote industrial stabilization through the collective bargaining agreement. . . . A major factor in achieving industrial peace is the inclusion of a provision for arbitration of grievances in the collective bargaining agreement.
> . . . arbitration is the substitute for industrial strife. . . .
> . . . the parties' objective in using the arbitration process is primarily to further the common goal of uninterrupted production under the agreement. . . .

Subsequently, the Court held that state courts that had theretofore heard breach of contract labor cases as well as federal tribunals were to retain jurisdiction over collective agreement disputes to articulate a uniform federal labor law of contract.[16] Under such federal labor

---

12 United Steelworkers v. American Mfg. Co., 363 U.S. 564 (1960); United Steelworkers v. Warrior & Gulf Navigation Co., 363 U.S. 574 (1960); United Steelworkers v. Enterprise Wheel & Car Corp., 363 U.S. 593 (1960).

13 353 U.S. at 455.

14 See Drake Bakeries, Inc. v. Local 50, American Bakery & Confectionery Workers, 370 U.S. 254, 261 n. 7 (1962); Local 721, United Packinghouse Workers v. Needham Packing Co., 376 U.S. 247 (1964).

15 363 U.S. at 578, 582.

16 Charles Dowd Box Co. v. Courtney, 368 U.S. 502 (1962); Teamsters, Local 174 v. Lucas Flour Co., 369 U.S. 95 (1962).

law, a union refusal to arbitrate could be remedied by damages in the instance of either a no-strike clause or a broad arbitration clause through which the no-strike obligation was implied.[17] But, if the federal labor policy was to encourage the peaceable resolution of industrial disputes and if the no-strike pledge and the grievance-arbitration machinery were properly viewed as an exchange as the Court had stated in *Lincoln Mills* and the *Steelworkers Trilogy*, the question whether an employer could obtain an injunction against the no-strike violation remained clouded. This was so because the Norris-LaGuardia Act, enacted by Congress in 1932, prohibited, except in enumerated instances, the issuance of injunctions by federal courts.[18] More specifically, Norris-LaGuardia provides that federal courts shall not have jurisdiction to issue an injunction in a "labor dispute" so as to prohibit any person from "[c]easing or refusing to perform any work or to remain in any relation of employment."[19]

In essence then, the federal judiciary was confronted with a fundamental dilemma in an attempt to reconcile two diverse statutes. Norris-LaGuardia, on the one hand, was representative of a strong congressional desire to remove the courts from labor disputes on the theory that they had acted in a biased and uninformed manner, thus exposing the judiciary to a disrespect and contempt that independent judges cannot afford in a democracy.[20] There had been serious abuses in connection with the issuance of such injunctions,[21] albeit for the most part outside the context of labor contract litigation. Moreover, it was thought important to take away from federal judges the power effectively to resolve labor disputes according to their own view of social and economic philosophy—

---

[17] Teamsters, Local 174 v. Lucas Flour Co., 369 U.S. 95 (1962). The British courts seem more cautious about the articulation of such judge-made law because there is no comparable statutory authority. See Ford Motor Co. v. Amalgamated Union of Eng'rs & Foundry Workers, [1969] 1 W.L.R. 339. But see Selwyn, *Collective Agreements and the Law*, 32 Mod. L. Rev. 377 (1969).

[18] 29 U.S.C. § 104.   [19] *Ibid.*

[20] *Compare* Bickel, The Supreme Court and the Idea of Progress (1970), *and* Bickel, The Least Dangerous Branch (1962), *with* Black, The People and the Court (1960).

[21] See Frankfurter & Greene, The Labor Injunction (1930); Aaron, *Labor Injunctions in the State Courts: Part II—A Critique*, 50 Va. L. Rev. 1147 (1964); Comment, *Labor Injunctions and Judge-Made Labor Law: The Contemporary Role of Norris-LaGuardia*, 70 Yale L.J. 70 (1960).

particularly where, as in the case of strikes, what purported to be temporary relief had the effect of finality.[22] As Mr. Justice Harlan said: ". . . this judge-made law of the late 19th and early 20th centuries was based on self-mesmerized views of economic and social theory."[23] But subsequent to Norris-LaGuardia, Congress had begun to move in another direction. The passage of the NLRA in 1935[24] had put the NLRB, and eventually the federal courts,[25] into the middle of industrial disputes. In effect, the policy of laissez faire —or "collective laissez faire," as Professor Kahn-Freund would have it[26]—was implicitly rejected by a statute that invoked the courts and which, particularly through its 1947 Taft-Hartley amendments of which § 301 was a prominent part, seemed to invite a measure of judicial activism. The approach taken by the Court in *Lincoln Mills* and the *Steelworkers Trilogy* accentuated the dilemma all the more. For these cases articulated the *quid pro quo* approach that meant, if it meant anything, that employers could enforce the no-strike obligation against unions. Despite the broad prohibitory language of Norris-LaGuardia, the Court had reconciled the statute with the grievance machinery of the Railway Labor Act (RLA) in *Brotherhood of Railroad Trainmen v. Chicago & Indiana R.R.*,[27] where it held that strikes called over an issue properly submitted to the National Railroad Adjustment Board (NRAB) could be enjoined. Thus, where the RLA was involved, the Norris-LaGuardia hurdle was not too high for the Court to jump in order to enjoin a strike.[28] In 1962 Mr. Justice Black, speaking for the Court, attempted to deal

---

[22] On the nature of the injunction, see FRANKFURTER & GREENE, note 21 *supra*, at 53–60.

[23] Brotherhood of Railroad Trainmen v. Jackson Terminal Co., 394 U.S. 369, 382 (1969). See also Marine Cooks v. Panama S.S. Co., 362 U.S. 365, 369 (1960).

[24] 49 Stat. 449 (1935).   [25] 29 U.S.C. § 160(f).

[26] Kahn-Freund, *Labor Law*, in LAW AND OPINION IN GREAT BRITAIN IN THE 20TH CENTURY 227 (Ginsberg ed. 1959). See also in this connection GRUNFELD, MODERN TRADE UNION LAW (1966); KAHN-FREUND, LABOR LAW; OLD TRADITIONS AND NEW DEVELOPMENTS (1968); WEDDERBURN, THE WORKER AND THE LAW (1965); WEDDERBURN & DAVIES, EMPLOYMENT GRIEVANCES AND DISPUTES PROCEDURE IN BRITAIN (1969).

[27] 353 U.S. 30 (1957).

[28] For an excellent analysis of this decision see Cox, *Current Problems of the Law of Grievance Arbitration*, 30 ROCKY MOUNT. L. REV. 247, 252 (1958). Subsequently, the Court declined the opportunity to undertake a more difficult accommodation in NLRB v. Drivers Local 639, 362 U.S. 274 (1960).

with the same problem in the context of the NLRA in *Sinclair Refining Co. v. Atkinson.*[29]

In *Sinclair*, by a 5 to 3 vote,[30] the Court rejected the argument that § 301 of the act could be said to have "impliedly repealed" § 4 of the "pre-existing Norris-LaGuardia Act." In that case the collective bargaining agreement provided for binding arbitration of "any difference regarding wages, hours or working conditions between the parties hereto or between the Employer and an employee covered by this working agrement which might arise within any plant or within any region of operations." The contract also imposed a flat prohibition upon slowdowns, strikes, or work stoppages for "any cause which is or may be the subject of a grievance."[31] The complaint alleged that a number of work stoppages and strikes had been undertaken in violation of the contract. The company claimed that in such circumstances there was no adequate remedy at law that would protect its contractual rights and therefore requested injunctive relief. The unions sought dismissal of the complaint on the ground that the controversy was a "labor dispute" within the meaning of the Norris-LaGuardia Act and that therefore a federal court was without jurisdiction to issue the injunction requested.

The majority opinion of the Court concluded that since the strike constituted a "labor dispute" within the meaning of Norris-LaGuardia, the statute barred an injunction. Conceding the argument that the injunction might be sensible and sound labor policy, Mr. Justice Black said for the majority:[32]

> We cannot ignore the plain import of a congressional enactment, particularly one which, as we have repeatedly said, was

---

[29] 370 U.S. 195 (1962). See *Report of Special Atkinson-Sinclair Committee*, 1963 ABA Section of Labor Relations Law, pt. II, 226–40.

[30] Mr. Justice Frankfurter did not participate. Mr. Justice Stewart was part of the *Sinclair* majority but switched his position in *Boys Market*. Mr. Chief Justice Burger, not a member of the Court at the time of *Sinclair*, was also a part of the *Boys Market* majority.

Chief Justice Burger had earlier indicated an impatience with stare decisis in the area of labor law by joining the concurring opinion of Mr. Justice White in Longshoremen v. Ariadne Co., 397 U.S. 195, 201–02 (1970), which announced a desire to reconsider some of the preemption doctrine. This opinion, together with the Chief Justice's concurring opinion in Taggart v. Weinacker's, Inc., 397 U.S. 223, 227–28 (1970), evoked a memorandum from Mr. Justice Harlan stressing adherence to prior judgments, even in those cases in which he had dissented.

[31] 370 U.S. at 197.   [32] *Id.* at 203.

> deliberately drafted in the broadest of terms in order to avoid
> the danger that it would be narrowed by judicial construction.
>   ... Upon consideration, we cannot agree with [the view that
> Norris-LaGuardia has been narrowed by the subsequent enact-
> ment of § 301] and agree instead with the view ... that § 301
> was not intended to have any such partially repealing effect
> upon such a longstanding carefully thought out and highly
> significant part of this country's labor legislation as the Norris-
> LaGuardia Act.

The Court stated that the failure of Congress expressly to repeal
Norris-LaGuardia when enacting § 301 made it unlikely that Congress intended to repeal the former statute's anti-injunction features
—particularly in light of the fact that Congress had repealed Norris-
LaGuardia for other purposes in the NLRA where it sought to
prohibit certain kinds of economic pressure by unions.[33] Moreover,
the Court rejected the employer argument that, even if Congress
did not intend to repeal Norris-LaGuardia, it was willing to confer
a power upon the courts to "accommodate" the provisions of
seemingly contrary statutes.

Mr. Justice Brennan, speaking also for Justices Douglas and Harlan, dissented in *Sinclair* and stated that the majority's conclusions
were inconsistent with the federal labor policy favoring arbitration
as articulated in *Lincoln Mills* and the *Steelworkers Trilogy*. Conceding the fact that Congress did not repeal Norris-LaGuardia
insofar as § 301 was concerned, Mr. Justice Brennan contended
that such a conclusion did not preclude judicial inquiry into the
question of accommodation. The dissenting opinion thus concluded
that merely because Congress did not wish to permit the wholesale
abandonment of Norris-LaGuardia in contract actions, it was not
necessarily logical to conclude that § 301 and its approach were to
be subservient to Norris-LaGuardia. Further, the dissenting opinion
stated that the anti-injunction features of Norris-LaGuardia were
not vital to the ends of federal labor policy where the underlying
dispute which gave rise to the strike was itself arbitrable and thus

---

[33] *Id.* at 204–05. The Court specifically referred to the fact that Congress had
amended Taft-Hartley and repealed Norris-LaGuardia so as to permit the board
some latitude to seek injunctions and the Attorney-General to enjoin national
emergency strikes. 29. U.S.C. §§ 160, 178. One obvious distinction between these
provisions and § 301 is that government rather than private employers requests
injunctive relief in the former situations. *Cf.* Sears, Roebuck & Co. v. Carpet Layers
Local 419, 397 U.S. 655 (1970).

capable of resolution through preferred procedures, *i.e.*, arbitration, as implied in the NLRA.[34]

Mr. Justice Brennan had other objections to the majority opinion in *Sinclair*. He noted that the practical effect of *Sinclair* forced on the Court the choice between two equally undesirable alternatives. On the one hand, the uniformity of federal labor law governing the collective agreement argued for the proposition that injunctive relief must be denied in state as well as federal courts. If the Court was to hold that federal and state courts were bound by the same rules, § 301 would then deprive employers of a state remedy that they had enjoyed prior to the passage of the 1947 amendments. This seemed inconsistent with § 301 because the statute had clearly been designed to create a greater contractual responsibility on the part of unions and the Court would thus be articulating a rule that would have the opposite effect.

On the other hand, if state courts were to retain the ability to issue injunctions where no state "baby" Norris-LaGuardia Acts were in existence,[35] state courts would then become the "preferred instruments to protect the integrity of the arbitration process."[36] Thus, the state judiciary would become dominant in an area of law that was to be both uniform and federal. Disparate rules of law that would result, depending upon the particular jurisdiction in which the strike took place, would be clearly inconsistent with the Court's prior pronouncements on the desirability of uniformity in labor-management contractual relationships.

Mr. Justice Brennan also noted that unions might attempt to remove such injunction suits to federal courts, although he was of the view that removal would not be allowed. But "if it is allowed, the result once again is that § 301 will have had the strange consequence of taking away a contract remedy available before its enactment."[37]

---

[34] "Final adjustment by a method agreed upon by the parties is declared to be the desirable method for settlement of grievance disputes arising over the application or interpretation of an existing collective-bargaining agreement." 29 U.S.C. § 173 (d).

[35] "Almost half the states have such provisions." Aaron, *Strikes in Breach of Collective Agreements: Some Unanswered Questions*, 63 Colum. L. Rev. 1027, 1036 n. 67 (1963). See also Bartosic, *Injunctions and Section 301: The Patchwork of Avco and Philadelphia Marine on the Fabric of National Labor Policy*, 69 Colum. L. Rev. 980, 1001–11 (1969).

[36] 370 U.S. at 226.   [37] *Id.* at 227.

And, indeed, in *Avco Corp. v. Aero Lodge No. 735*[38] the majority of the Court approved removal.

In *Avco* the complaint stated that employees were engaging in work stoppages and a walkout because of disputes "allegedly subject" to the grievance procedure in the face of a no-strike clause. The state court issued an *ex parte* injunction. The respondents then moved in the federal district court for removal of the case. Mr. Justice Douglas, speaking for the Court,[39] held that the action was removable. He said, however, that "the nature of the relief available after jurisdiction attaches is, of course, different from the question whether there is jurisdiction to adjudicate the controversy."[40] Thus, the power of federal courts as well as the question whether state court injunctions were to be dissolved in such removal proceedings was left open. Similarly, the Court avoided the question of state court authority to issue injunctive relief, independent of the removal question, in light of *Sinclair*. Mr. Justice Stewart, concurring, joined by Justices Harlan and Brennan, said: "[T]he Court expressly reserves decision on the effect of *Sinclair* in the circumstances presented by this case. The Court will, no doubt, have an opportunity to reconsider the scope and continuing validity of *Sinclair* upon an appropriate future occasion."[41]

That future occasion turned out to be the case of *Boys Market*. Appropriately, the task of delivering the majority opinion fell to Mr. Justice Brennan, who had written the dissent in *Sinclair*. In *Boys Market*, the union protested the assignment of certain work to the employer's supervisors and other nonbargaining unit employees. The union representative insisted that certain food cases be stripped of all merchandise placed there by such non-unit employees and restocked by workers whom the union represented. When the employer resisted this demand, the union called a strike despite a broad arbitration clause that purportedly covered the dispute in question. A separate clause, entitled "work stoppages," stated that "matters subject to the procedures of this Article shall be settled and resolved in the manner provided herein," and went on to prohibit

---

[38] 390 U.S. 557 (1968). Cf. Lesnick, *State-Court Injunctions and the Federal Common Law of Labor Contracts: Beyond Norris-LaGuardia*, 79 HARV. L. REV. 757 (1966).

[39] Mr. Justice Douglas had previously reiterated his views on the *Sinclair* problem in Local 1219, ILA v. Philadelphia Marine Trade Ass'n, 389 U.S. 64, 77 (1967).

[40] 390 U.S. at 561.   [41] *Id.* at 562.

stoppages or lockouts except where "the other party refuses to perform any obligations under this Article or refuses to abide by, accept or perform a decision or award of an arbitrator or board."[42]

The employer, upon seeking a temporary restraining order in a state court, simultaneously sought to invoke the grievance and arbitration procedures so as to resolve the underlying dispute. The state court issued both a temporary restraining order forbidding continuation of the strike and an order to show cause why a preliminary injunction should not be granted. The union then removed this action to federal district court and made a motion to quash the state court's temporary restraining order. The employer, in turn, moved for an order compelling arbitration and enjoining the continuation of the strike.

The federal district court ordered the parties to arbitrate and enjoined the strike, but the Ninth Circuit reversed upon the authority of *Sinclair*.[43] The Supreme Court, in *Boys Market*, undertook to "re-examine" the *Sinclair* holding and concluded that "*Sinclair* was erroneously decided and that subsequent events have undermined its continuing validity."[44]

II. The Activist Rationale of Boys Market

The primary reason given for such a re-examination was the fact that *Sinclair* "stands as a significant departure from our otherwise consistent efforts upon the congressional policy to promote the peaceful settlement of of labor disputes through arbitration."[45] But a preliminary question not touched by any of the opinions in *Boys Market* is whether the Court's efforts in the *Steelworkers Trilogy* had made any contribution to the achievement of industrial peace and, thus, whether abandonment of the stare decisis principle could be justified in terms of the overriding importance of § 301 as a central part of national labor policy. Although the impact of the law upon industrial relations is quite difficult to measure in most instances, the argument that the Court's work is irrelevant to the presence of work stoppages, if accepted, would make rejection of the prohibitory language of Norris-LaGuardia all the more difficult. If it were, accommodation between the two statutes would be hardly worth the candle.

---

42 398 U.S. at 239 n.3.

43 416 F.2d 368 (1969).

44 398 U.S. at 238.

45 *Id*. at 241.

Professor Wellington made such an argument. He contended that the increased number and percentage of strikes recently occurring during the terms of labor contracts prove that the *Trilogy* has "had no effect" in contributing to labor peace.[46] Moreover, he continued, where there are issues that are critical to the parties, they are simply postponed for resolution through warfare subsequent to the expiration of the contract. One can hardly dispute the existence of an extreme tenacity by the parties which is sufficient in a number of instances merely to postpone the confrontation to a later date. The subcontracting issue in the automobile industry provides a more than adequate example.[47] The United Automobile Workers Union has continuously attempted to restrict managerial authority in this area through both arbitration and contract negotiation.

This thesis of despair, however, ignores the fact that the contractual strike prohibition may serve as a cooling-off period and thus lend a measure of rationality to the resolution of disputes. The allocation of a specific time for disputes, *i.e.*, the expiration of the collective agreement, releases the union from pressure to threaten the stoppage over every grievance that arises, improves management's ability to meet business orders and delivery dates and, if one can judge from the British experience, probably induces a better atmosphere for productivity increases.[48]

Moreover, the fact that breach-of-contract stoppages appear to be on the upswing since the *Trilogy* hardly proves Professor Wellington's point. In the first place, *Sinclair*—the governing law for the past eight years—deprived management of its most effective remedy for breach of a no-strike clause. It is at least possible that *Boys Market* may have improved this situation to some extent and thus made breach-of-contract stoppages less likely. But, more important, an analysis of the *Trilogy* and strike statistics that fails to take account of other factors operating during the past decade is necessarily superficial. The most obviously relevant consideration is the phenomenon of relatively full employment and inflation—both of which may

---

[46] Wellington, Labor and the Legal Process 119–20, 353–54 n.62 (1968).

[47] See Ford Motor Co., 42 Lab. Arb. 220 (1964). Ford Motor Co., unreported (June 9, 1967). See, most recently, on the subject, Erikson, *Ford's Contract Workers Come under Fire*, Detroit News, Aug. 1, 1970, p. 5A, col. 5.

[48] See Donovan Report; Flanders, Collective Bargaining: Prescription for Change (1967); Flanders, Industrial Relations: What Is Wrong with the System? (1965).

encourage restiveness under a contract of fixed duration or, for that matter, under any other system.[49] And it would be interesting to speculate (and it would be no more speculative than the attack upon the *Trilogy* under discussion) about the extent to which the very considerable number of rank and file rejections of negotiated contracts during recent years would have taken the form of wildcat or breach-of-contract strikes if the no-strike obligation did not have some legal sanctions behind it.[50] Explosive discontent in the work place may have been channeled into another forum that appears to be less disruptive. If so, one can find the § 301 rationale substantially intact, thus justifying the reconciliation of the no-strike mandate to its purposes.

Because Mr. Justice Black had assented to both *Lincoln Mills* and the *Steelworkers Trilogy*,[51] the above rationalization would not have been to his liking—although it must be pointed out that Mr. Justice Black has remained the most consistent critic of the Court's decisions in the arbitration area.[52] Stymied by the industrial peace objectives interpretation previously placed upon § 301, Mr. Justice Black apparently felt obliged to focus his attack on the weak points of the majority opinion of Mr. Justice Brennan in *Boys Market*.

At the outset of the majority opinion, the Court brushed aside the doctrine of stare decisis as a rule that did not necessitate mechanistic adherence to prior decisions. As Mr. Justice Stewart said in a separate concurring opinion quoting Mr. Justice Frankfurter: "Wisdom

---

[49] For a more detailed critique of Professor Wellington's views, see Gould, *Book Review*, 16 WAYNE L. REV. 384 (1969); Shapiro, *Book Review*, 22 STAN. L. REV. 657 (1970).

[50] See Salpukas, *Young Workers Raising Voices for Factory and Union Changes*, N.Y. Times, June 1, 1970, p. 23, col. 1, where it is indicated that younger workers wish to remove the no-strike clause, "want faster changes and sometimes bypass their own union leaders and start wildcat strikes." The 1970 Steelworkers convention also demonstrated a growing demand for the elimination of no-strike clauses. See Conti, *U.S.W. Convention Echoes with Strike Talk for Next July*, Wall St. J., Oct. 2, 1970, p. 8, col. 2.

[51] Indeed, Mr. Justice Black joined with Mr. Justice Douglas in his dissenting opinion in Association of Westinghouse Salaried Employees v. Westinghouse Elec. Corp., 348 U.S. 437 (1965), in a view which was eventually to become the majority opinion in *Lincoln Mills*.

[52] See Mr. Justice Black's dissenting opinions in Teamsters Local 174 v. Lucas Flour Co., 369 U.S. 95 (1962); Smith v. Evening News Association, 371 U.S. 195, 201 (1962); Carey v. Westinghouse Elec. Corp., 375 U.S. 261, 273 (1964); Vaca v. Sipes, 386 U.S. 171, 203 (1967); Republic Steel Corp. v. Maddox, 379 U.S. 650, 659 (1965).

too often never comes, and so one ought not to reject it merely because it comes late."[53] Moreover, the Court stated that the mere
silence of Congress was an insufficient reason to refuse to reconsider
Sinclair. The most important factor in the Court's decision was the
Steelworkers Trilogy and its policy in favor of arbitration. Said
the Court: "Furthermore, in light of developments subsequent to
Sinclair, in particular a decision in *Avco Corp.*, . . . it has become
clear that the *Sinclair* decision does not further but rather frustrates
realization of an important goal of our national labor policy."[54] Mr.
Justice Brennan then noted that "*Avco*, viewed in the context of
Lincoln Mills and its progeny, . . . produced an anomalous situation
which . . . makes urgent the reconsideration of *Sinclair*."[55]

The urgency resulted from the destruction of state court jurisdiction over breach of no-strike clause cases. Since *Avco* permitted
removal and *Sinclair* precluded federal district court injunctions,
said the Court, the state courts were now effectively ousted from
this field. But this, in turn, was inconsistent with the Court's previously announced holding that federal jurisdiction for breach of contract cases was to supplement the pre-existing jurisdiction of state
courts and not to intrude upon this area.[56] Said the Court: "It is
ironic indeed that the very provision which Congress clearly intended to provide additional remedies for breach of collective-bargaining agreements has been employed to displace previously existing state remedies."[57] Mr. Justice Brennan agreed that labor law
issues could not be "administered identically in all courts," but,
where so significant a remedial device as the injunction was involved, "its availability or non-availability in various courts will not
only produce rampant forum-shopping and maneuvering from one
court to another, but will also greatly frustrate any relative uniformity in the enforcement of arbitration agreements."[58] Since some
state courts permitted injunctions to be issued in the *Sinclair–Boys*

---

[53] 398 U.S. at 255. Frankfurter's statement quoted by Mr. Justice Stewart is from
a dissenting opinion in Henslee v. Union Planters Bank, 335 U.S. 595, 600 (1949).

[54] 398 U.S. at 241.   [55] *Id.* at 244.

[56] "The clear implication of the entire record of the congressional debate in both
1946 and 1947 is that the purpose of conferring jurisdiction upon the federal courts
was not to displace, but to supplement, the thoroughly considered jurisdiction of
the courts of the various States over contracts made by labor organizations." Charles
Dowd Box Co. v. Courtney, 368 U.S. 502, 511 (1962).

[57] 398 U.S. at 245.   [58] *Id.* at 246.

Market type of cases,[59] and since this had obviously created forum-shopping,[60] the Court's observations seem to have been well justified.

Mr. Justice Brennan, however, was not content to rest on lack of uniformity and the implications of *Avco*. The *Boys Market* opinion further stated—in response to the argument that *Sinclair* should be made applicable to the states so as to avoid the uniformity problem[61]—that such a resolution of the dilemma would have "devastating implications," since, under such a scheme, equitable remedies would not be available in any forum. Said the Court: "Any incentive for employers to enter into such an [arbitration and no-strike] arrangement is necessarily dissipated if the principal and most expeditious method by which the no-strike obligation can be enforced

---

[59] See, for instance, Perry & Sons v. Robilotto, 39 Misc.2d 147 (N.Y. Sup. Ct. 1963); McCarroll v. Los Angeles County District Council of Carpenters, 49 Cal.2d 45 (1957). The argument was made, however, that § 301 and the Court's decision in *Sinclair* precluded the issuance of injunctions in labor disputes by state courts because *Sinclair* was federal substantive labor law. See Shaw Elec. Co. v. IBEW, Local 98, 418 Pa. 1, (1965). The cases are collected in Bartosic, note 35 *supra*, at 1102, nn. 136, 137, 138. The Supreme Court had reserved decision on this matter both in *Avco*, 390 U.S. at 560 n.2; and in *Dowd Box*, 368 U.S. at 514 n.8. *Cf.* Ruppert v. Engelhofer, 3 N.Y.2d 576 (1958).

[60] American Dredging Co. v. Local 25, Int'l Union of Operating Eng'rs, 338 F.2d 837 (3d Cir. 1964). For a thorough and excellent discussion of this matter see Bartosic, note 35 *supra*, at 987–96.

[61] Presumably state courts may issue injunctions under appropriate circumstances in labor disputes even without statutory authorization. Of course, the employer may circumvent any difficulties on this score by simply filing a request for injunctive relief under *Boys Market* in federal district court. But the rule ought to be the same in state courts—even in those jurisdictions which have baby Norris-LaGuardia Acts—so as to preserve both federal and state jurisdiction and to reduce the incentive to utilize only federal tribunals. In effect, *Boys Market* ought to require a second accommodation at the level between § 301 and state statutes. See Teamsters Local 174 v. Lucas Flour Co., 369 U.S. 95 (1962); Charles Dowd Box Co. v. Courtney, 368 U.S. 502 (1962). But see McCarroll v. Los Angeles County Dist. Council of Carpenters, 49 Cal. 2d 45 (1957). This would delimit both the automatic issuance of injunctions without consideration of such factors as whether the dispute itself was arbitrable, see, *e.g.*, Construction & Gen. Laborers Local 246 v. Jordan Co., 75 L.R.R.M. 2201 (Ga. 1970) as well as mandate the modification of "baby" Norris-LaGuardia statutes to conform with *Boys Market*. Professor St. Antoine does not appear to be so certain. See St. Antoine, *Interventionism, Laissez-Faire, and Stare Decisis*, Address before ABA Section of Labor Relations Law, Aug. 10, 1970. The federal courts will probably revise state court injunctions at variance with *Boys Market* requirements. See Holland Construction Co., Inc. v. International Union of Operating Engr's., 74 L.R.R.M. 3087 (D. Kan. 1970). *Cf.* Atlantic Coast Line R.R. v. Locomotive Engineers, 398 U.S. 281 (1970).

is eliminated."[62] The Court did not, however, cite any empirical data or authority to support this proposition. Most probably, this portion of the Court's rationale falls short of the mark since all evidence is that arbitration clauses have gained increasingly wider acceptance during the past eight years, *i.e.*, since *Sinclair* has been the law.[63] Thus, this aspect of the *Boys Market* rationale, though its logic is sound, is not in tune with the practicalities of industrial relations.

Mr. Justice Brennan hedged against the possibility of such criticism when he stated that even if management were not encouraged to resist arbitration agreements by *Sinclair*, it was improperly deprived of the most effective weaponry to deal with no-strike violations. The Court's opinion did not assess the effectiveness of the more traditional remedies utilized by management, *i.e.*, discharge and discipline, nor did it deal with the possibility of encouraging parties voluntarily to adopt "quickie" or expeditious grievance-arbitration machinery equipped to deal with stoppages, perhaps through the use of a permanent umpire rather than an ad hoc arbitrator.[64] But the Court did address itself to the availability of damages under § 301 and state breach-of-contract cases:[65]

> While it is of course true, as respondent contends, that all other avenues of redress, such as an action for damages, would remain open to an aggrieved employer, an award with damages after a dispute has been settled is no substitute for an immediate halt to an illegal strike. Furthermore, an action for damages prosecuted during or after a labor dispute would only tend to aggravate industrial strife and delay an early resolution of the difficulties between employer and union.

Here the Court is on undeniably sound ground. Employers are unlikely to sue and certainly not to continue such legal action subse-

---

[62] 398 U.S. at 248.

[63] Approximately 94 percent of the collective bargaining agreements negotiated between unions and employers contain arbitration clauses. U.S. Bureau of Labor Statistics, BULL. No. 1425-1, *Grievance Procedures*, p. 1 (1964). It would appear that the *Sinclair* rule did not deter employers from entering into contracts with arbitration clauses. See also Jones & Smith, *Management and Labor Appraisals and Criticisms of the Arbitration Process: A Report with Comments*, 62 MICH. L. REV. 1115 (1964).

[64] But see 398 U.S. at 244 n. 10.   [65] *Id.* at 248.

quent to a strike settlement.[66] Indeed, the price of settlement is often a promise by management to withdraw damage suits that are pending or about to be instituted. A contrary practice would detract from the achievement of sound industrial relations.[67] Moreover, the measure of damages to which the employer is entitled is vague and debatable.[68]

If, however, the injunction is indeed the most effective remedy and the damage actions will simultaneously produce the discord that is so antithetical to our national labor policy, the Court was nevertheless still left with the problem of the Norris-LaGurdia bar against enjoining "labor disputes." The Court concluded that since congressional emphasis in dealing with labor unions had changed from the days of Norris-LaGuardia as labor organizations "grew in strength and developed toward maturity,"[69] equitable remedies that protected collective bargaining procedures and arbitration could be accommodated by Norris-LaGuardia. Indeed, said the Court, since the purpose of Norris-LaGuardia was to encourage and foster the growth of labor organizations, equitable remedies of the kind articulated in *Boys Market* were hardly inconsistent with the "core purpose"[70] of that statute.

In dissent, Mr. Justice Black stated that stare decisis, while not of overbearing importance in the constitutional arena where ultimate responsibility rests with the Court, ought to foreclose re-examination of past decisions where the primary responsibility lies with Congress, unless there were exceptional circumstances presented.[71]

---

[66] See *Report of Special Atkinson-Sinclair Committee*, note 29 *supra*, at 242; Cox, note 28 *supra*, at 255; Warren, C. J., dissenting, in UAW v. Russell, 356 U.S. 634, 647 (1958).

[67] This practice prevails in Great Britain as well. See WEDDERBURN & DAVIES, note 26 *supra*, at 49. At the same time, it should be noted that the possibility of a damage action has some deterrent effect. And equally important is the fact that some of the courts have imposed bonds upon unions that cannot be negotiated away at the bargaining table. See Tanker Service Committee, Inc. v. Masters Local 14, 269 F. Supp. 551 (E.D. Pa. 1967), *aff'd* 394 F.2d 160 (3d Cir. 1968); Ormet Corp. v. United Steelworkers, 72 L.R.R.M. 2268 (W.D. Pa. 1969), *injunction suspended pending appeal*, 72 L.R.R.M. 2510 (3d Cir. 1969). An obvious benefit to be derived from this conditional damage remedy is speed. But, query, is this reconcilable with Drake Bakeries v. Bakery Local 50, 370 U.S. 254 (1962), which remits damage questions to arbitration?

[68] See cases cited *infra*, at note 126. See Cox, note 28 *supra*. But see, *e.g.*, International Brotherhood of Teamsters Local 25 v. W. L. Mead, Inc., 230 F.2d 576 (1st Cir. 1956); United Steelworkers of America v. CCI Corp., 395 F.2d 529 (10th Cir. 1968).

[69] 398 U.S. at 251.   [70] *Id.* at 253.   [71] *Id.* at 255.

Mr. Justice White relied upon the majority opinion in *Sinclair* in his separate dissent.[72]

Perhaps, where highly volatile and controversial issues like strikes and labor contracts are involved, Congress should be charged with final responsibility to adjust the delicate balance after the Court has placed interpretative gloss upon the statute as it did in *Sinclair*. Trade unionists who regard *Boys Market* as a logical extension of the *Steelworkers Trilogy* (and there are many such union advocates) might have hoped to fashion a political compromise in Congress that would have removed some of the Taft-Hartley amendments far more onerous to organized labor. Such an approach, however, overlooks the argument that error—particularly an error which is an egregious departure from national labor policy articulated by the Court—ought to be corrected. Moreover, if the criticism is made that the Court has become too activist and usurped the authority of Congress, it would seem that that kind of critique is more properly leveled at *Lincoln Mills* and its rather extraordinary assumption of authority to fashion federal labor law.[73] There must be no mistake about the fact that *Boys Market* is judicial policy making. But it was *Lincoln Mills* that called upon the courts to make use of their "judicial inventiveness."[74] And I should think that, in terms of both legislative intent and judicial precedent, the foundation of *Boys Market* is more firmly established than that upon which *Lincoln Mills* rested. In 1947 Congress was most concerned to discipline trade unions which exhibited a lack of contractual responsibility.[75]

The Court, having made its quantum jump in *Lincoln Mills* hardly could have retained a doctrine that was contrary to the direct implications of that decision as well as the *Trilogy*. After all, it was *Lincoln Mills* that properly assumed the applicability of § 301 to labor unions. The difficult question, decided affirmatively in that case, was whether liability was to be imposed upon

---

[72] *Id.* at 261.

[73] Mr. Justice Douglas said in *Lincoln Mills:* "The legislative history of § 301 is somewhat cloudy and confusing. But there are a few shafts of light that illuminate our problem." 353 U.S. at 452. See Bickel & Wellington, note 11 *supra*.

[74] 353 U.S. at 457. For an application of this approach to another area of labor arbitration, see Gould, *Labor Arbitration of Grievances Involving Racial Discrimination*, 118 U. PA. L. REV. 40 (1969). See also in this regard Shapiro, *Some Thoughts on Intervention before Courts, Agencies and Arbitrators*, 81 HARV. L. REV. 721 (1968).

[75] 398 U.S. at 245 n.12. See the discussion of legislative history in *Lincoln Mills*, 353 U.S. at 452–57.

employers as well. Moreover, as the majority noted in *Boys Market*, primary reliance upon damages (as well as the unmentioned remedy of discharge and discipline) is most often an irritant, inappropriate to mature union-employer relationships, and thus at odds with the national labor policy that favors the achievement of industrial peace. *Boys Market* can then be said to be in step with a common law of labor relations that is "dynamic and adaptable to changing times [predicated upon] legislatively based principles . . . to the extent it is in the law developed during the more than thirty years of administering our most comprehensive national labor scheme, the National Labor Relations Act."[76]

One other factor not mentioned by the Court in *Boys Market* is that an employer who sought damages or disciplinary action would normally proceed to arbitration. This course of action is required by the Court's decision in *Drake Bakeries*[77] handed down at the time of *Sinclair*. If the hearing were to take place in the midst of the stoppage or while the underlying issue which had given rise to it was still unresolved, the setting would more often be counterproductive than not. In the midst of a strike or its immediate aftermath, emo-

---

[76] 394 U.S. at 383.

[77] 370 U.S. 254 (1962). In *Drake Bakeries*, the Court held that the proper forum for adjudication of a no-strike violation was arbitration rather than the courts. *Cf.* Atkinson v. Sinclair Refining Co., 370 U.S. 238 (1962). The Court also held that a strike in violation of the contract did not necessarily repudiate the arbitration clause through which the alleged no-strike violation might be heard. See Local 721, United Packing House, Food & Allied Workers v. Needham Packing Co., 376 U.S. 247 (1964). On the *Drake Bakeries* rule, see generally, Fluor Corp. v. Carpenters District Council, 424 F.2d 283 (5th Cir. 1970); Johnson Builders, Inc. v. United Bhd. of Carpenters and Joiners, 422 F.2d 137 (10th Cir. 1970); Howard Elec. Co. v. IBEW, Local 570, 423 F.2d 164 (9th Cir. 1970); Local 748, IUE v. Jefferson City Cabinet Co., 314 F.2d 192 (6th Cir. 1963); Los Angeles Paper Bag Co. v. Printing Specialties and Paper Products Union, 345 F.2d 757 (9th Cir. 1965); District 50, United Mine Workers of America v. Chris-Craft Corp., 385 F.2d 946 (6th Cir. 1967). For cases granting stay of proceedings pending arbitration, see IT&T v. Communication Workers, 422 F.2d 77 (2d Cir. 1970); Scalizitti Co. v. Operating Eng'rs., Local 150, 351 F.2d 576 (7th Cir. 1965); Franchi Construction Co. v. Hod Carriers, Local 560, 248 F. Supp. 134 (D. Mass. 1965); United States Steel Corp. v. Seafarers, 237 F. Supp. 529 (E.D. Pa. 1965); Clothing Workers v. United Garment Mfg. Co., 338 F.2d 195 (8th Cir. 1964); Fifth Ave. Coach Lines v. Transport Workers, 235 F. Supp. 842 (S.D. N.Y. 1964); Swartz & Funston v. Bricklayers, 319 F.2d 116 (3d Cir. 1963); Gilmour v. Lathers Union, Local 74, 223 F. Supp. 236 (N.D. Ill. 1963); Yale & Towne Mfg. Co. v. Local 1717, IAM, 299 F.2d 882 (3d Cir. 1962). For cases denying stay of proceedings pending arbitration, see G. T. Schjeldahi Co. v. Local 1680, IAM, 393 F.2d 502 (1st Cir. 1968); Simonds Construction Co. v. Hod Carriers, Local 1330, 315 F.2d 291 (7th Cir. 1963); Boeing Co. v. UAW, 234 F. Supp. 404 (E.D. Pa. 1965).

tions run high. Here again, *Sinclair*, by permitting the strike to continue, could be viewed as an aberration.

Nevertheless, the unease with which many both in and out of the house of labor view *Boys Market* has substantial historical basis. One must recall that the issuance of an injunction as a result of *Boys Market* is dependent upon the existence of an arbitrable grievance that gave rise to the strike. The Court's holding is a "narrow one." As Mr. Justice Brennan said in dissent in *Sinclair:*[78]

> . . . the employer should be ordered to arbitrate, as a condition of his obtaining an injunction against the strike. Beyond this, the District Court must, of course, consider whether issuance of an injunction would be warranted under ordinary principles of equity—whether breaches are occurring and will continue, or have been threatened and will be committed; whether they have caused or will cause irreparable injury to the employer and whether the employer will suffer more from the denial of an injunction than the union will from its issuance.

Labor experience with injunctions before 1932 was extremely bad.[79] Among the abuses were frequent use of *ex parte* injunctions against strikes and picketing, issuance of injunctions on the basis of vague and generalized affidavits, and general unwillingness by the judiciary to reverse, at the permanent injunction stage, a decision already made by the judge in issuing a temporary restraining order. Once the injunction was handed down, contempt penalties were often meted out against individual strikers as well as union representatives by the same judge who had issued the decree at the outset.[80] Moreover, prior to Norris-LaGuardia, judicial intervention

---

[78] 370 U.S. at 228. See Teamsters, Local 795 v. Yellow Transit Freight Lines, 370 U.S. 711 (1962), and General Electric Co. v. Local 191, IUE, 398 U.S. 436 (1970), *vacating and remanding* 413 F.2d 964 (5th Cir. 1969), where the underlying disputes were not arbitrable. On the *Sinclair* debate prior to *Boys Market*, see generally Aaron, note 35 *supra;* Bartosic, note 35 *supra;* Isaacson, *The Grand Equation: Labor Arbitration and the No-Strike Clause,* 48 A.B.A.J. 914 (1962); Dunau, *Three Problems in Labor Arbitration,* 55 Va. L. Rev. 427 (1969); Givens, *Section 301, Arbitration and the No-Strike Clause,* 11 Lab. L. J. 1005 (1960); Wellington, *The No-Strike Clause and the Labor Injunction: Time for a Re-Examination,* 30 U. Pitt. L. Rev. 293 (1968); Keene, *The Supreme Court, Section 301 and No-Strike Clauses: From Lincoln Mills to Avco and Beyond,* 15 Vill. L. Rev. 32 (1969); Stewart, *No-Strike Clauses in the Federal Courts,* 59 Mich. L. Rev. 673 (1961).

[79] See generally, Frankfurter & Greene, note 21 *supra;* Wellington & Albert, *Statutory Interpretation and the Political Process: A Comment on Sinclair v. Atkinson,* 72 Yale L.J. 1547 (1963).

[80] On the right to trial by jury as it may relate to contempt proceedings in *Boys Market* injunctions, see Bloom v. Illinois, 391 U.S. 194 (1968); Frank v. United

in labor disputes carried with it the so-called objectives test. This test, through which the courts could evaluate the legitimacy of the objectives of strikers, was used by a heavy-handed and pro-employer judiciary to suppress worker protest without remedying the serious injustices that were to be found in the employer-employee relationship. Its apogee was *Duplex Printing Press Co. v. Deering*,[81] where the Court enjoined a secondary boycott in the teeth of the supposedly ameliorative provisions of the Clayton Act.[82] Norris-LaGuardia was the answer to such abuses, destroying federal court jurisdiction in the labor dispute arena.

A short answer to this forecast of doom based on history is that the Court's holding in *Boys Market* is not one-sided. The employer must demonstrate a willingness to arbitrate the underlying dispute. Further, accommodations between antitrust legislation and Norris-LaGuardia are undertaken elsewhere in order to reconcile two statutory policies.[83] The task of harmonizing Title VII of the Civil Rights Act of 1964 as well as other civil rights legislation on employment[84] with the NLRA and the RLA policies against work stoppages has been undertaken by the judiciary.[85] And while con-

States, 395 U.S. 147 (1969); Duncan v. Louisiana, 391 U.S. 145 (1968). See also *In re* Green, 369 U.S. 689 (1962). The early summary contempt cases often involved the unions. See *In re* Debs, 158 U.S. 564 (1895); Gompers v. United States, 233 U.S. 604 (1914).

81 254 U.S. 443 (1921). See also, in this regard, Loewe v. Lawlor, 208 U.S. 274 (1908); Lawlor v. Loewe, 235 U.S. 522 (1915). The British analogue appears to be Taff Vale Ry. v. A.S.R.S., [1901] A.C. 426.

82 15 U.S.C. §§ 12 *et seq.* Apparently the Clayton Act, rather than restricting the injunction, stimulated its use. See FRANKFURTER & GREENE, note 21 *supra*, at 99. "This [the Clayton Act] introduces no new principle into the equity jurisprudence of those courts. It is merely declaratory of what is the best practice always." American Foundries v. Tri-City Council, 257 U.S. 184, 203 (1921).

83 Note, *Accommodation of Norris LaGuardia Act to Other Federal Statutes*, 72 HARV. L. REV. 354 (1958). See Apex Hosiery Co. v. Leader, 310 U.S. 469 (1940); United States v. Hutcheson, 312 U.S. 219 (1941); Allen Bradley v. Local 3, IBEW, 325 U.S. 797 (1945); Amalgamated Meat Cutters v. Jewel Tea Co., 381 U.S. 676 (1965); Ramsey v. UMW, 416 F.2d 655 (6th Cir. 1969), *cert. granted*, 397 U.S. 1006 (1970).

84 See 42 U.S.C. § 1981. *Cf.* Jones v. Alfred H. Mayer Co., 392 U.S. 409 (1968); Waters v. Wisconsin Steel Works, 2 FEP Cases 574 (7th Cir. 1970). See also Exec. Order No. 11246, 3 C.F.R. 339 (1964–65).

85 See Gould, *Black Power in the Unions: The Impact upon Collective Bargaining Relationships*, 79 YALE L.J. 46 (1969). *Cf.* NLRB v. Tanner Motor Livery Ltd., 419 F.2d 216 (9th Cir. 1969). On the accommodation issue, see especially Waters v. Wisconsin Steel Works, note 84 *supra*.

ceding the revived threat of judicial decrees based upon personal philosophy, Professor Cox has said: "Making an exception [to Norris-LaGuardia] for strikes in breach of contract would carry out fairly specific legislative enactment without inviting judicial determination of labor policy."[86]

Most significant is the improved position in which labor unions now find themselves in the United States. The relationship between organized labor and capital can no longer be generalized into one involving unequal parties in an atmosphere of bitter social strife.[87] Indeed, in some instances, it is the unions which now hold the cards of power.[88] The labor movement cannot evade the responsibility of contractual sanctions when it has voluntarily entered into the collective agreement for the benefit of its members. And the fact of the matter is that the abuses that prompted Norris-LaGuardia had little to do with breach of contract stoppages or the interpretation of collective agreements.

At the same time, it must be acknowledged that the injunctive power now in the hands of federal and state courts in labor disputes in all parts of the country may contain a potential for abuse that Norris-LaGuardia was devised to correct, particularly where unions are weak. This is less an argument against *Boys Market* than it is a call upon the federal courts to draw upon that "judicial inventiveness" which Mr. Justice Douglas prescribed in *Lincoln Mills*. Special rules upon which *Boys Market* injunctions are to be conditioned must be enunciated by the Court.[89] And finally, the good sense of the *Boys Market* conclusion is also demonstrated by the fact that, despite Norris-LaGuardia, injunctions have been issued against both employers and unions so that a substantial number of limitations upon Norris-LaGuardia have already been set forth by the courts. The order of specific enforcement in *Lincoln Mills* was one in-

---

[86] Cox, note 28 *supra*, at 256.

[87] For a description of the situation in 1930, see FRANKFURTER & GREENE, note 21 *supra*, at 81.

[88] See COX, LAW AND THE NATIONAL LABOR POLICY 48–52 (1960); *cf.* Gould, *Taft-Hartley Revisited: The Contrariety of the Collective Bargaining Agreement and the Plight of the Unorganized*, 13 LABOR L.J. 348 (1962).

[89] For instance, in the preemption area, the Court in Linn v. United Plant Guard Workers, Local 114, 383 U.S. 53 (1966), borrowed from the constitutional rules articulated in New York Times Co. v. Sullivan, 376 U.S. 254 (1964). Thus, the Court in *Linn* held that state jurisdiction over libel actions arising out of labor disputes could be maintained where the statement was made with deliberate or reckless untruth. See also note 80 *supra*.

stance.[90] And, under the RLA, a similar order was entered against an employer who refused to recognize the lawful representative of its workers.[91] The duty of fair representation (now carried over into the NLRA)[92] was imposed upon the unions through equity.[93] Most recently, stoppages by white workers aimed at perpetuating racially discriminatory practices have been enjoined.[94]

Nor has the injunctive power been utilized only against stoppages for racial discrimination or for enforcement of recognition rights. In *Chicago River*,[95] Chief Justice Warren, speaking for a unanimous Court, held that where a minor dispute under the RLA involving the interpretation of the labor contract was submitted to the NRAB, the Court might lawfully enjoin the union from striking to defeat the jurisdiction of the board. The Court stated that the Norris-La-Guardia Act could not be read alone when dealing with matters under the RLA. The Court differentiated the controversy arising under Railway Labor Act machinery from the kinds of labor disputes that had triggered Norris-LaGuardia: "Such controversies, therefore, are not the same as those in which the injunction strips labor of its primary weapon without substituting any reasonable alternative."[96] As Professor Cox has said: " . . . there is much the same kind of conflict between the Norris-LaGuardia Act's blanket restriction and the policy of Section 301 as there was in the *Chicago*

---

[90] "The kinds of acts which had given rise to abuse of the power to enjoin are listed in § 4. The failure to arbitrate was not a part and parcel of the abuses against which the act was aimed. Section 8 of the Norris-LaGuardia Act does, indeed, indicate a congressional policy to a settlement of labor disputes by arbitration, for it denies injunctive relief to any person who has failed to make 'every reasonable effort' to settle the dispute by negotiation, mediation, or 'voluntary arbitration.'. . . we see no justification in policy for restricting § 301 (a) to damages suits, leaving specific performance of the contract to arbitrate grievance disputes to the inapposite procedural requirements of the Act." Douglas, J., in *Lincoln Mills*, 353 U.S. at 458.

[91] Virginia R. Co. v. System Federation, 300 U.S. 515 (1937); *cf.* Texas & N. O. R.R. v. Brotherhood of Ry. & S.S. Clerks, 281 U.S. 548 (1930).

[92] NLRB v. Local 1367, ILA, 368 F.2d 1010 (5th Cir. 1966); Local 12, United Rubber Workers v. NLRB, 368 F.2d 12 (5th Cir. 1966).

[93] Graham v. Brotherhood of Locomotive Fireman & Enginemen, 338 U.S. 232 (1949).

[94] State v. Baugh, 2 FEP Cases 271 (W.D. Wash. 1969); United States v. Local 189, United Papermakers & Paperworkers, 282 F. Supp. 39 (E.D. La. 1968); Central Contractors Ass'n v. Local 46, IBEW, 2 FEP Cases 189 (W.D. Wash. 1969); United States v. Building & Const. Tr. Coun. of St. Louis, 271 F. Supp. 447 (E.D. Mo. 1966).

[95] Brotherhood of R.R. Trainmen v. Chicago River & Indiana R. Co., 353 U.S. 30 (1957).

[96] *Id.* at 41.

River case between the blanket restrictions of the Norris-LaGuardia Act and the obligation to submit grievances to the Adjustment Board. From the standpoint of practical labor relations the two situations are exact parallels."[97]

The majority opinion in *Boys Market* relied heavily upon *Chicago River*. In *Sinclair*, the Court had held that *Chicago River* was distinguishable from § 301 contract law for two reasons: (1) the "affirmative duty" imposed upon unions under the RLA which compelled submission of disputes to the NRAB as an "exclusive method"; (2) the rejection by Congress of a Norris-LaGuardia repeal in the case of no-strike violations under the NLRA.[98] But *Boys Market* treated the *Chicago River* doctrine as "equally applicable" to § 301. To the arguments put forth by Mr. Justice Black in *Sinclair*, Mr. Justice Brennan responded thus:[99]

> To be sure, *Chicago River* involved arbitration procedures established by statute. However, we have frequently noted, in such cases as *Lincoln Mills*, the *Steelworkers Trilogy*, and *Lucas Flour*, the importance which Congress has attached generally to the voluntary settlement of labor disputes without resort to self-help and more particularly to arbitration as a means to this end.

Thus, the *Chicago River* principle of accommodation governs § 301 as well. As noted above, the distinction between the RLA and NLRA articulated by *Sinclair* has always seemed strange. For, aside

---

[97] Cox, note 28 *supra*, at 255.   [98] 370 U.S. at 210–12.

[99] 398 U.S. at 52.

Professor St. Antoine has pointed out that the Court's language in *Boys Market* can be interpreted so as to permit injunctions where grievance procedures exist without arbitration. See St. Antoine, note 61 *supra*. Section 203 of the NLRA, although it does not mention arbitration speaks of "final adjustment." It is therefore possible that an employer can convince a court that final adjustment which places authority in the employer's hands short of arbitration is consistent with the *quid pro quo* concept for *Boys Market* purposes.

Query, can the employer and union agree in their collective bargaining agreement to permit the employer to obtain a *Boys Market* injunction even where the underlying dispute is non-arbitrable? May the parties widen the accommodation between Norris-LaGuardia and § 301 and thus in effect confer jurisdiction upon the court under § 301 contract law? This is obviously quite different from a situation where the parties might seek to oust the court of jurisdiction. Cf. United Electrical Radio & Machine Workers of America v. NLRB, 409 F.2d 150 (D.C. Cir. 1969). See also IUE v. General Elec. Co., 407 F.2d 253, 259 (2d Cir. 1968), on the question whether the parties may nullify by collective agreement the *Warrior* presumption on arbitrability. Prior to *Boys Market* the courts held that the parties were able to confer jurisdiction for injunctive relief under *Sinclair*, albeit there in the context of grievance-arbitration machinery. See cases in note 115 *infra*. Moreover, it is possible

from the fact that resort to the NRAB is specifically provided by the statute, neither statutory procedure may be properly said to be more compulsory or exclusive than the other. Under the RLA—as is the case under the NLRA—one party must trigger machinery in order to have it utilized. Moreover, just as the Court in *Boys Market* has indicated that an employer unwilling to proceed to arbitration cannot obtain the fruits of the injunctive decree against a labor union, so also under the RLA there is doubt that the *Chicago River* doctrine is applicable where a submission has not been made to NRAB.[100] Because *Boys Market* relied so heavily upon *Chicago River* as well as "ordinary principles of equity" in the issuance of injunctions, the attention of the courts confronted with requests for injunctive relief under § 301 will undoubtedly focus upon experience to date under the Railway Labor Act.

A. STATUS QUO IN EMPLOYMENT CONDITIONS

Probably, one of the first issues to be presented will be whether the employer has an obligation to freeze existing working conditions

---

for a party to waive meritorious objections in equity. See McCLINTOCK ON EQUITY, 101-02 (2d ed. 1948). The case would be the least compelling where the union had only grievance machinery and not an arbitration clause available to it or where the arbitration clause was carefully circumscribed. Moreover, it is possible that the court may focus upon the question whether the no-strike clause itself is arbitrable, Stroehmann Bros. Co. v. Local 427, 74 L.R.R.M. 2957 (M.D. Penna. 1970), inasmuch as meritorious defenses to the no-strike obligation would be raised, or whether the matter in dispute is susceptible to arbitration as part of an actual employment condition that is involved in the employment relationship. An obvious example of a case not susceptible to arbitration, but which ought to be a leading candidate for *Boys Market* injunctive relief where the parties have so provided by contract, is where a union engages in stranger picketing and the dispute is unrelated to the employment relationship of the workers at that particular plant. See, generally, Johnson Builders, Inc. v. United Brotherhood of Carpenters, 422 F.2d 137 (10th Cir. 1970); Carney & Florsheim, *The Treatment of Refusals to Cross Picket Lines: "Bypaths and Indirect Crookt Ways,"* 55 CORN. L. REV. 940 (1970); Comment, *Picket Line Observance: The Board and the Balance of Interest,* 79 YALE L.J. 1369 (1970). All of this would comport with national labor policy insofar as it emphasizes freedom of contract considerations. See NLRB v. Insurance Agents' International Union, 361 U.S. 477 (1960); NLRB v. American Nat. Ins. Co., 343 U.S. 395 (1952). Cf. Phelps Dodge Corporation, 184 N.L.R.B. No. 106 (1970). On the question of waiver through management rights and zipper clauses, see note 133 *infra*, and Long Lake Lumber Co., 182 N.L.R.B. No. 65 (1970); see Standard Trucking Co., 183 N.L.R.B. No. 67 (1967); Cello-Foil Products, Inc., 178 N.L.R.B. No. 103 (1969); Century Electric Motor Co., 180 N.L.R.B. No. 174 (1970).

100 Cf. Manion v. Kansas City Terminal Ry., 353 U.S. 927 (1957); Louisville & N. R.R. v. Brown, 252 F.2d 149 (5th Cir. 1958).

pending the outcome of the arbitration proceeding. In *Brotherhood of Locomotive Engineers v. Missouri-Kansas-Texas Railroad Co.*,[101] the Court dealt with the question whether a *Chicago River* injunction might be granted which conditioned its enforcement upon the employer's preservation of the status quo in working conditions. The Court, in *M-K-T*, held that a district court is empowered to exercise the "typical" powers of a court of equity and therefore may, in appropriate circumstances, require the maintenance of the status quo by the employer. A contrary result, said the Court, could only be justified by an abuse of discretion by the trial court when balancing the equities or by the "clearest legislative direction," inasmuch as such relief was sometimes "essential to insure that extraordinary equitable remedies [injunctions against strikes] will not become the engines of injustice."[102]

Since § 301 contains no legislative guidance to the contrary, it would appear that *Boys Market* may justify federal court intervention in the underlying dispute that gave rise to the stoppage at the time of the request for injunction. Indeed, the lower courts operating under § 301, and anticipating an issue which *M-K-T* did not resolve,[103] have issued temporary injunctive relief against employers,

---

101 363 U.S. 528 (1960). See generally Comment, 60 COLUM. L. REV. 381 (1960); cf. Elgin, J. & E. Ry. Co. v. Burley, 325 U.S. 711 (1945); Order of Conductors v. Pitney, 326 U.S. 561 (1946); Slocum v. Delaware, L. & W.R. Co., 339 U.S. 239 (1950); Order of R.R. Telegraphers v. Chicago & North Western Ry. Co., 362 U.S. 330 (1960). See Meltzer, *The Chicago & North Western Case: Judicial Workmanship and Collective Bargaining*, 1960 SUPREME COURT REVIEW 113.

102 363 U.S. at 532.

103 In *M-K-T* the Court said: "We did not decide in *Chicago River*, and we do not decide here, whether a federal court can, during the pendency of a dispute before the Board, enjoin a carrier from effectuating the changes which gave rise to and constitute the subject matter of the dispute, *independent'y of any suit by the railroad for equitable relief*. As we read the order of the District Court, this case does not involve independent relief for the union." *Id.* at 531 n. 3. (Emphasis added.)

Lower courts have, however, granted injunctions requested by unions to preserve the status quo pending resolution of the merits by the NRAB. See Railroad Yardmasters v. St. Louis–San Francisco Ry., 231 F. Supp. 986 (N.D. Tex. 1964), *app. dismissed*, 345 F.2d 18 (5th Cir. 1965); Spokane, P. & S. Ry. v. Order of Ry. Conductors & Brakemen, 265 F. Supp. 892 (D.D.C. 1967). And see Westchester Lodge 2186 v. Railway Express Agency, Inc., 329 F.2d 748 (2d Cir. 1964). Relief has been denied where there is no evidence of irreparable injury. Brotherhood of R.R. Trainmen v. Boston & Maine R.R., 244 F. Supp 378 (D. Mass. 1965).

For cases arising under the NLRA involving remedial authority of the board, see NLRB v. Tidee Products, Inc., 426 F.2d 1243 (D.C. Cir. 1970); United Steel-

independent of any request for relief against a strike, where preservation of the status quo was necessary to protect the union and employees from irreparable injury.[104] For instance, where an employer sought to remove certain operations from Washington, D.C., to Chicago, temporary relief to the union was granted pending the outcome of arbitration, since the balance of convenience was weighted in favor of the employees.[105] In this connection, the court noted that "human considerations" were to be carefully taken into account.[106] Moreover, without considering the contract provisions relied upon by the union, the court noted that the employer's delay in selecting the arbitration panel, albeit a "plausible" and "perfectly reasonable one," caused potential harm to the workers since the arbitration process could not be completed prior to the contemplated business rearrangement. Thus, a preliminary injunction was granted by the court. Still another court, without discussing contract provisions, preserved the status quo where an employer planned to move to an-

---

workers v. NLRB, 74 L.R.R.M. 2747 (D.C. Cir. 1970); cf. NLRB v. Gissel Packing Co., 395 U.S. 575 (1969), and see note 104 *infra*.

On the problem of the status quo in the context of federal government employment, see United States v. Plasch, 75 L.R.R.M. 2331 (7th Cir. 1970).

[104] Local 38, RWDSU v. American Bakeries Co., 305 F. Supp. 624 (W.D. N.C. 1969); Local 328, IBT v. Armour & Co., 294 F. Supp. 168 (W.D. Mich., 1968); International Union, UAW v. Seagrave Fire Apparatus Division, 56 L.R.R.M. 2874 (S.D. Ohio 1964); Local Div. 1098, Amalgamated Ass'n of St. Elec. Ry. & Motor Coach Employees of America, AFL-CIO v. Eastern Greyhound Lines, 225 F. Supp. 28 (D. D.C. 1963); International Union, UAW, Local 408 v. Crescent Brass & Pin Co., 46 L.R.R.M. 2975 (E. D. Mich. 1960). But see Wolko v. Highway Truck Drivers, 232 F. Supp. 594 (E.D. Pa. 1964); Electrical Workers v. General Elec. Co., 332 F.2d 485 (2d Cir. 1964). On some of the general remedial problems in labor law, see St. Antoine, *A Touchstone for Labor Board Remedies,* 14 Wayne L. Rev. 1039 (1968). Under the RLA there is a status quo requirement for so called "major" disputes; the minor disputes are referred to the National Railroad Adjustment Board. See Detroit & Toledo Shore Line R.R. v. United Transportation Union, 396 U.S. 142 (1969). Cf. Bhd. Locomotive Fireman v. Bangor & Aroostook Railroad Co., 420 F.2d 77 (D.C. Cir. 1969); Chicago & N.W. Ry. Co. v. UTU, 422 F.2d 979 (7th Cir. 1970); Piedmont Aviation, Inc. v. Air Line Pilots Ass'n, 416 F.2d 633 (4th Cir. 1969). The question of status quo arrangements for employment conditions is under debate in Great Britain. See Hanna, *Scanlon Key to Pact or Chaos,* Sunday Times (London), June 28, 1970, p. 54, col. 4; Shakespeare, *Engineering "Summit" on Labour Dispute,* The Times (London), June 19, 1970, p. 23, col. 1; Shakespeare, *Engineering Disputes Row Vital to Future,* The Times (London), Apr. 24, 1970, p. 23, col. 4.

[105] Amalgamated Ass'n of St. Elect. Ry. & Motor Coach Employees v. Eastern Greyhound Lines, 225 F. Supp. 28 (D.D.C. 1963).

[106] See also Slote, Termination: The Closing at Baker Plant (1969).

other state.[107] Because the inconvenience to the employer in this case was more than "a few weeks delay" in moving facilities, thus entailing "substantial monetary losses," injunctive relief would be denied, said the court, if the company furnished a bond in the amount of $400,000 to protect the union should it prevail in arbitration.

Where an injunction is issued under *Boys Market*, the argument on behalf of a status quo arrangement as the price of enjoining the union's stoppages becomes more compelling. But the range of cases may be relatively narrow. Presumably, cases where management is engaging in a plant closure[108]—a large subcontracting operation, or massive discharges or layoffs of workers where that is protested— present the kind of situation in which the *M-K-T* remedy may be appropriate.

There are two principal difficulties with this approach. First, it will be contended that federal courts will become unduly enmeshed in the merits of labor disputes, a result which was heartily condemned by the Court in the *Steelworkers Trilogy*. The Court's answer to this allegation that in effect the authority of the arbitrator— or in the case of the RLA, the NRAB—would be usurped, is only partially satisfactory:[109]

> It is true that a District Court must make some examination of the nature of the dispute before conditioning relief since not all disputes coming before the Adjustment Board threaten irreparable injury and justify the attachment of a condition. . . . But this examination of the nature of the dispute is so unlike that which the Adjustment Board will make of the merits of the same dispute, and is for such a dissimilar purpose, that it could not interfere with the later consideration of the grievance by the Adjustment Board.

The federal courts operating under § 301 have been successful in avoiding this pitfall. Moreover, the standard for judicial examination may be somewhat instructive for federal and state courts in determining whether the strike should be enjoined.[110]

A second, related consideration is that, where substantial interference with managerial prerogatives and economic decisions is involved, the courts may be reluctant to act. Indeed, Professor Kroner

---

[107] International Union, UAW v. Seagrave Fire Apparatus Division, 56 L.R.R.M. 2874 (S.D. Ohio 1964).

[108] But see Textile Workers Union v. Darlington Mfg. Co., 380 U.S. 263 (1965); *cf.* Fibreboard Paper Products Corp. v. NLRB, 379 U.S. 203 (1964).

[109] 363 U.S. at 533–34.   [110] See text *infra*, at notes 125–38.

has asserted that this has been the experience under the RLA.[111] And in many respects the cases arising under the RLA are the most attractive candidates for status quo relief since delays before the NRAB have been scandalously long. The federal judiciary may approach the question of enjoining plant removals and subcontracting with a great deal of trepidation. Despite the fact that reinstatement of employees improperly discharged is an appropriate and common remedy, the courts may be somewhat reluctant to impose this kind of relief pending the outcome of arbitration, especially where there is a personal employer-employee relationship.[112]

Moreover, such a utilization of *Boys Market*, in anything less than the most extreme kind of case involving arbitrary action by an employer, runs against the grain of a substantial amount of arbitral precedent which has been evolved over the past twenty-five years. The conventional wisdom remains that management has the authority to move first and that it is the union's function to challenge but not to interfere with a decision before it is made.[113] Thus, the broad latitude of the *M-K-T* principle might put the courts on a collision course with the everyday expectations of management and labor. On the other hand, it may be said that injunctions against strikes arising out of labor disputes are so extraordinary because of Norris-LaGuardia, that equally unusual decrees are well justified. Yet, the courts may be reluctant to condition the injunction in the absence of some procedure to protect the employer against burdensome delay and consequent economic injury. The dilemma is perhaps best demonstrated by the facts of *Boys Market* itself. For, in that case,

---

[111] Kroner, *Interim Injunctive Relief under the Railway Labor Act: Some Problems and Suggestions*, 18TH ANNUAL N.Y.U. CONFERENCE ON LABOR 179; Kroner, *Minor Disputes under the Railway Labor Act: A Critical Appraisal*, 37 N.Y.U. L. REV. 41 (1962). See also Comment, note 101 *supra*.

[112] Proposals have been put forward (and have been incorporated in some collective bargaining agreements) to the effect that unless the discharge involves some particularly troublesome offense such as stealing, dishonesty, drunkenness on the job, etc., the employee should be permitted to work until the discharge is resolved in arbitration. Alternatively, it has been advocated that if management is in error about the discharge and the arbitrator holds that some other penalty such as a suspension was the proper method of dealing with the worker, full back pay as well as reinstatement be provided. The theory is that the power to discharge and to await the outcome of a lengthy arbitration proceeding places too much authority in the hands of management, may deter employees from engaging in legitimate activity, and places all of the burden of inconvenience upon the worker.

[113] Of course, this is especially true where employees are given orders to follow. See Fleming, *Arbitrators and the Remedy Power*, 48 VA. L. REV. 1199, 1222 (1962).

if union allegations prove accurate, workers are being deprived of employment to which they are entitled. Over a period of time during which final adjudication is pending, damages can be substantial. But, in my judgment, it would be difficult to convince most judges that the situation is unusual enough to warrant relief of the *M-K-T* variety.

All of this then suggests an alternative scope of inquiry under the *Boys Market* doctrine hinted at by some of the § 301 cases that have granted injunctions to preserve the status quo. The judicial experience with so-called "quickie" arbitration procedures may be instructive. Before such an examination of the relationship between the law on this subject and status quo remedies, it is necessary to examine the law that had developed in this area prior to *Boys Market* and the implications of the Court's decision in that case for such cases.

B. "QUICKIE" ARBITRATION ON THE STRIKE IN BREACH OF CONTRACT

In *New Orleans Steamship Association v. General Longshore Workers*,[114] an employers' association brought an action to enforce an arbitration award directing two local unions and their members to cease and desist work stoppages in violation of a collective bargaining agreement. The arbitrator, serving as one of six permanent arbitrators selected by the parties for the duration of the contract, was notified by the employer that the local unions had engaged in work stoppages and was requested to hold a hearing within seventy-two hours as provided by the contract. Within seventy-two hours a hearing commenced which lasted four days and an award was entered approximately two months later in which the arbitrator found that the stoppages had occurred in violation of the agreement. The arbitrator therefore directed the unions, their officers, agents, representatives, and members to cease and desist from work stoppages in violation of their contract. The district court dismissed the complaint which sought an enforcement of the award, relying principally upon *Sinclair* and its interpretation of the Norris-LaGuardia Act. In effect, the district court held, as did other federal courts,[115]

---

[114] 389 F.2d 369 (5th Cir. 1968).

[115] See Marine Transport Lines, Inc. v. Curran, 65 L.R.R.M. 2095 (S.D. N.Y. 1967); Gulf & South American S.S. Co. v. National Maritime Union, 360 F.2d 63 (5th Cir. 1966). But see Philadelphia Marine Trade Ass'n v. Local 1291, ILA 368 F.3d 932 (3d Cir. 1966), *rev'd on other grounds*, 389 U.S. 64 (1967); Pacific Maritime Ass'n v. International Longshoremen & W. U., 304 F. Supp. 1315 (N.D. Cal.

that the employer was attempting to gain indirectly that which *Sinclair* declared unobtainable because of Norris-LaGuardia. Under this view, enforcement of the arbitration award was regarded as a kind of injunctive decree which was prohibited by *Sinclair*.

A unanimous Fifth Circuit reversed. The court stated that, if an arbitrator were to issue such a ruling "absent jurisdiction," one would be confronted with an attempt to gain a federal injunction against a work stoppage contrary to the *Sinclair* rule. But the court refused to find that such a situation was to be found in the facts of *New Orleans Steamship Association*. The court correctly noted that *Sinclair* did not involve an arbitration award but rather an injunction to enforce a no-strike clause where "strikes were ensuing but where there had been no arbitration."[116] Therefore, said the court, *Sinclair* did not govern the precise issue involved. The court then turned to *Lincoln Mills* and the *Steelworkers Trilogy* and the interpretation of § 301 of the NLRA given in those cases. Not to enforce the award by injunction, said the court, would be to discourage arbitration. The no-strike clause and arbitration were a *quid pro quo* and the parties having submitted their dispute to arbitration under a specified procedure with articulated remedies, the losing party might—absent the injunction—ignore the award and continue the stoppage. This case, said the court, was distinguishable from *Sinclair*. Such a result could not be imputed to Congress:[117]

> In this case the parties agreed to the remedy of a desist order by the arbitrator. Such an order was entered and breached. The court in enforcing such order or award, although injunctive in nature, would be doing no more than enforcing the agreement of the parties. This not unusual action on the part of the court will lie unless the court has been deprived of jurisdiction by the Norris-LaGuardia Act.
>
> . . . We have before us a contract wherein the parties have ceded their remedy of self-help in a labor dispute to arbitration

---

1969); Ruppert v. Engelhofer, 3 N.Y.2d 576 (1958); *In re* Local 28, Sheet Metal Workers, 53 L.R.R.M. 2590 (N.Y. Sup. Ct., N.Y. Co., 1963); F & M Schaefer Brewing Co. v. Hoh, 72 L.R.R.M. 2529 (N.Y. Sup. Ct., Kings Co. 1969); Ford Motor Co. Chicago Stamping Plant, 41 Lab. Arb. 619 (1963); *In re* Ford Motor Company, 41 Lab. Arb. 621 (1963). See generally, Givens, *Injunctive Enforcement of Arbitration Awards Prohibiting Strikes*, 17 LAB. L.J. 292 (1966); McDermott, *Enforcing No-Strike Provisions via Arbitration*, 18 LAB. L.J. 579 (1967). The quickie arbitration clause is a mandatory subject of bargaining within the meaning of § 8(a)(5), § 8(b)(3), and § 8(d) of the act. See United Electrical Radio and Machine Workers of America v. NLRB, 409 F.2d 150 (D.C. Cir. 1969).

[116] 389 F.2d at 371.   [117] *Id.* at 372.

even to the point of permitting the arbitrator to grant a desist order.

The force of Mr. Justice Brennan's reasoning in *Boys Market* applies in even greater measure to the *New Orleans Steamship* fact situation. A contrary result would have been inconsistent with a policy supporting voluntry arbitration. Even if, contrary to what was asserted in *Boys Market*, employers might not be renouncing arbitration procedures because of a failure to obtain adequate remedies to enforce the *quid pro quo*, it is difficult to envisage any inducement for employers to negotiate quickie arbitration procedures with all the inconvenience and hardship involved for both parties, if the union or dissident workers might flaunt the award without fear of its judicial enforcement and contempt penalties. The Fifth Circuit's holding must therefore be viewed as more nearly harmonious with the national labor policy than the opposing position urged upon that tribunal.

The rules articulated in *New Orleans Steamship*, however, present both pitfalls and opportunities for the courts confronted with *Boys Market* applications for injunctions. On the negative side is the real likelihood that impatient employers may run to the courts and thus bypass arbitration and, perhaps even more important, the negotiation of expeditious no-strike procedures. This availability of the judicial avenue may, exaggerated by other factors besides the *Boys Market* result, prove too attractive to employers. The unions too may be moved away from quickie arbitration—at least as it applies to the strike issue—because the Supreme Court has held that an injunction is appropriate only in the case of an arbitrable dispute. But the no-strike clause itself is generally not so limited,[118] and there was no indication in the Fifth Circuit's opinion that the enforcement of an arbitrable award had any such qualifications.[119] If it is possible that an employer might obtain relief under a quickie or

---

[118] There are, however, many exceptions to the broad prohibitions contained in no-strike provisions. See U.S. BUREAU OF LABOR STATISTICS, BULL. No. 1425-1, *Arbitration Procedures* 56 (1966). The limited nature of many no-strike clauses was a point emphasized in brief for the AFL-CIO, as amicus curiae, in *Boys Market* case, at pp. 21–23.

[119] See Gulf & South American Steamship Co. v. National Maritime Union, 360 F.2d 63, 65 (5th Cir. 1966), where the court refused enforcement of an arbitration award prohibiting a strike where it was clear that the underlying issue which triggered the stoppage was arbitrable but was not decided by the arbitrator.

seventy-two-hour arbitration procedure without regard to the question whether the underlying dispute is arbitrable, unions will soon shun the arbitral route because management's resort to the judiciary will produce a better result in this regard under *Boys Market, i.e.,* an injunction only in the case of an arbitrable dispute that triggered the stoppage. *Boys Market* provides for arbitration of this issue almost simultaneous with injunctive relief against the union. Indeed, for reasons enumerated below,[120] equity might well dictate a judicial decree requiring a speedy arbitral resolution of the issue that caused the strike or an order that arbitration with regard to both the underlying and no-strike issue proceed simultaneously. Here again, labor unions will benefit by channeling the strike issue to the courts rather than the arbitrator.

This then would be an undesirable and obviously unintended by-product of *Boys Market*. It is antithetical to the doctrine of a limited role for the judiciary in labor arbitration matters stated by the Court in the *Steelworkers Trilogy*. And, ironically, if the situation were to develop as stated above, the criticism echoes that which the Court itself gave to *Sinclair* in the *Boys Market* opinion, *i.e.*, that the former case was an inconsistent departure from § 301 as interpreted by the Court. The effect of *Boys Market* could produce an anomaly of equal proportions, *i.e.*, to discourage the utilization of voluntary arbitration procedures.

To counter such a situation, the ruling in *New Orleans Steamship* might be modified so as to comport with *Boys Market*. The argument against this is that the parties themselves have provided both a no-strike obligation and arbitration as well as the remedy which the arbitrator is to impose through the collective bargaining process. According to this view, cease and desist orders might issue in enforceable form in those instances where the parties themselves have provided for them. Otherwise, both freedom to bargain collectively and the growth of arbitration are obstructed through any approach that would impose judge-made rules of law.[121] On balance, it seems that such considerations are outweighed by the imminent erosion of arbitral adjudication of no-strike issues. Here judicial involvement

---

[120] See text *infra*, at note 124.

[121] This, of course, is not to say that judge-made rules of law are entirely inappropriate. See *Lucas Flour Co.*, 369 U.S. 95 (1962). See generally Summers, *Collective Agreements and the Law of Contracts*, 78 YALE L.J. 525 (1969). *Cf.* Gulf & South American Steamship v. National Maritime Union, 360 F.2d 63, 65 (5th Cir. 1966).

contains within it the seeds of abuse and error.[122] It ought to be effectively limited—to the extent possible—in the spirit of the *Steel-workers Trilogy*.

At the same time, two factors remain unaltered by the re-evaluation of *New Orleans Steamship* described above. Employers will feel more secure moving to the courts for injunctive relief rather than to arbitration, even where expeditious procedures are available. In part, this explains the absence of any clear pattern of arbitration procedures to deal with the strike in breach of contract. Management is fearful of the tendencies of arbitrators in this area. And, as the facts in *New Orleans Steamship* demonstrate, arbitrators, sensitive to industrial tensions and factors such as morale and productivity in the plant community, are reluctant to put themselves in the position of commanding unusual remedies that might interfere with the parties' traditional expectations.[123] To some extent, this reluctance may be charged to arbitrators' alleged concern with their own self-preservation.[124] But this reluctance can be more easily understood when one recalls the status quo controversy and the *M-K-T* remedy. In the absence of the most clearly articulated grant of authority, an arbitrator would not require an employer to retain a worker on the payroll during an interim period while the merits of his discharge were resolved. As noted above, the expectation is that management has the authority to act subject, of course, to the union's challenge. In sensitive areas like this and the strike issue, arbitrators are cautious.

The unions, generally, have not been favorably impressed by the process. Although a speedy cease and desist order can often relieve the union of the hard and unpopular task of urging an aroused membership back to work, the union is faced with the one-sidedness of the procedure. There are inherent difficulties in explaining to the rank and file the reason for a special procedure to deal with strikes different from other breaches of the contract[125] even if the fact is

---

[122] See text *infra*, at notes 128–41.

[123] "In general, caution should certainly be the password on arbitral inventiveness in this area." Fleming, note 113 *supra*. For a discussion of this problem, see Gould, note 74 *supra*.

[124] See Hays, Labor Arbitration: A Dissenting View (1966). *Cf.* Fleming, The Labor Arbitration Process (1965).

[125] I am somewhat skeptical of the view that simply because the stoppage is a wildcat, the union will be willing and anxious to attempt to get the workers back

that other alleged contract violations, which may also entail the issuance of extraordinary remedies, require a more lengthy hearing, and detailed investigation and analysis.

At this point, analysis of *M-K-T* and *New Orleans Steamship* tends to converge. As Professor Kroner has noted, the small number of reported decisions imposing temporary injunctive relief where employer conduct has produced irreparable injury to workers reflects a deep-seated reluctance to interfere with managerial decisions that involve substantial business rearrangements motivated by economics. Moreover, as the Court properly noted in *M-K-T*, the function of the judiciary is not to examine the merits but only to determine whether expeditious relief is necessary. The inescapable problem is that the employer has no remedy for interference with efficiency and other factors, even though management's position may eventually prevail on the merits. This, of course, enforces the reluctance to move into this area where long delays and interference with implementation of such managerial decisions are involved.

The issuance of an injunction is not, however, an automatic process.[126] It is a function of judicial discretion and involves considerations of equity. Where the union may suffer irreparable injury as a result of employer action involving, for instance, plant closures or removal, it may be inequitable to enjoin the strike in violation of contract even though arbitration will be required and the award will issue long after the action has been taken, thus making it increasingly unlikely that the union can obtain a meaningful remedy as a practical matter. Taking a cue from *M-K-T*, courts—where equities are balanced properly and the unions are not themselves guilty of footdragging in pursuing grievance-arbitration machinery—might pose this alternative to the employer: (1) the status quo until arbitration is completed; (2) speedy arbitration procedures[126a] on

---

on the job. At the same time the union may adopt this posture so as to avoid a potential for damages liability. See Bartosic, note 35 *supra;* Dunau, note 78 *supra.*

[126] *Cf.* Crestwood School District v. Crestwood Education Ass'n, 382 Mich. 577 (1969); School District for the City of Holland v. Holland Education Ass'n, 380 Mich. 314 (1968). See 398 U.S. at 253–54.

[126a] Judge Frankel in American Tel. & Tel. Co. v. Communications Workers, 75 L.R.R.M. 2178 (S.D. N.Y. 1970), ordered the parties to select an arbitrator from the very day of the no-strike injunction and further ordered that the "arbitrator so selected shall be required by the parties in the submission to render his award by noon on Aug. 24, 1970 [six days after his selection]." *Id.* at 2180. Although such speed is unusual in the arbitration process, the arbitrator was selected according

the underlying issues as well as discharge, discipline, and damages issues that may arise out of the violation of the no-strike clause itself. Presumably, management would opt for the latter and this would then have the desirable effect of encouraging the use of voluntary arbitration procedures that are expeditious. More important, if this kind of rule is articulated as a matter of federal labor law, the parties might begin to address themselves to speedy arbitration measures concerning both no-strike issues and, at least, substantial managerial rearrangements. This would then take both the no-strike and other underlying issues away from the courts and put them into the hands of the arbitrators. The inducement for the unions would be that relief would be forthcoming on matters that seriously affect workers' security. The employers would avoid the distasteful status quo requirement of substantial duration as the price of judicially obtained remedies. This would make the courts a less inviting place to proceed and presumably would encourage the peaceful resolution of labor disputes by more appropriate processes.

III. The Judicial Role

In the *Steelworkers Trilogy* the Court instructed federal district courts to order parties to arbitrate unless it could be said with positive assurance that the matter was not arbitrable. In one of these three landmark cases, *United Steelworkers v. American Mfg. Co.*,[127] the Court, in rationalizing this doctrine, examined the no-strike clause and said: "There is no exception to the 'no-strike' clause and none therefore should be read into the grievance clause, since one is *quid pro quo* for the other."[128]

As previously noted, however, a literal application of the *quid pro quo* approach has not found favor with the Court. Further, where the no-strike clause is not unqualified as it was in *American Manufacturing*, the courts have not altered their analysis from that employed in the *Steelworkers Trilogy* in determining whether arbitration ought to be compelled.[129] This in itself undermines the simplistic view that would resolve all doubts in favor of enjoining

---

to the court order and the award appears to have been rendered within the deadline. See American Tel. & Tel. Co., Daily Lab. Rep. 170 (1970).

[127] 363 U.S. 564 (1960).   [128] *Id.* at 567.

[129] See, *e.g.*, Akron Typographical Union 182 v. The Beacon Journal Publishing Co., 72 L.R.R.M. 2362 (N.D. Ohio 1968), *aff'd*, 416 F.2d 969 (6th Cir. 1969); IUE v. General Elec. Co., 332 F.2d 485 (2d Cir. 1964); Lodge 913, IAM v. General Elec.

strikes on the theory that the same judicial attitude must be taken to both portions of the exchange between labor and management rather than having the courts reserve such decrees for issuance only where it can be said with reasonable certainty that the no-strike obligation is being violated. The first of these two paths would produce an indiscriminate reliance upon the injunctive process that would indeed nullify the purpose of Norris-LaGuardia as well as give an aura of legitimacy to the notion that the judiciary is inherently biased in labor disputes. But, as the Court has said in *Boys Market*, injunctions are to be issued with care. One is not confronted with an exception to the rule that the equities are to be balanced. On the other hand, if one does not resolve all doubts in favor of judicial intervention, as in the *Steelworkers Trilogy*, the courts are faced with what was so artfully avoided in those cases, contract interpretation.

The dangers involved, at least with regard to no-strike issues, have been somewhat exaggerated.[130] First, it should be a relatively easy matter for a judge to determine whether a stoppage, or a strike or slowdown or other kind of interruption of production contrary to the union's commitment to industrial peace, has taken place and is prohibited by the contract. The evidentiary hearing will not be lengthy in most cases. Moreover, in those few instances where the employer will have been found to have repudiated the no-strike clause through violations of the contract, including the arbitration provisions, the courts are not adrift, since the issue has been before them in connection with motions to compel arbitration.[131] If the Court holds that the *Lucas Flour* rule establishing an implied no-strike liability on the basis of a broad arbitration clause is carried over, the effort of a trial court ought to be, in these kinds of cases, a relatively simple one.

The web becomes a bit more tangled when the courts are confronted with the numerous conditional no-strike clauses. For instance, the collective agreement may state that the union and/or employee cannot strike unless and until grievance procedure has

---

Co., 57 L.R.R.M. 2526 (S.D. Ohio 1964); IUE v. Westinghouse Elec. Corp., 53 L.R.R.M. 2923 (S.D. N.Y. 1963); United Steelworkers of America, AFL-CIO v. General Elec. Co., 211 F. Supp. 562 (N.D. Ohio 1962).

[130] See Dunau, note 78 *supra*, at 466 n.105.

[131] See especially United Packinghouse Workers v. Needham Packing Co., 376 U.S. 247 (1964); Ice Cream Drivers v. Borden, Inc., 75 L.R.R.M. 2481 (2d Cir. 1970).

been exhausted. The NLRB, although not primarily concerned with contract interpretation, has faced up to this issue.[132] The courts are not so unequipped as to disqualify them outright for a similar role.[133] If the arbitrator finds that the conditions do not prohibit the strike, the injunction must be dissolved. The same holds true where the

---

[132] On the board's authority, see NLRB v. Strong Roofing & Insulating Co., 393 U.S. 357 (1969); NLRB v. Acme Indus. Co., 385 U.S. 432 (1967); NLRB v. C & C Plywood Corp., 385 U.S. 421 (1967). The board's authority over unfair labor practices is plenary. See Carey v. Westinghouse Elec. Corp., 375 U.S. 261, 268 (1964); Smith v. Evening News Ass'n, 371 U.S. 195, 197–98 (1962); *cf.* United Steelworkers v. American Int'l Aluminum Corp., 334 F.2d 147 (5th Cir. 1964); Amalgamated Ass'n of St. Employees v. Trailways of New England, Inc., 232 F. Supp. 608 (D. Mass. 1964), *aff'd,* 343 F.2d 815 (1st Cir. 1965). The board must interpret conditional no-strike clauses. See, *e.g.,* Young Spring & Wire Corp., 138 N.L.R.B. 643 (1962); Mid-West Metallic Prods., Inc., 121 N.L.R.B. 1317 (1958).

The board's considerations of strikes during the term of a contract generally arise under § 8(d) prohibitions against a strike or lockout to terminate or modify the terms of a collective bargaining agreement without providing proper notice prior to contract expiration. Speaking about this statutory provision, the board has said: "Our interpretation preserves the right to strike in all circumstances where the parties have provided in their agreement for negotiating substantial changes in its provisions—if the statutory requirements of § 8(d) are met. Moreover, our decision has no bearing on the right to strike for reasons and purposes other than to obtain contract modification or termination." Lion Oil Company, 109 N.L.R.B. 680, 684 (1954), *aff'd,* NLRB v. Lion Oil Company, 352 U.S. 282 (1957). See also Mastro Plastics v. NLRB, 350 U.S. 270, 284–89 (1956); United Furniture Workers of America v. NLRB, 336 F.2d 738 (D.C. Cir. 1964); McLeod v. Compressed Air, 292 F.2d 358 (2d Cir. 1961). The § 8(d) "cooling off" period for which notice must be given may not be waived by the parties' contract. See Rocky Mountain Prestress, Inc., 172 N.L.R.B. No. 87 (1968). The question whether a stoppage is arrived at to enforce a different interpretation of the contract is a difficult one to resolve. See General Elec. Co., 181 N.L.R.B. No. 111 (1970); International Union, UMW v. NLRB, 257 F.2d 211 (D.C. Cir. 1958); Kaynard v. Communications Workers of America, 72 L.R.R.M. (E.D. N.Y. 1969). The scope of bargaining during the term of the contract remains wide. See NLRB v. C & C Plywood Corp., 385 U.S. 421 (1967); UAW v. General Motors Corp., 381 F.2d 265 (D.C. Cir. 1967); NLRB v. Jacobs Mfg. Co., 196 F.2d 680 (2d Cir. 1952); Equitable Life Ins. Co., 133 N.L.R.B. 1675 (1961); Proctor Mfg. Corp., 131 N.L.R.B. 1166 (1961); *cf.* Tidewater Associated Oil Co., 85 N.L.R.B. 1096 (1949); LeRoy Mach. Co., 147 N.L.R.B. 1431 (1964); New York Mirror, 151 N.L.R.B. 834 (1965). See generally Cox & Dunlop, *Regulation of Collective Bargaining by the National Labor Relations Board,* 63 HARV. L. REV. 389 (1950). Where a stoppage during the term of the agreement is in breach of contract, the strikers are subject to discharge and discipline inasmuch as their conduct is unprotected activity. See NLRB v. Sands Mfg. Co., 306 U.S. 332 (1939); Artim Transportation System, Inc. v. NLRB, 396 F.2d 359 (7th Cir. 1968); Sillbaugh v. NLRB, 74 L.R.R.M. 2955 (D.C. Cir. 1970); A. Borchman & Sons Co., 174 N.L.R.B. No. 38 (1969); McLean Trucking Company, 175 N.L.R.B. No. 66 (1969).

[133] See, *e.g.,* Forrest Industries, Inc. v. Local 3-436, Int'l Woodworkers of America, 381 F.2d 144 (9th Cir. 1967); Rothlain v. Armour & Co., 268 F. Supp. 545 (W.D. Pa. 1967); General Elec. Co. v. Local 761, IUE, 62 L.R.R.M. 2782 (W.D. Ky. 1966).

arbitrator determining the question of arbitrability for himself[134] holds that the underlying dispute is not arbitrable. Yet, this problem becomes more complicated and the sanctions less attractive when, for instance, certain subject matter is exempted from the no-strike obligation. In the automobile industry, production standards and the pay rates for new jobs, health and safety matters, are all outside the strictures of the no-strike clause.[135] But much to the consternation of employers, such clauses often act as stalking horses for dissatisfaction over other issues or protests where two or more are inescapably intertwined. This is the kind of no-strike case that can be difficult to sort out, especially for a court. Although the problem grows in the automobile industry, the companies have been reluctant to press the issue in arbitration. But a legal remedy may prove more tempting to management now that the Court has spoken in *Boys Market*. Here again, one notes the movement away from arbitration into the courts, an undesirable result from the vantage point of preserving industrial self-government.

Such problems are troublesome, but hardly insurmountable. In the first place, while the court is required to determine whether the strike is in breach of contract, such a ruling ought not to foreclose a hearing de novo on the strike issue before an arbitrator. Since a number of arbitrators have held that damages may be awarded under the contract in the case of a no-strike violation,[136] the issues relating to contract interpretation, including union responsibility for the stoppage, could be raised anew at that time. Here again, the theme

---

134 In the *Warrior* case the arbitrator considered the question of arbitrability anew. See Warrior & Gulf Navig. Co., 36 Lab. Arb. 695 (1961). Of course, the courts must also examine under the *Warrior* standard in the first instance. See Atkinson v. Sinclair Refining Co., 370 U.S. 238, 241 (1962); Wiley v. Livingston, 376 U.S. 543 (1964).

135 See, *e.g.*, Agreement between Ford Motor Company and UAW (Oct. 25, 1967), pp. 24, 56, which exempts production standards, health and safety, and new job rates from the no-strike clause subsequent to the exhaustion of the grievance procedure. See Agreement between Chrysler Corp. and UAW (Nov. 10, 1967), pp. 7–8, 41–42. Agreement between General Motors Corp. and UAW (Dec. 15, 1967), pp. 85–87, 36–40.

136 On damages for no-strike clause violations, see Drake Bakeries, Inc. v. Local 50, 370 U.S. 254, 265–66 (1962). See Roger J. Air & Son, Inc., unreported (May, 1970); Vulcan Mold & Iron Co., 53 Lab. Arb. 869 (1969); Forest City Publishing Co., 50 Lab. Arb. 683 (1968); Pinchaven Sanitarium, Inc., 49 Lab. Arb. 991 (1967); Cleveland Newspaper Publishers Ass'n, 49 Lab. Arb. 1043 (1967); Bradlees Family Circle Stores, 47 Lab. Arb. 567 (1966); American Pipe & Construction Co., 43 Lab. Arb. 1126 (1964); Publishers Ass'n of New York, 42 Lab. Arb. 95 (1964); Booth Newspapers, Inc., 43 Lab. Arb. 785 (1964). See also Fleming, note 113 *supra*.

is one previously expressed in connection with both status quo relief for unions and the conclusory nature of the court's adjudication of the arbitrability question. An injunction issued under the authority of *Boys Market* is essentially temporary relief for the employer because of both irreparable injury and the inadequacy of alternate remedies. This and the clear thrust of the *Steelworkers Trilogy* mean that arbitrators ought to review both arbitrability and the no-strike violation and the courts must keep entirely clear of the merits on both issues when one party seeks to enforce an award or to dissolve the injunctions as the result of the arbitrator's holding. This the court cannot do upon request for temporary relief under *Boys Market*. Accordingly, the price of the Court's holding is that a union may have imposed upon it (for a considerable period of time unless more speedy arbitration processes are devised) an injunctive decree because, in the court's view, it can be said with reasonable certainty that the no-strike clause has been violated—and the union is thereby restrained from use of its most effective weapon until the arbitrator has rendered an award to the contrary. Of course, one should not fudge and say that the treasuries of the unions are exposed to employer actions only in the instance of arbitration. Quite obviously, resistance to the *Boys Market* injunction can produce contempt sanctions—and where the injunction must be dissolved subsequent to an arbitrator's award, the resulting inequities are particularly glaring. Obstreperous trade unionists have discovered that, in cases where Norris-LaGuardia prohibitions have not been found to be applicable, judicially imposed fines can be substantial indeed.[137] If the courts may issue injunctions under *Boys Market*, their decrees will have to be enforced.

---

[137] Both the United Mine Workers and its former president, John L. Lewis, were fined large sums for contempt of court. See United States v. UMW, 330 U.S. 258 (1947). See also N.Y. Times, Aug. 4, 1970, p. 27, col. 6, and see *id.*, Aug. 5, 1970, p. 38, col. 1, for account that the union and officers were fined $25,000 per day for contempt for a stoppage directed against an arbitrator's award. In this case, however, the company bargained away the contempt fine. The trial judge then asked that criminal contempt proceedings be brought against the union. See Whitney, *U.S. Acts on Union in Parcel Strike*, N.Y. Times, Sept. 24, 1970, p. 61, col. 1. Criminal contempt proceedings raise the problem of right to jury trial. See cases cited in note 80 *supra*. Moreover, the specter of both civil and criminal contempt sanctions is present even where the injunction is later found to be invalid. See Walker v. City of Birmingham, 388 U.S. 307, 316 n. 6 (1967). The Court has held, however, that if state jurisdiction had been preempted, the injunction can be properly defied if there is an attempt to challenge the injunction's validity. *In re* Green, 369 U.S. 689 (1962).

At the same time, the federal law of labor injunctions under § 301 can be articulated so as to guard against the judicial abuses of the past. The Court has borrowed from constitutional law principles to determine the extent to which state courts may entertain suits for libel in cases arising from labor disputes.[138] There is no reason why the same cannot be done in connection with labor injunctions. For instance, the Court has held that, where First Amendment rights are involved, restraining orders cannot be issued *ex parte* and without a full hearing on the merits.[139] The Court would be wise to adopt a similar rule for both federal and state judges in the case of § 301 injunctions. This is in the spirit of *Boys Market*. The uniform federal labor law of § 301 must provide adequate safeguards against repetition of our experience with judicial abuses in connection with labor injunctions, even if, as the Court in *Boys Market* has noted, unions have matured and gained strength and the judicial treatment of labor cases is far more progressive than it was forty years ago.

The difficulty inherent in judicial involvement grows where the courts must not merely interpret the no-strike clause, but also other portions of the contract as well. In the pristine *Boys Market* case, the question whether the underlying dispute is arbitrable can be resolved within the guidelines set forth in the *Steelworkers Trilogy*. But suppose that the parties then proceed to the arbitration, and the arbitrator renders an award, the effect of which the parties disagree about. The union might then strike to enforce its interpretation of the award. Indeed, the no-strike provision in *Boys Market* itself states that "this [no strike] limitation shall not be binding upon either party hereto if the other party [refuses to arbitrate] . . . or fails to abide by, accept or perform a decision or award of an arbitrator or board."[140] In such a case, the parties' clear preference is to resolve the refusal to abide by an award or the disagreement as to its interpretation through industrial warfare. This then, unlike the situation in *New Orleans Steamship*, where the Fifth Circuit was able to enjoin a stoppage because of the reconciliation of such action with the parties' intent, or the *Boys Market* litigation

---

[138] See Linn v. United Plant Guard Workers, Local 114, 383 U.S. 53 (1966).

[139] See Carroll v. President & Comm'rs of Princess Anne, 393 U.S. 175 (1968), which held unconstitutional temporary restraining orders issued without notice or opportunity to be heard, on the ground that it denied the First Amendment right to speak.

[140] 398 U.S. at 239 n.3.

where the no-strike clause appeared to cover the dispute in question, since the employer wished to invoke the grievance-arbitration machinery, poses a more difficult question for the courts.

Where the parties, as in *Boys Market*, indicate quite clearly that an exception to the no-strike clause is intended where one of the parties refuses to abide by the award, the argument in favor of not issuing an injunction becomes a strong one. After all, the parties have themselves designated the method of dispute resolution. Moreover, the courts would be deciding whether the parties had complied with the award in the teeth of a mandate against judicial intervention.

Suppose, however, that there is no contract provision such as that contained in the *Boys Market* agreement. Should the result be the same? The parties have not bargained their way out of the courts, but the difficulties involved in determining compliance remain. The Third Circuit, in *Philadelphia Marine Trade Association v. ILA, Local 1219*,[141] held that where stoppages were called to protest an arbitrator's award, confirmed in that case in a federal district court, the union could be enjoined from thwarting enforcement of the award by the imposition of contempt sanctions. But the question whether the union is actually resisting the award—before or after its confirmation in court[142]—is more difficult than determining whether the court ought to enforce the award itself. There is a risk of erroneously construing the arbitrator's award in terms of the particular work stoppage engaged in. It would seem proper, therefore, and compatible with Norris-LaGuardia (especially where there are any exceptions to the scope of the no-strike clause which make the lawfulness of the strike an important issue), to enjoin the stoppage only where it is patent that its intent or effect is to undermine the award. In the absence of such a finding, a court of equity might well refer the matter back to the arbitrator to obtain further clarification or, alternatively, order the parties to proceed to arbitration on the merits of the issue or the scope of the no-strike clause or both. Where, however, there is no issue about the no-strike aspect, an injunction would undoubtedly issue under the standards of the *Boys Market* doctrine.

---

[141] 365 F.2d 295 (3d Cir. 1966), 368 F.2d 932 (3d Cir. 1966), *rev'd on other grounds*, 389 U.S. 64 (1967).

[142] See Dunau, note 78 *supra*, at 476–77.

IV. Some Public Law Problems

The NLRA prohibits employer discharge or discipline of workers when they engage in protected concerted activity to protest working conditions.[143] The Supreme Court has held that where strike action is prohibited by collective bargaining agreement, a stoppage during the term of that contract is unprotected and the worker is therefore exposed to the penalties of discharge and discipline.[144] The Court stated in *Mastro Plastics v. NLRB*,[145] however, that where the contract does not specifically provide to the contrary a broad no-strike clause cannot be interpreted to preclude a strike called in protest against "serious" unfair labor practices.[146] The *Mastro Plastics* opinion noted that the unfair practices presented in that case were at odds with the "foundations" of the negotiated labor contract.[147] Thus, there are circumstances where federal labor legislation carves out statutory exceptions to the contractually negotiated no-strike provisions of the contract.

Accordingly, when an employer seeks to enjoin a strike allegedly in violation of the contract under the *Boys Market* doctrine, the union may contend that the employer's unfair labor practices have triggered the stoppage and it is thus protected activity under the NLRA within the meaning of *Mastro Plastics*. Although the board, in determining whether a particular stoppage is protected or unprotected activity, is not resolving the question whether an injunction should issue, it would nevertheless be anomalous as a matter of federal labor policy to permit the courts to enjoin stoppages where workers have a protected status for striking under § 7.

---

[143] See NLRB v. Washington Aluminum Co., 370 U.S. 9 (1962). See generally Cox, *The Right to Engage in Concerted Activities*, 26 IND. L.J. 319 (1951); Getman, *The Protection of Economic Pressure by Section 7 of the National Labor Relations Act*, 115 U. PA. L. REV. 1195 (1967).

[144] NLRB v. Sands Mfg. Co., 306 U.S. 332 (1939).

[145] 350 U.S. 270 (1956).

[146] *Id.* at 281–83; Arlan's Department Store, 131 N.L.R.B. 802 (1961). But see Ford Motor Co., 133 N.L.R.B. 1462 (1961). See NLRB v. Wagner Iron Works, 220 F.2d 126 (7th Cir. 1955); NLRB v. Buitoni Foods Corp., 298 F.2d 169 (3d Cir. 1962); Wrought Originals, 139 N.L.R.B. 1435 (1962).

[147] Mr. Justice White has characterized *Mastro Plastics* as a case which "involved a flagrant unfair labor practice by the company threatening the very existence of the union itself." Drake Bakeries, 370 U.S. at 265.

While there is considerable disagreement among arbitrators as to the wisdom of their reliance upon law as well as contract,[148] the responsibility for the interpretation of the law, of course, lies with the courts.[149] Still, the matter is not quite so simple. For the Supreme Court has stated that, at least insofar as unfair labor practice jurisdiction is concerned, the NLRB has primary jurisdiction.[150] In the *Boys Market* context of an employer request for injunctive relief, the board will not have passed on the issue in contention. Therefore, review of the matter by a federal district court under § 301, provides for examination of the issues without the board's involvement. But the Court has held that, though an issue may be within the exclusive jurisdiction of the board, a breach of contract brings it under the jurisdiction of the federal courts under § 301.[151] Where employers request *Boys Market* injunctions, the federal courts cannot avoid their duty. But they would be wise to request an amicus brief from the agency charged with primary responsibility whether that is the NLRB or, in a Title VII matter, the Equal Employment Opportunity Commission. For collective agreements should not be read to defeat important rights derived from either Title VII or the NLRA.

The courts have also held that a walkout to protest unsafe working conditions constitutes a statutory exception to the no-strike clause under § 502 of the act.[152] Here again, requests for *Boys*

---

[148] See generally Howlett, *The Arbitrator, the N.L.R.B. and the Courts*, in Proceedings of the Twentieth Annual Meeting of the National Academy of Arbitrators 67 (1967); Meltzer, *Ruminations About Ideology, Law and Labor Arbitration, id.* at 1; Mittenthal, *The Role of Law in Arbitration*, in Proceedings of the Twenty-first Annual Meeting of the National Academy of Arbitrators 42 (1968); Meltzer, *The Role of Law in Arbitration: Rejoinders, id.* at 58.

[149] See, *e.g.,* Monroe Sander Corp. v. Livingston, 377 F.2d 6, 13 (2d Cir. 1967) (dictum); McGuire v. Humble Oil & Refining Co., 355 F.2d 352, 358 (2d Cir. 1966); Local 95 UAW v. W. M. Chase Co., 262 F. Supp. 114, 117–19 (E.D. Mich. 1966); Glendale Mfg. Co. v. Local 520, ILGWU, 283 F.2d 936, 938–39 (4th Cir. 1960).

[150] San Diego Building Trades Council v. Garmon, 359 U.S. 236 (1959).

[151] Smith v. Evening News Ass'n, 371 U.S. 195 (1962).

[152] See NLRB v. Knight Morley Co., 251 F.2d 753 (6th Cir. 1957); Philadelphia Marine Trade Ass'n v. NLRB, 330 F.2d 492 (3d Cir. 1964); NLRB v. Fruin-Colnon Construction Co., 330 F.2d 885 (8th Cir. 1964). If the employer condones a strike in breach of contract, subsequent discharge of the strikers may be unlawful. *Cf.* Plasti-Line, Inc. v. NLRB, 278 F.2d 482 (6th Cir. 1960); Dubo Manufacturing Corp., 148 N.L.R.B. 1114 (1964), *enf'd*, 353 F.2d 157 (6th Cir. 1965); Complete Auto Transit, 134 N.L.R.B. 652 (1961); Ohio Stove Company, 180 N.L.R.B. No. 134 (1970); Need-

Market injunctions may involve consideration of this substantive issue. In *U.S. Steel v. United Mine Workers*,[153] a federal district court granted coal mine operators an injunction restraining a strike where the workers refused to work on the grounds of lack of safety precautions in the mines. The court was confronted with an interpretation of both the NLRA and the recently enacted Federal Coal Mine Health and Safety Act.[154] It was requested to issue a writ of mandamus against the Secretary of Interior to enforce the provisions of the latter statute. Without discussing the impact of law upon a private contract, the court came to the questionable conclusion that since the Federal Coal Mine Health and Safety Act was passed subsequent to the negotiation of the contract, it could not be "incorporated into the agreement" inasmuch as the statute was not known to the parties at the time they executed their contract. Therefore, said the court, "this Act of Congress cannot abrogate or change the existing collective bargaining agreements."[155] The district court said that a remedy existed as part of the contract, since the matter was subject to arbitration, and held that it was the court's "duty" to enjoin the stoppage. Five days later the Third Circuit reversed.[156]

The Third Circuit, noting that injunctions under the *Boys Market* doctrine are not automatic, set aside the district court's order because no finding was made (1) as to whether the dispute was properly within the settlement procedures of the Federal Coal Mine Health and Safety Act of 1969, (2) as to whether the stoppage was authorized by any union authority, (3) as to the presence or absence of a "dangerous condition," and (4) whether that was a proper subject for arbitration or whether the stoppage was called against abnormally dangerous conditions which would, under § 502 of the NLRA, immunize workers against no-strike contractual prohibitions. Therefore, the circuit court summarily reversed and remanded to the district court for a hearing de novo on the application for a preliminary injunction.

---

ham Packing Co., Inc., 180 N.L.R.B. No. 159 (1970); Poloron Products of Indiana, Inc., 177 N.L.R.B. No. 54 (1969); W. R. Grace & Co., 179 N.L.R.B. No. 81 (1969); American River Constructors, 163 N.L.R.B. No. 67 (1968); Packers Hide Association, 152 N.L.R.B. 655, *enf'd*, 360 F.2d 59 (8th Cir. 1966).

[153] 74 L.R.R.M. 2607 (W.D. Pa. 1970), *rev'd*, 74 L.R.R.M. 2611 (3d Cir. 1970).

[154] 83 Stat. 742, 30 U.S.C. § 801 (1969).

[155] 74 L.R.R.M. at 2609.   [156] 74 L.R.R.M. 2611 (3d Cir. 1970).

The correctness of the Third Circuit's view highlights some of
the misgivings that supporters of the old *Sinclair* rule may have had.
For, quite clearly, the district court in *U.S. Steel Corp.* was wrong-
headed in its application of *Boys Market* and inexpert in its handling
of both fact and law in this labor dispute. Such judicial deficiencies
are all the more worrisome in light of the growing racial tensions
in the American industrial community and the relatively recent
phenomena of stoppages, in some instances wildcat or unauthorized, called to protest alleged racially discriminatory practices. For
instance, suppose a black caucus or group of black militants inside
the plant are dissatisfied with the demands that the union has made
for a holiday pay provision. The black caucus insists that the company offer a holiday for Martin Luther King's birthday. Suppose
there is a walkout to secure this demand. Or suppose that the demand of the black caucus is for so-called inverse seniority which
would require the employer to lay off, in times of economic stress
or in the case of a reduction of work force, the more senior workers who, more often than not, will be white.[157] Or suppose that
black workers insist upon wearing Black Power buttons in the
plant, and that an employer prohibits such activity because of its
allegedly disruptive impact upon the work force. An arbitrator
agrees with the employer's position, but a walkout is triggered to
protest the award. If the employer sought confirmation of the award
in federal or state court, the judge would be called upon to deal
with the issue whether the wearing of such buttons could be regarded as § 7 activity and whether a collective agreement could
lawfully waive such a § 7 right for the affected black workers.[158]
Quite clearly the same evaluation must be made by the court when
the dispute arises in the form of a prayer for *Boys Market* relief.
All these questions are complicated and will strain the resources of
the courts in *Boys Market* injunction cases. While the full sweep
of the legal issues is beyond the scope of this article,[159] such cases
raise at least two issues: (1) the extent to which Title VII and
other laws dealing with racial discrimination in employment as
well as public policy may serve to immunize workers who engage

---

[157] See Gould, note 85 *supra*.

[158] See Gould, *The Question of Union Activity on Company Property*, 18 VAND.
L. REV. 73 (1964). *Cf.* United Aircraft Corp. v. Canel Lodge No. 700, I.A.M., 74
L.R.R.M. 2518 (D. Conn. 1970).

[159] See Gould, note 85 *supra*.

in stoppages to protest racial discrimination; (2) the circumstances under which workers may engage in such activity independent of union authorization at any level despite the principle of exclusive bargaining representative articulated in the NLRA.[160]

For instance, although the board has struggled to articulate an approach which would protect racial wildcat strikes in certain circumstances, I have observed:[161]

> In terms of the relationship between black dissidents and exclusive bargaining agents the Board's approach . . . has it all backwards. In cases involving walkouts which arise from discrimination or unconscionable practices, the Board should not strain to discover a rapport between the union and the workers, for in most cases no such rapport exists in fact. Rather, such walkouts should be presumed to be protected under Section 7 of the National Labor Relations Act *because they are disruptive of the role played by the exclusive representative.* If the union behaves properly in such cases, it is the agent through which conflicts should properly emerge. Where the activities of the unions are so unresponsive as to require blacks to act on their own, the necessity of ending discrimination requires that they be protected. If, on the other hand, a union is in accord with the workers on the racial issue and would support the protest, the conduct of the black employees should be unprotected. In such circumstances, there is no justification for bypassing the exclusive representative. The question to be answered, of course, is how to determine the nature of the union's policy.

Where workers engage in such stoppages, are discharged or disciplined, and the arbitrator upholds such managerial action (especially in those many instances where the arbitrator does not take into account public law considerations),[162] the courts are inevitably confronted with these issues if one party seeks either to confirm or to upset the arbitration award in a federal or state court. Thus, these questions, while new both to the courts and to the agencies, are not foreign to what would have been the judicial experience even without *Boys Market.* While *U.S. Steel Corp.* is an example

---

[160] See, *e.g.,* NLRB v. Draper, 145 F.2d 199 (4th Cir. 1944); NLRB v. Sunbeam Lighting Co., 318 F.2d 661 (7th Cir. 1963); NLRB v. R. C. Carr Co., 328 F.2d 974 (5th Cir. 1964); NLRB v. Tanner Motor Livery Ltd., 419 F.2d 216 (9th Cir. 1969). Compare the approach taken under the RLA in National Airlines, Inc. v. IAM, 416 F.2d 998 (5th Cir. 1969); *decision on remand,* 73 L.R.R.M. 2163 (S.D. Fla. 1970), *rev'd on appeal,* 74 L.R.R.M. 2833 (5th Cir. 1970).

[161] Gould, note 85 *supra,* at 67.   [162] Note 148 *supra.*

of blundering by the judiciary, the fact that the courts would have had these issues in any event, makes it clear that judicial consideration of such matters is not something which is created by *Boys Market* inasmuch as it does not involve the courts in what would otherwise be unexplored territory.

There is one final issue which will undoubtedly come before the courts more often in the future. This is the question of union responsibility for the stoppage and the standard to be imposed upon the union under contract language in existence.[163] This is a most important issue in terms of guarding or raiding (depending upon one's vantage point) the union treasury, but also because, if union responsibility is not established, the courts are up against the most untidy consequence of *Boys Market*: the enforcement of judicial decrees against individual workers or groups of workers (which may constitute a dissident organization) who call or are involved in unauthorized stoppages.

It has been said that the principal contribution of *Boys Market* is that the decision will make available the more potent remedy of injunction to deal with wildcat or unauthorized stoppages.[164] In one sense, this assessment of the Court's decision is an accurate one in that union leaders will find it easier to stand up to the rank and file and to adhere to contract commitments. The court issuing the injunction becomes the political scapegoat rather than the international or local union officers. With rank and file protests on the upswing, *Boys Market* may provide a much needed palliative to cope with the unauthorized stoppages in breach of contract. Yet, this analysis is superficial for a number of reasons.

In the first place, a collective bargaining agreement may impose a mere passive responsibility on the part of the international or local union, *i.e.*, the union must not sanction or encourage the stoppage. Thus, the no-strike clause may simply require the union not

---

[163] See Fairweather, Employer Actions and Options in Response to Strikes in Breach of Contract 129 (1966). *Compare* United Constr. Workers v. Haislip Baking Co., 223 F.2d 872 (4th Cir. 1955), *with* United Textile Workers v. Newberry Mills, 238 F. Supp. 366 (W.D. S.C. 1955). See Cox, *Some Aspects of the Labor Management Relations Act, 1947*, 61 Harv. L. Rev. 274, 302–12 (1948).

[164] See Unkovic, *Enforcing the No-Strike Clause*, 21 Lab. L.J. 387 (1970). Of course, if rank and file pressure makes a substantial impact upon union leadership, the price of the no-strike clause itself as well as other costs imposed upon the employer may go higher. I am advised of one situation where the union relinquished wage increase demands in order to obtain removal of the no-strike clause and the *Boys Market* remedy.

to encourage such unauthorized activity rather than to impose a
more severe affirmative action obligation to see that the stoppage
is discontinued. Perhaps the courts will read no-strike clauses broadly so as to require the union to engage in a good faith effort to get
the workers to return to the job.[165] Broad contract construction
would be compatible with the policy of federal labor law of encouraging industrial peace in the *quid pro quo* concept which
might otherwise be thwarted by irresponsible rank and file activities. And it would not conflict with either the standard previously
advocated for a judicial finding of no-strike violation, *i.e.*, that the
violation be reasonably clear, or final adjudication of liability and
violation questions by the arbitrator.

Even if the union is responsible for bringing an end to the stoppage, difficulties remain. The union cannot be regarded as a guarantor to supply labor in all instances.[166] Some of these problems are
highlighted by Judge Judd's recent opinion in *REA Express v.*

---

[165] For the variety of no-strike clauses and arbitral awards regarding them, see,
e.g., Vulcan Mold & Iron Co., 53 Lab. Arb. 869 (1969); Forest City Publishing Co.,
50 Lab. Arb. 683 (1968); Merchant's Frozen Foods Div., 34 Lab. Arb. 607 (1960);
Cleveland Newspapers Ass'n, 49 Lab. Arb. 1043 (1967); Master Builders Ass'n, 49
Lab. Arb. 1157 (1967); Electric Autolite Co., 40 Lab. Arb. 522 (1963); Crawford
Clothes, Inc., 12 Lab. Arb. 1104 (1949); Motor Products Corp., 12 Lab. Arb. 49
(1949). *Cf.* GOULDNER, WILDCAT STRIKE (1965); Leahy, *Arbitration, Union Stewards
and Wildcat Strikes*, 25 ARB. J. 150 (1970). The court order must be based upon contract. *Cf.* Cox, note 163 *supra*, at 311.

[166] *Cf.* NLRB v. Norfolk Shipbuilding & Drydocking Corp., 195 F.2d 632, 636
(4th Cir. 1952). Even if the affirmative action obligation is not present, the union's
withdrawal of support has some impact upon employee action: "By pledging that
it will not support a wildcat strike a Union makes it clear that it will not make
[strike assistance] . . . payments. A contract usually allows the employer to stop
paying the premiums for employee insurance coverage during the strike, and so the
Union pays the premiums to keep the coverage intact. In a no-support type no-strike
pledge, however, the Union makes it clear that it will not finance such premiums.
Most importantly, in a no-support type clause the Union pledges that it will not use
its talent and resources in planning and waging any strike that occurs. Often an
international union gives a strike a whole new dimension by contacting the cus-
tomers of a struck employer with whom it has collective bargaining relationships
and asking them, in consideration of their good relationship, to discontinue purchasing from the struck employer during the strike. This cannot happen where the
international has pledged no support. Nor can an international use its often extensive
communications media in aid of a strike where it has signed a promise of no support.
The international may not plan strategy or tactical moves to assist the strikes in
their resort to self-help. Finally, the international may not use its very considerable
strength with other international unions to solicit financial and tactical support for
the strikers." Brief for International Union, UAW and Local Union No. 758, pp.
44–45, in Vulcan Mold & Iron Co., 53 Lab. Arb. 869 (1969).

Brotherhood of Railway, Airline & Steamship Clerks,[167] where the court issued an injunction against the international union as well as the local. Although the international had not authorized the strike, the international had not taken disciplinary action against those responsible for the stoppage. Said the court:[168]

> There is no evidence that BRAC [the international union] ever took any action to penalize those responsible for illegal work stoppages. The penalties in the BRAC constitution for illegal strikes may be so severe that they are reluctant to apply them. The only specific penalties mentioned are expulsion of participating members, which it is the duty of the local Lodge to enforce promptly, and revocation of the charter of any lodge which does not proceed with the members transferred to other lodges. . . . BRAC should be able, however, to find some powers lurking in the 171 pages of constitution, statutes, and protective laws which it could use to protect itself against violations by its members of obligations which it has assumed as the bargaining agent for all employees.

In effect, this is the approach that the Trades Union Congress has agreed to undertake to regulate "unofficial" stoppages in Great Britain.[169] But it is much easier to talk about such actions than to impose them, for the political facts of life may make it difficult

---

[167] 74 L.R.R.M. 2346 (E.D. N.Y. 1970).

[168] *Id.* at 2439. But see Boeing v. Local Lodge 751 and IAM, 91 F. Supp. 596 (W.D. Wash. 1950), where it was held that the international was subject to several rather than joint liability where both the international and local were party to the collective agreement. Thus, unless stated to the contrary, the contract does not automatically obligate the international for the local's conduct. Section 301 makes federal labor law dependent upon traditional rules of agency. *Cf.* United Broth. of Carpenters and Joiners v. United States, 330 U.S. 395 (1947); UMW v. Gibbs, 383 U.S. 715, 736 (1966); Flaherty v. McDonald, 178 F. Supp. 544, 548 (S.D. Cal. 1959). One kind of international union discipline is placing the local under trusteeship. But this raises problems under § 302 of Landrum Griffin. See Jolly v. Gorman, 74 L.R.R.M. 2706 (5th Cir. 1970). Whether the union violates § 8(b)(1)(A) of the NLRA when it disciplines nonstriking members seems to turn on whether the union stoppage is lawful. Thus a strike in breach of contract by the union makes the collection of union imposed fines unlawful "restraint" and "coercion." See National Grinding Wheel Company, Inc., 176 N.L.R.B. No. 89 (1969); Stark Glass, Inc., 177 N.L.R.B. No. 37 (1969); Rocket Freight Lines Co. v. NLRB, 74 L.R.R.M. 2452 (10th Cir. 1970); *cf.* National Tea Company, 181 N.L.R.B. No. 116 (1970).

[169] See Wood, *Anti-Strike Bill Abandoned by Wilson: Agreement Heals Breach in the Labour Movement,* The Times (London), June 19, 1969, p. 1, col. 1. See also note 4 *supra;* Carr, *The Unions: What the Tories Would Put in Place of Strife,* Sunday Times (London), June 1, 1969, p. 12, col. 1; Shanks, *Reforming the Unions by*

for internationals to penalize local union officers who may then be tempted to move to another union in competition for the same members. Although such considerations are tempered by the very judicial intervention which has been temporarily rejected in Britain, these problems are now exaggerated in this country by the withdrawal of the UAW and International Brotherhood of Teamsters from the AFL-CIO and the consequent potential for increased raiding among the unions.[170] And much the same factors are present where the local union moves against individual workers. These workers may opt for a more politically acceptable choice in the form of a rival union. On the other hand, if the court is requiring the international or local officers to take action of a fairly reasonable nature, *i.e.*, trusteeship rather than expulsion or fines, and the instances in which such sanctions are imposed remains limited to cases in which there is defiance of court orders, or a strong potential for such, damage to both organized labor and the courts may be minimized. And perhaps it may be said that even the transferral of allegiance to another union may be desirable from the point of view of public policy if the competing union decides to behave properly. But, of course, the price or by-product of such success may be the irrational resolution of grievances, exorbitant and inflationary settlements (in the case of interest disputes), or an indiscriminate sanction of employee claims—all of which are risks whenever reduction of strikes becomes a primary goal in labor-management policy.

If legal action against the unions is unsuccessful, there is only one other approach that could be taken through the courts, *i.e.*, an employer suit against the individual striker or groups of strikers. This approach has been adopted in Sweden,[171] but employers rarely sue individual employees because of the disruptive effect upon a harmonious industrial relations policy. Moreover, the Swedish statute specifically limits the amount of damages that can be collected to a relatively small amount, thus striking the same kind of

Contract, The Times (London), Nov. 13, 1967, p. 21, col. 3. For some of the recent decisions by British courts on the right to strike, see Daily Mirror Newspapers v. Gardner, [1968] Q.B. 762; Torquay Hotel Co. v. Cousins, [1968] 3 W.L.R. 540; Stratford & Son v. Lindley, [1965] A. C. 269; Rookes v. Barnard, [1964] A.C. 1129.

[170] See Loftus, *AFL-CIO Drops Automobile Union for Dues Arrears*, N.Y. Times, May 17, 1968, p. 1, col. 3; Janson, *U.A.W. and Teamsters Form Political and Organizing Team*, N.Y. Times, July 24, 1968, p. 51, col. 1.

[171] See SCHMIDT, THE LAW OF LABOUR RELATIONS IN SWEDEN 117 (1962).

contorted balance adopted by the New York legislature in 1967 in the Taylor Law[172] with regard to public employees. Whether injunctive decrees or damage suits may be maintained against employees pursuant to § 301 has not yet been resolved by the Supreme Court. The Court has held, in *Atkinson v. Sinclair Refining Co.*,[173] that union agents may not be sued individually under § 301 inasmuch as the act was intended to render the union liable as an entity for breach of contract. But *Atkinson* dealt with suits against individuals where the responsibility belonged to the union and therefore the relief sought against union agents was essentially duplicative. In *Atkinson*, the Court specifically reserved ruling on the question whether damage suits against individuals may be entertained under § 301.[174]

V. Conclusion

> An enforced shut-down caused by a strike in a small plant in a quite different part of the country may hit the earnings of . . . a highly capitalised firm very hard. Its willingness to accept the risks of heavy investment in the production of specialised products dependent on the chain of other operations will be influenced by the view that it takes of the reliability of the engagements made by its suppliers of essential goods and services. If the flow is constantly subject to unpredictable interruption, business initiative in important fields of activity is likely to be discouraged. There is also the effect on wage-earnings; the demand for total autonomy by a work group

---

[172] N.Y. Civ. Serv. Law, § 200 *et seq.* (McKinney Supp. 1969), imposes penalties upon individual workers, § 210(2)(f) (one year's probation while serving without tenure); § 210(2)(g) (payroll deduction of twice daily rate for each day in violation of act); § 210(3)(g) (no compensation paid to those engaged in strike).

[173] 370 U.S. 238, 246–49 (1962).

[174] *Id.* at 249 n.7. See also in this connection Louisville & N.R.R. v. Brown, 252 F.2d 149 (5th Cir. 1958); Givens, *Responsibility of Individual Employees for Breaches of No-Strike Clauses*, 14 IND. & LAB. REL. REV. 595 (1961); Comment, *Liability of Employees under State Law for Damages Caused by Wildcat Strike: The Brown Case*, 50 COLUM. L. REV. 177 (1959); Gilmour v. Wood Wire & Metal Lathers International Union, Local 74, 223 F. Supp. 236 (N.D. Ill. 1953). But two state courts have enjoined strike activity by individuals. See American Device Mfg. Co. v. Machinists, 105 Ill. App.2d 299 (1969); Armco Steel Corp. v. Perkins, 411 S.W.2d 935 (Ky. Ct. App. 1967). Query, does an injunction against individuals raise constitutional questions? See International Union, UAWA v. W.E.R.B., 336 U.S. 245, 259 (1949); Dorchy v. Kansas, 272 U.S. 306, 311 (1926). See also Hughes v. Superior Court, 339 U.S. 460, 465 (1950).

which has banded together to stop or slow down production in one place results in the loss of wages and the disruption of the working lives of many times their number elsewhere. These workers and their employers both have a right to expect the effective intervention of trade unions in plants where labour is organised, to ensure that frivolous or minor disputes are not allowed to cause excessive damage.[175]

So said Andrew Shonfield, in a Note of Reservation to Great Britain's Donovan Report of 1968. In effect, the arbitration system in the United States is an answer to the problem to which Mr. Shonfield was addressing himself in Britain, although the American system's success may be extolled beyond actual practice in the plant.[176] Of course, it is axiomatic that the democratic society cannot eliminate strikes, whether they occur during the term of the contract or at its expiration. As a matter of fact, the short-run impact of *Boys Market* may actually increase the incidence of stoppages over the terms of a new contract in industries like auto and steel where the rank and file rumblings about elimination of the no-strike clause during the term of the agreement are the greatest. *Boys Market* could impel union leadership to press hard for the removal of the strike prohibition even to the point of striking for this demand at the expiration of the contract. But the interdependent nature of a technologically advanced economy requires modernized industrial relations and this necessitates changes which may be abrasive to private parties.[177] The labor unions do not stand immune from that rule of life. (Indeed, the labor movement's willingness to obey Taft-Hartley national emergency dispute injunctions indicates its recognition of this.) Section 301, as interpreted by the Court in *Lincoln Mills* and its progeny, seeks to make the law responsive to these conditions.

And yet, to paraphrase Santayana, one cannot ignore history and risk repetition of its mistakes. Mr. Justice Frankfurter's dissent in *Lincoln Mills* was largely undercut by the *Steelworkers Trilogy*.

---

[175] Donovan Report, 288, 289. See also the expansive approach taken toward enjoining jurisdictional stoppage in the United States (partially on the authority of *Boys Market*), in Plasterers Local Union No. 79 v. NLRB, 74 L.R.R.M. 2575 (D.C. Cir. 1970).

[176] See KUHN, BARGAINING IN GRIEVANCE SETTLEMENT (1961).

[177] See GALBRAITH, THE NEW INDUSTRIAL STATE (1967); CROSLAND, THE FUTURE OF SOCIALISM (1956).

But his views loom larger when one considers the problems bound up with *Boys Market*. The nature of judicial scrutiny in connection with the injunction gives Frankfurter's dissenting opinion a more prophetic quality. Nevertheless, while conceding the existence of a specter now somewhat enlarged, on balance, I am of the view that judicial resiliency is sufficient to evade most of the traps that once brought the unions to distrust so severely the law and the courts.